Stuttgart, Germany

Sam Ni

Contents

Articles

Overview of Germany

History of Germany

History of Germany

This article is part of **a series**
Early History
Germanic peoples
Migration Period
Frankish Empire
Medieval Germany
East Francia
Kingdom of Germany
Holy Roman Empire
Eastward settlement
Early Modern period
Sectionalism
18th century
Kingdom of Prussia
Unification of Germany
Confederation of the Rhine
German Confederation & Zollverein
German Revolutions of 1848
North German Confederation

The German Reich
German Empire
World War I
Weimar Republic Saar, Danzig, Memel, Austria, Sudeten
Nazi Germany
World War II Flensburg government
Germany since 1945
Occupation + Ostgebiete
Expulsion of Germans
FRG, Saar & GDR
German reunification
reunified Germany
Topics
Military history of Germany
Territorial changes of Germany
Timeline of German history
Germany Portal

The concept of Germany as a distinct region in central Europe can be traced to Roman commander Julius Caesar, who referred to the unconquered area east of the Rhine as *Germania*, thus distinguishing it from Gaul (France), which he had conquered. The victory of the Germanic tribes in the Battle of the Teutoburg Forest (AD 9) prevented annexation by the Roman Empire. Following the fall of the Roman Empire, the Franks subdued the other West Germanic tribes. When the Frankish Empire was divided among Charlemagne's heirs in 843, the eastern part became East Francia, ruled by Louis the German. Henry the Fowler became the first king of Germany in 919. In 962, Henry's son Otto I became the first emperor of what historians refer to as the Holy Roman Empire, the medieval German state.

In the High Middle Ages, the dukes and princes of the empire gained power at the expense of the emperors, who were elected by the princes and crowned by the pope. The northern states became Protestant in the early 16th century, while the southern states remained Catholic. Protestants and Catholics clashed in the Thirty Years' War (1618–1648), which left vast areas depopulated. The Peace of Westphalia of 1648 marked the effective end of the Holy Roman Empire and the beginning of the modern nation-state system. The Habsburg family continued to use the title "emperor", but ruled only in Austria.

After the Napoleonic Wars (1803–1815), an Austrian-led German Confederation of 39 states was formed. Nationalist sentiment led to the unsuccessful 1848 March Revolution. A German Empire that excluded Austria was formed in 1871 under the leadership of Prussia and its "Iron Chancellor", Otto von Bismarck. Although there was an elected Reichstag, or parliament, it had little authority compared to the chancellor and the Bundesrat, who were appointed by the emperor and the princes. Unification was followed by an industrial revolution. By 1900, Germany's economy was by far the largest in Europe (and second only to the U.S. in the world). In World War I (1914–1918), Germany was defeated by an alliance of Russia, Britain, France and America. As a result, the Empire was replaced by the democratic Weimar Republic (1918–1933).

The Great Depression (1929–1933) caused unemployment to soar and led to a loss of confidence in the government. German politics polarized and there was an upsurge of support for the Communists on the left and Nazis on the right. In 1933, the Nazis under Adolf Hitler gained power and promptly imposed a totalitarian regime. Jews were rounded up and killed in the Holocaust. In World War II (1939–1945), Germany was again defeated, but this time divided between democratic West Germany and Communist East Germany. In the Cold War, West Germany joined NATO, a military alliance led by the United States, while East Germany was a member of the rival Warsaw Pact, led by the Soviet Union. Communism collapsed in 1989 and East Germany was reunited with West Germany soon afterwards. Germany has become increasingly integrated into the European Union, notably with the "Europe 1992" effort to create a unified market and adoption of the euro, a Europe-wide currency, in 2002.

Pre-history

The earliest hominid fossils found in what is now Germany are Homo heidelbergensis (500,000 years old) and the Steinheim Skull (300,000 years old). The Neanderthals, named for Neander Valley, flourished around 100,000 years ago. The region was glaciated from 30,000 years ago to about 10,000 years ago. The Nebra sky disk, dated 1600 BC, is one of the oldest known astronomical instruments found anywhere. Northern Germany experienced the Nordic Bronze Age from 1700BC to 450BC and thereafter the Pre-Roman Iron Age. Differences between artifacts from northern Germany and those from southern Germany suggest the beginning of differentiation between the Germanic and Celtic peoples. In the 1st century BC, the Germanic tribes began expanding south, east, and west.

Early history (56 BC to 260 AD)

Main articles: Germanic peoples and Germania

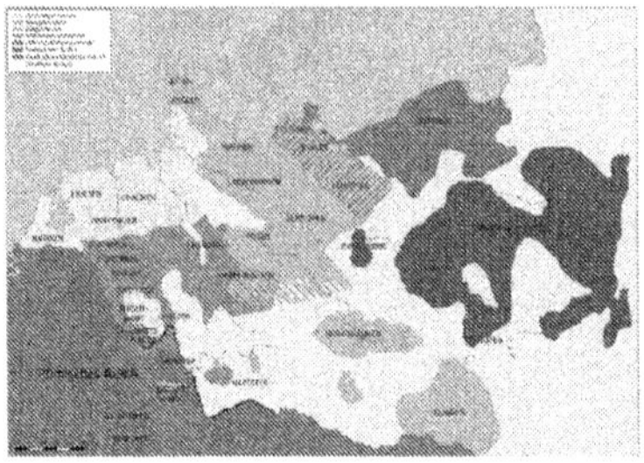

Germanic tribes in 50 AD (not including most of Scandinavia)

Early Old High German runic inscription on the Pforzen buckle

Germany entered recorded history in June 56 BC, when Roman commander Julius Caesar crossed the Rhine. His army built a huge wooden bridge in only ten days. He retreated back to Gaul upon learning that the Suevi tribe was gathering to oppose him. The English word "Germany" is derived from the Latin *Germania*, a word first recorded in Caesar's writings.

Under Augustus, the Roman General Publius Quinctilius Varus began to invade Germania (to the Romans, an area running roughly from the Rhine to the Ural Mountains), and it was in this period that the Germanic tribes became familiar with Roman tactics of warfare while maintaining their tribal identity. In AD 9, three Roman legions led by Varus were defeated by the Cheruscan leader Arminius in the clades Variana ("Battle of the Teutoburg Forest"). Arminius later suffered a defeat at the hands of the Roman general Germanicus at the Battle of the Weser River or Idistaviso in AD 16, but the Roman victory was not followed up after the Roman Emperor Tiberius recalled Germanicus to Rome in AD 17. Tiberius wished that the Roman frontier with Germania be maintained along the Rhine. Modern Germany, as far as the Rhine and the Danube, thus remained outside the Roman Empire. By AD 100, the time of Tacitus' *Germania*, Germanic tribes settled along the Rhine and the Danube (the Limes Germanicus), occupying most of the area of modern Germany. The 3rd century saw the emergence of a number of large West Germanic tribes: Alamanni, Franks, Chatti, Saxons, Frisians, Sicambri, and Thuringii. Around 260, the Germanic peoples broke through the Limes and the Danube frontier into Roman-controlled lands.

See also: List of meanings of countries' names

The Stem Duchies & Marches

The Stem Duchies (tribal duchies) in Germany was mainly the areas of the old German tribes of the region. These strains were originally the Franks, the Saxons, the Alemanni, the Burgundians, the Thuringians, and the Rugians. In the 5th Century the Burgundians moved into Roman territory and would have been in 443 and 458 in the area, then Lower Burgundy. The area they had occupied in Germany, along with the Saxons, was occupied by the Franks. The Rugians which Odoacer destroyed in 487 formed a new confederation of Germans in their place, the Bavarians. All of these strains in Germany were finally subdued by the Franks, the Alamanni in 496 and 505, the Thuringia in 531, the Bavarians after a certain point 553, and then the Saxons, in a lengthy campaign of Charles himself, from 804. When Germany finally separated as the East Francia, took over the tribal areas of new identities as the subdivisions of the Empire, joining Lorraine (right Francia Media). For the ruler of this ancient Roman title dux ("the leader") was adopted. It was originally a Roman frontier military commander used. In German, however, the corresponding title, Herzog, more like a translation of a Greek, , stratêlatês, "army" (stratos) "leader" (elaunein, "to lead"). Thus, the Old High German title of herizoho, from heri, "army," and ziohan, "to lead." This looks very much like a similar title,voivode, maybe a translation into Slavic languages.

Frankish Empire

Main article: Frankish Empire

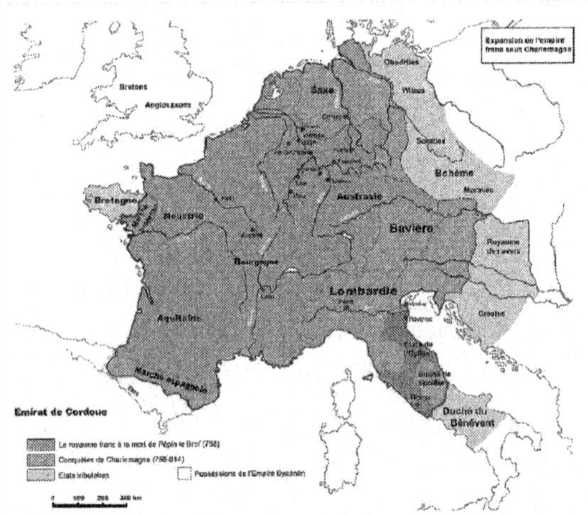

Frankish Empire: Realm of Pippin III in 758 (blue), expansion under Charlemagne until 814 (red), marches and dependencies (yellow)

After the fall of the Western Roman Empire the Franks created an empire under the Merovingian kings and subjugated the other Germanic tribes. Swabia became a duchy under the Frankish Empire in 496, following the Battle of Tolbiac. Already king Chlothar I ruled the greater part of what is now Germany and made expeditions into Saxony while the Southeast of modern Germany was still under influence of the Ostrogoths. In 531 Saxons and Franks destroyed the Kingdom of Thuringia. Saxons inhabit the area down to the Unstrut river. During the partition of the Frankish empire their German territories were a part of Austrasia. In 718 the Franconian Mayor of the Palace Charles Martel made war against Saxony, because of its help for the Neustrians. The Franconian Carloman started in

743 a new war against Saxony, because the Saxons gave aid to Duke Odilo of Bavaria. In 751 Pippin III, mayor of the palace under the Merovingian king, himself assumed the title of king and was anointed by the Church. The Frankish kings now set up as protectors of the Pope, Charlemagne launched a decades-long military campaign against their heathen rivals, the Saxons and the Avars. The Saxons (by the Saxon Wars (772-804)) and Avars were eventually overwhelmed and forcibly converted, and their lands were annexed by the Carolingian Empire.

Middle Ages

Main article: Holy Roman Empire

The prince-electors of the Holy Roman Empire. (left to right: Archbishop of Cologne, Archbishop of Mainz, Archbishop of Trier, Count Palatine, Duke of Saxony, Margrave of Brandenburg and King of Bohemia)

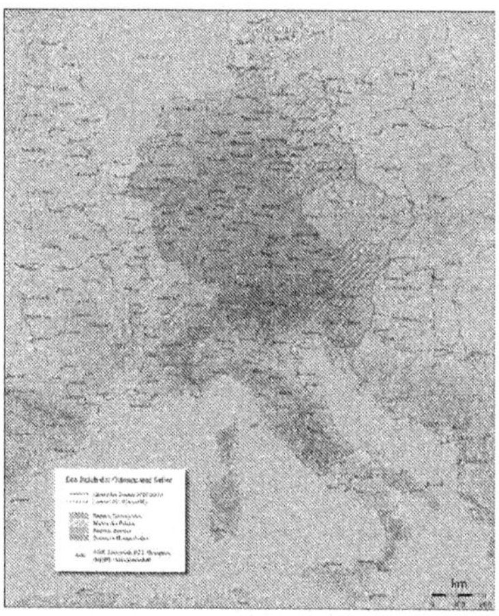

Holy Roman Empire, 10th century

Marienburg (Malbork) castle of the Teutonic Knights

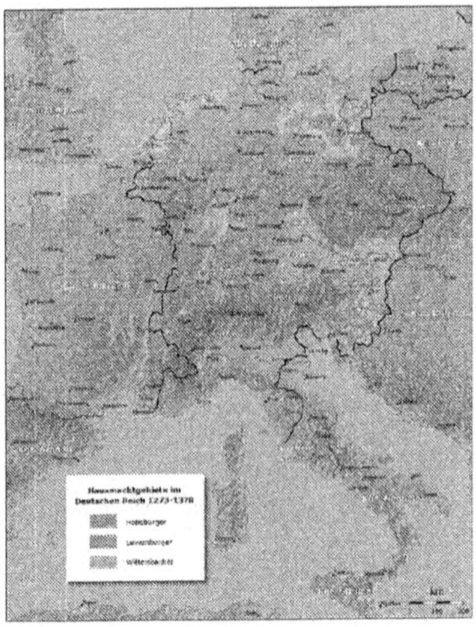

Holy Roman Empire, 14th century

In 768 the Frankish king died, leaving his kingdom to his two sons—Charles and Carloman. When Carloman suddenly died in 771, Charles seized his brother's lands and made them part of his own kingdom. During the next two years, Charles consolidated his control over his kingdom and became more commonly known as "Charles the Great" or "Charlemagne". From 771 until his death in 814, Charlemagne extended the Carolingian empire into northern Italy and the territories of all west Germanic peoples, including the Saxons and the Bajuwari (Bavarians). In 800, Charlemagne's authority was confirmed by his coronation as emperor in Rome. The Frankish empire was divided into counties, and its frontiers were protected by border marches. Imperial strongholds (*Kaiserpfalzen*) became economic and cultural centres (Aachen being the most famous).

Between 843 and 880, after fighting between Charlemagne's grandchildren, the Carolingian empire was partitioned into several parts in the Treaty of Verdun (843), the Treaty of Meerssen (870) and the Treaty of Ribemont The German region developed out of the East Frankish kingdom, East Francia. From 919 to 936 the Germanic peoples (Franks, Saxons, Swabians and Bavarians) were united under Duke Henry of Saxony, who took the title of king. For the first time, the term Kingdom (Empire) of the Germans ("Regnum Teutonicorum") was applied to a Frankish kingdom, even though Teutonicorum at its founding originally meant something closer to "*Realm of the Germanic peoples*" or "*Germanic*

Realm" than realm of the Germans.

Otto the Great

In 936 , Otto I the Great was crowned at Aachen. He strengthened the royal authority by re-asserting the old Carolingian rights over ecclesiastical appointments. Otto wrested from the nobles the powers of appointment of the bishops and abbots, who controlled large land holdings. Additionally, Otto revived the old Carolingian program of appointing missionaries in the border lands. Otto continued to support the celibacy rule for the higher clergy. Thus, the ecclesiastical appointments never became hereditary. By granting land to the abbotts and bishops he appointed, Otto actually made these bishops into "princes of the Empire" (*Reichsfürsten*). In this way, Otto was able to establish a national church. In 951 Otto the Great married the widowed Queen Adelheid, thereby winning the Lombard crown. Outside threats to the kingdom were contained with the decisive defeat of the Magyars of Hungary near Augsburg at the Battle of Lechfeld in 955. The Slavs between the Elbe and the Oder rivers were also subjugated. Otto marched on Rome and drove John XII from the papal throne and for years controlled the election of the pope, setting a firm precedent for imperial control of the papacy for years to come. In 962, Otto I was crowned emperor in Rome, taking the succession of Charlemagne, and this also helped establish a strong Frankish influence over the Papacy.

During the reign of Conrad II's son, Henry III (1039 to 1056), the Holy Roman Empire supported the Cluniac reform of the Church - the Peace of God, the prohibition of simony (the purchase of clerical offices) and the celibacy of priests. Imperial authority over the Pope reached its peak. In the Investiture Controversy which began between Henry IV and Pope Gregory VII over appointments to ecclesiastical offices, the emperor was compelled to submit to the Pope at Canossa in 1077, after having been excommunicated. In 1122 a temporary reconciliation was reached between Henry V and the Pope with the Concordat of Worms. The consequences of the investiture dispute were a weakening of the Ottonian church (*Reichskirche*), and a strengthening of the Imperial secular princes.

The time between 1096 and 1291 was the age of the crusades. Knightly religious orders were established, including the Templars, the Knights of St John and the Teutonic Order .

Towns

From 1100, new towns were founded around imperial strongholds, castles, bishops' palaces and monasteries. The towns began to establish municipal rights and liberties (see German town law), while the rural population remained in a state of serfdom. In particular, several cities became Imperial Free Cities, which did not depend on princes or bishops, but were immediately subject to the Emperor. The towns were ruled by patricians (merchants carrying on long-distance trade). The craftsmen formed guilds, governed by strict rules, which sought to obtain control of the towns. Trade with the East and North intensified, as the major trading towns came together in the Hanseatic League, under the leadership of Lübeck.

Wars and expansion

The German colonisation and the chartering of new towns and villages began into largely Slav-inhabited territories east of the Elbe, such as Bohemia, Silesia, Pomerania, and Livonia (see also Ostsiedlung).

Henry V, great-grandson of Conrad II became Holy Roman Emperor in 1106 upon the death of his father, Henry IV. Henry V's reign was born into a civil war which had continued from his fathers' reign. Hoping to gain complete control over the church inside the Empire, Henry V appointed Adalbert of Saarbruken as archbishop of Mainz in 1111 However, like Becket in England some fifty years later, once appointed as archbishop, Adalbert began to take his position seriously and began to assert the powers of the Church against secular authorities, that is, the Emperor. This precipitated the "Crisis of 1111". Henry, Duke of Bavaria, known as Henry the Proud, became heir to the duchy of Saxony, making him the most powerful lord in the kingdom, as well as the logical successor of Lothair as the Holy Roman Emperor. However in 1137 the magnates turned back to the Hohenstaufen family for a candidate, Conrad III. Conrad III tried to Henry the Proud of his two duchies, leading to war in southern Germany as the Empire divided into two factions. The first faction called themselves the "Welfs" after Henry the Proud's family name which was the ruling dynasty in Bavaria. The other faction was known as the "Waiblings." In this early period, the Welfs generally represented ecclesiastical independence under the papacy plus "particularism" (a strengthening of the local duchies against the central imperial authority). The Waiblings on the other hand stood for control of the Church by a strong central Imperial government.

Between 1152 and 1190, during the reign of Frederick I (Barbarossa), of the Hohenstaufen dynasty, an accommodation was reached with the rival Guelph party by the grant of the duchy of Bavaria to Henry the Lion, duke of Saxony. Austria became a separate duchy by virtue of the Privilegium Minus in 1156. Barbarossa tried to reassert his control over Italy. In 1177 a final reconciliation was reached between the emperor and the Pope in Venice.

In 1180 Henry the Lion was outlawed and Bavaria was given to Otto of Wittelsbach (founder of the Wittelsbach dynasty which was to rule Bavaria until 1918), while Saxony was divided.

From 1184 to 1186 the Hohenstaufen empire under Barbarossa reached its peak in the *Reichsfest* (imperial celebrations) held at Mainz and the marriage of his son Henry in Milan to the Norman princess Constance of Sicily. The power of the feudal lords was undermined by the appointment of "ministerials" (unfree servants of the Emperor) as officials. Chivalry and the court life flowered, leading to a development of German culture and literature (see Wolfram von Eschenbach).

Between 1212 and 1250 Frederick II established a modern, professionally administered state in Sicily. He resumed the conquest of Italy, leading to further conflict with the Papacy. In the Empire, extensive sovereign powers were granted to ecclesiastical and secular princes, leading to the rise of independent territorial states. The struggle with the Pope sapped the Empire's strength, as Frederick II was excommunicated three times. After his death, the Hohenstaufen dynasty fell, followed by an interregnum during which there was no Emperor.

Beginning in 1226 under the auspices of Emperor Frederick II, the Teutonic Knights began their conquest of Prussia after being invited to Chelmno Land by the Polish Duke Konrad I of Masovia. The native Baltic Prussians were conquered and Christianized by the Knights with much warfare, and numerous German towns were established along the eastern shore of the Baltic Sea. From 1300, however, the Empire started to lose territory on all its frontiers.

The failure of negotiations between Emperor Louis IV with the papacy led in 1338 to the declaration at Rhense by six electors to the effect that election by all or the majority of the electors automatically conferred the royal title and rule over the empire, without papal confirmation.

Between 1346 and 1378 Emperor Charles IV of Luxembourg, king of Bohemia, sought to restore the imperial authority.

Around 1350 Germany and almost the whole of Europe were ravaged by the Black Death. Jews were persecuted on religious and economic grounds; many fled to Poland.

Around the middle of the 14th century, the Black Death ravaged Germany and Europe. From the Dance of Death by Michael Wolgemut (1491)

The Golden Bull of 1356 stipulated that in future the emperor was to be chosen by four secular electors (the King of Bohemia, the Count Palatine of the Rhine, the Duke of Saxony, and the Margrave of Brandenburg) and three spiritual electors (the Archbishops of Mainz, Trier, and Cologne).

After the disasters of the 14th century, early-modern European society gradually came into being as a result of economic, religious and political changes. A money economy arose which provoked social discontent among knights and peasants. Gradually, a proto-capitalistic system evolved out of feudalism. The Fugger family gained prominence through commercial and financial activities and became financiers to both ecclesiastical and secular rulers.

The knightly classes found their monopoly on arms and military skill undermined by the introduction of mercenary armies and foot soldiers. Predatory activity by "robber knights" became common. From 1438 the Habsburgs, who controlled most of the southeast of the Empire (more or less modern-day Austria and Slovenia, and Bohemia and Moravia after the death of King Louis II in 1526), maintained a constant grip on the position of the Holy Roman Emperor until 1806 (with the exception of the years between 1742 and 1745). This situation, however, gave rise to increased disunity among the Holy Roman Empires territorial rulers and prevented sections of the country from coming together and forming nations in the manner of France and England.

During his reign from 1493 to 1519, Maximilian I tried to reform the Empire: an Imperial supreme court (*Reichskammergericht*) was established, imperial taxes were levied, the power of the Imperial Diet (*Reichstag*) was increased. The reforms were, however, frustrated by the continued territorial fragmentation of the Empire.

Early modern Germany

Lutheranism

Luther's Seal

Book of Concord

- Apostles' Creed
- Nicene Creed
- Athanasian Creed
- Augsburg Confession
- Apology of the Augsburg Confession
- Luther's Small Catechism
- Luther's Large Catechism
- Smalcald Articles
- Treatise on the Power and Primacy of the Pope
- Formula of Concord

Theology

- Justification
- Law and Gospel
- Sola gratia
- Sola scriptura
- Christology
- Sanctification
- Two Kingdoms
- Priesthood of all believers
- Divine Providence
- Marian theology
- Theology of the Cross
- Sacramental Union

Sacraments & Rites

- The Sacrament of Holy Baptism
- The Sacrament of the Eucharist
- Holy Absolution
- Confirmation
- Holy Matrimony
- Holy Orders
- Anointing of the Sick

Globally

- Confessional Evangelical Lutheran Conference
- International Lutheran Council
- Lutheran World Federation
- List of Lutheran church-bodies

History

- Protestant Reformation
- The start of the Reformation
- Reformation in Denmark-Norway and Holstein
- Reformation in Finland
- Reformation in Germany
- Reformation in Iceland
- Reformation in Sweden
- Lutheran Orthodoxy
- Gnesio-Lutherans
- Pietists
- Haugeans
- Laestadians
- Finnish Awakening
- Old Lutherans
- Neo-Lutherans
- High Church Lutherans
- Confessional Lutherans

Missionaries

- John Campanius
- Bartholomäus Ziegenbalg
- Hans Egede
- Johann Heinrich Callenberg
- Johann Phillip Fabricius
- Paul Henkel
- John Christian Frederick Heyer
- Karl Graul
- Martti Rautanen
- Wilhelm Sihler
- F. C. D. Wyneken
- Hans Paludan Smith Schreuder
- Lars Olsen Skrefsrud
- Ludwig Ingwer Nommensen
- Onesimos Nesib
- Paul Olaf Bodding
- Johann Flierl
- Christian Keyser

Theologians
• Martin Luther
• Wife: Katharina Luther
• Philipp Melanchthon
• Johannes Bugenhagen
• Johannes Brenz
• Justus Jonas
• Lucas Cranach the Elder
• Hans Tausen
• Laurentius Petri
• Olaus Petri
• Mikael Agricola
• Matthias Flacius
• Johann Gerhard
• Abraham Calovius
• Johannes Andreas Quenstedt
• Johann Wilhelm Baier
• David Hollaz
• Henry Muhlenberg
• Lars Levi Læstadius
• Charles Porterfield Krauth
• C. F. W. Walther

Lutheranism portal	

Main articles: Early Modern history of Germany and 18th century history of Germany

see List of states in the Holy Roman Empire for subdivisions and the political structure

Reformation and Thirty Years War

Around the beginning of the 16th century there was much discontent in the Holy Roman Empire caused by abuses such as indulgences in the Catholic Church and a general desire for reform.

In 1515 the Frisian peasants rebellion took place. Led by Pier Gerlofs Donia and Wijard Jelckama, thousands of Frisians (a Germanic race) fought against the suppression of their lands by Charles V. The hostilities ended in 1523 when the remaining leaders were captured and decapitated.

Martin Luther, 1529

In 1517 the Reformation began with the publication of Martin Luther's 95 Theses; he had posted them in the town square, and gave copies of them to German nobles, but it is debated whether he nailed them to the church door in Wittenberg as is commonly said. The list detailed 95 assertions Luther believed to show corruption and misguidance within the Catholic Church. One often cited example, though perhaps not Luther's chief concern, is a condemnation of the selling of indulgences; another prominent point within the 95 Theses is Luther's disagreement both with the way in which the higher clergy, especially the pope, used and abused power, and with the very idea of the pope.

Statue of Pier Gerlofs Donia, self acclaimed "King of all Frisians". Famous rebel and freedom fighter of legendary strength and size.

In 1521 Luther was outlawed at the Diet of Worms. But the Reformation spread rapidly, helped by the Emperor Charles V's wars with France and the Turks. Hiding in the Wartburg Castle, Luther translated the Bible from Latin to German, establishing the basis of the German language.

In 1524 the German Peasants' War broke out in Swabia, Franconia and Thuringia against ruling princes and lords, following the preachings of Reformist priests. But the revolts, which were assisted by war-experienced noblemen like Götz von Berlichingen and Florian Geyer (in Franconia), and by the theologian Thomas Münzer (in Thuringia), were soon repressed by the territorial princes. It is estimated that as many as 100,000 German peasants were massacred during the revolt, usually after the battles had ended. With the protestation of the Lutheran princes at the *Reichstag* of Speyer (1529) and rejection of the Lutheran "Augsburg Confession" at Augsburg (1530), a separate Lutheran church emerged.

From 1545 the Counter-Reformation began in Germany. The main force was provided by the Jesuit order, founded by the Spaniard Ignatius of Loyola. Central and northeastern Germany were by this time almost wholly Protestant, whereas western and southern Germany remained predominantly Catholic. In 1547, Holy Roman Emperor Charles V defeated the Schmalkaldic League, an alliance of Protestant rulers.

The Peace of Augsburg in 1555 brought recognition of the Lutheran faith. But the treaty also stipulated that the religion of a state was to be that of its ruler (Cuius regio, eius religio).

In 1556 Charles V abdicated. The Habsburg Empire was divided, as Spain was separated from the Imperial possessions.

In 1608/1609 the Protestant Union and the Catholic League were formed.

From 1618 to 1648 the Thirty Years' War ravaged in the Holy Roman Empire. The causes were the conflicts between Catholics and Protestants, the efforts by the various states within the Empire to increase their power and the Emperor's attempt to achieve the religious and political unity of the Empire. The immediate occasion for the war was the uprising of the Protestant nobility of Bohemia against the emperor (Defenestration of Prague), but the conflict was widened into a European War by the intervention of King Christian IV of Denmark (1625–29), Gustavus Adolphus of Sweden (1630–48) and France under Cardinal Richelieu, the regent of the young Louis XIV (1635–48). Germany became the main theatre of war and the scene of the final conflict between France and the Habsburgs for predominance in Europe. The war resulted in large areas of Germany being laid waste, a loss of approximately a third of its population, and in a general impoverishment.

The war ended in 1648 with the Peace of Westphalia, signed in Münster and Osnabrück: Imperial territory was lost to France and Sweden and the Netherlands left the Holy Roman Empire after being de facto seceded for 80 years already. The imperial power declined further as the states' rights were increased.

End of the Holy Roman Empire

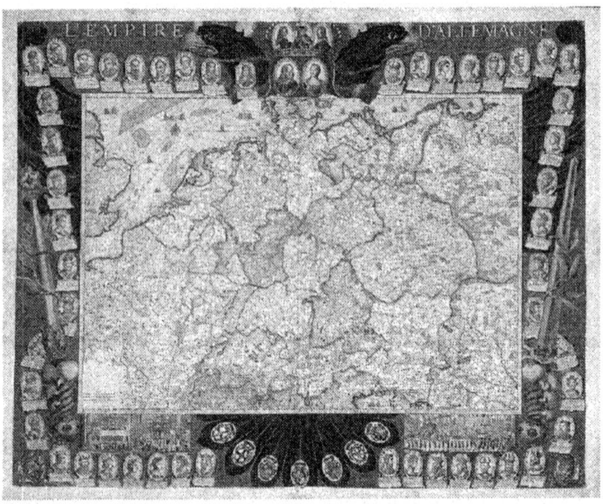

The German Empire in 1705, map "L'Empire d'Allemagne" from Nicolas de Fer

After the Peace of Hubertsburg in 1763, Prussia became a European great power. The rivalry between Prussia and Austria for the leadership of Germany began

From 1640, Brandenburg-Prussia had started to rise under the Great Elector, Frederick William. The Peace of Westphalia in 1648 strengthened it even further, through the acquisition of East Pomerania. A system of rule based on absolutism was established.

In 1701 Elector Frederick of Brandenburg was crowned "King *in* Prussia". From 1713 to 1740, King Frederick William I, also known as the "Soldier King", established a highly centralised state.

Meanwhile Louis XIV of France had conquered parts of Alsace and Lorraine (1678–1681), and had invaded and devastated the Palatinate (1688–1697) in the War of Palatinian Succession. Louis XIV benefited from the Empire's problems with the Turks, which were menacing Austria. Louis XIV ultimately had to relinquish the Palatinate.

In 1683 the Ottoman Turks were defeated outside Vienna by a Polish relief army led by King Jan Sobieski of Poland while the city itself was defended by Imperial and Austrian troops under the command of Charles IV, Duke of Lorraine, accompanied by Prince Eugene of Savoy and elector Maximilian Emanuel of Bavaria, the "liberator of Belgrade". Hungary was reconquered, and later became a new destination for German settlers. Austria, under the Habsburgs, developed into a great power.

In the War of Austrian Succession (1740–1748) Maria Theresa fought successfully for recognition of her succession to the throne. But in the Silesian Wars and in the Seven Years' War she had to cede Silesia to Frederick II, the Great, of Prussia. After the Peace of Hubertsburg in 1763 between Austria, Prussia and Saxony, Prussia became a European great power. This gave the start to the rivalry between Prussia and Austria for the leadership of Germany.

From 1763, against resistance from the nobility and citizenry, an "enlightened absolutism" was established in Prussia and Austria, according to which the ruler was to be "the first servant of the state". The economy developed and legal reforms were undertaken, including the abolition of torture and the improvement in the status of Jews; the emancipation of the peasants slowly began. Education began to be enforced under threat of compulsion.

In 1772-1795 Prussia took part in the partitions of Poland, occupying western territories of Polish-Lithuanian commonwealth, which led to centuries of Polish resistance against German rule and persecution.

The French Revolution began in 1789. In 1792, Prussia and Austria were the first countries to declare war on France. By 1795, the French had overrun the Austrian Netherlands and the left bank of the Rhine and Prussia had dropped out of the war. Austria continued to fight until 1797 when it was defeated by Napoleon Bonaparte in Italy and signed the Treaty of Campo Formio, whereby it gave up Milan and recognised the loss of the Austrian Netherlands and the left bank of the Rhine, but gained Venice.

In 1799, hostilities with France resumed in the War of the Second Coalition. The conflict terminated with the Peace of Luneville in 1801. In 1803, under the *"Reichsdeputationshauptschluss"* (a resolution of a committee of the Imperial Diet meeting in Regensburg), Napoleon abolished almost all the ecclesiastical and the smaller secular states and most of the imperial free cities. New medium-sized states were established in southwestern Germany. In turn, Prussia gained territory in northwestern Germany.

In 1805, the War of the Third Coalition began. The main Austrian army under general Karl Mack was trapped at Ulm by Napoleon and forced to capitulate. The French then occupied Vienna, and routed a combined Austrian and Russian army at Austerlitz in December 1805. Afterwards, Austria ceded Venice and the Tirol to France and recognised the independence of Bavaria.

The Holy Roman Empire was formally dissolved on 6 August 1806 when the last Holy Roman Emperor Francis II (from 1804, Emperor Francis I of Austria) resigned. Francis II's family continued to be called Austrian emperors until 1918. In 1806, the Confederation of the Rhine was established under Napoleon's protection, which comprised all the minor states of Germany.

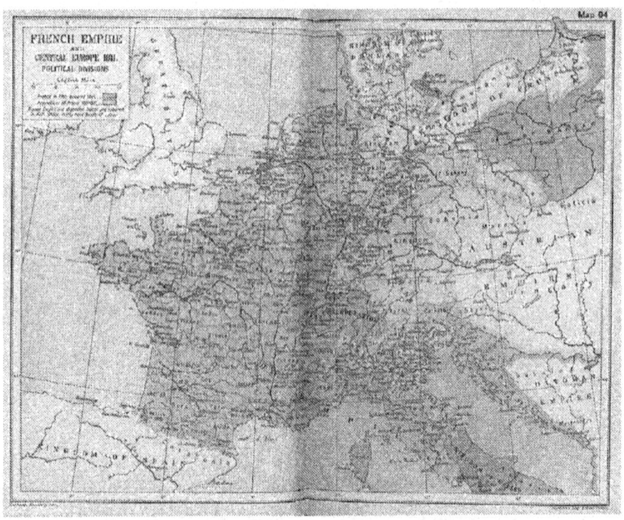

French provinces, kingdoms and dependencies in Germany during the Napoleonic Wars

Prussia now felt threatened by the large concentration of French troops in Germany and demanded their withdrawal. When France refused,

Prussia declared war. The result was a disaster. The Prussian armies were routed at Auerstedt and Jena. The French occupied Berlin and crossed east into Poland. When the Treaty of Tilsit terminated the war, Prussia had lost 40% of its territory, including its recently acquired section of Poland, and had to reduce its army to 45,000 men. There was no popular uprising against the French invasion, and the Prussian populace in fact showed complete apathy.

From 1808 to 1812 Prussia was reconstructed, and a series of reforms were enacted by Freiherr vom Stein and Freiherr von Hardenberg, including the regulation of municipal government, the liberation of the peasants and the emancipation of the Jews. These reforms were designed to encourage the spirit of nationalism in the people and give them something worth fighting for. A reform of the army was undertaken by the Prussian generals Gerhard von Scharnhorst and August von Gneisenau. The army was brought out of the 18th century. Mercenary troops were discarded, and discipline made more humane. Soldiers were encouraged to fight for their country and not merely because a commanding officer told them to.

In 1813 the Wars of Liberation began, following the destruction of Napoleon's army in Russia (1812). After the Battle of the Nations at Leipzig, Germany was liberated from French rule. The Confederation of the Rhine was dissolved.

In 1815 Napoleon was finally defeated at Waterloo by the Britain's Duke of Wellington and by Prussia's Gebhard Leberecht von Blücher. Prussia was considerably expanded after the war, gaining a large part of western Germany, including much of the Rhineland. In the east, it absorbed most of Saxony and also got back some of the Polish territory that had been lost in 1806, although the central part of Poland was left under Russian control.

German Confederation

Restoration and Revolution

Main articles: German Confederation and Revolutions of 1848 in the German states

After the fall of Napoleon, European monarchs and statesmen convened in Vienna in 1814 for the reorganisation of European affairs, under the leadership of the Austrian Prince Metternich. The political principles agreed upon at this Congress of Vienna included the restoration, legitimacy and solidarity of rulers for the repression of revolutionary and nationalist ideas.

Frankfurt 1848

On the territory of the former "Holy Roman Empire of the German Nation", the German Confederation (*Deutscher Bund*) was founded, a loose union of 39 states (35 ruling princes and 4 free cities) under Austrian leadership, with a Federal Diet (*Bundestag*) meeting in Frankfurt am Main. While this was a great improvement over the 300+ political entities that comprised the old Holy Roman Empire, it was still not satisfactory to many nationalists, and within a few decades, the advent of industrialisation made the German Confederation unworkable. Moreover, not everyone was satisfied with Austria's leading role in the Confederation. Some argued that it made sense as Austria had been the most powerful German state for more than 400 years, but others said that it was too much of a polyglot nation to be acceptable for such a role, and that Prussia was the natural leader of Germany.

In 1817, inspired by liberal and patriotic ideas of a united Germany, student organisations gathered for the "Wartburg festival" at Wartburg Castle, at Eisenach in Thuringia, on the occasion of which reactionary books were burnt.

In 1819 the student Karl Ludwig Sand murdered the writer August von Kotzebue, who had scoffed at liberal student organisations. Prince Metternich used the killing as an occasion to call a conference in Karlsbad, which Prussia, Austria and eight other states attended, and which issued the Karlsbad Decrees: censorship was introduced, and universities were put under supervision. The decrees also gave the start to the so-called "persecution of the demagogues", which was directed against individuals who were accused of spreading revolutionary and nationalist ideas. Among the persecuted were the poet Ernst Moritz Arndt, the publisher Johann Joseph Görres and the "Father of Gymnastics" Ludwig Jahn.

In 1834 the Zollverein was established, a customs union between Prussia and most other German states, but excluding Austria. As industrialisation developed, the need for a unified German state with a uniform currency, legal system, and government became more and more obvious.

Growing discontent with the political and social order imposed by the Congress of Vienna led to the outbreak, in 1848, of the March Revolution in the German states. In May the German National Assembly (the Frankfurt Parliament) met in St. Paul's Church in Frankfurt to draw up a national German constitution.

But the 1848 revolution turned out to be unsuccessful: King Frederick William IV of Prussia refused the imperial crown, the Frankfurt parliament was dissolved, the ruling princes repressed the risings by military force and the German Confederation was re-established by 1850.

The 1850s were a period of extreme political reaction. Dissent was vigorously suppressed, and many Germans emigrated to America following the collapse of the 1848 uprisings. Frederick William IV became extremely depressed and melancholy during this period, and was surrounded by men who advocated clericalism and absolute divine monarchy. The Prussian people once again lost interest in politics. In 1857, the king had a stroke and remained incapacitated until his death in 1861. His brother William succeeded him. Although conservative, he was far more pragmatic and rejected the superstitions and mysticism of Frederick.

William I's most significant accomplishment as king was the nomination of Otto von Bismarck as chancellor in 1862. The combination of Bismarck, Defense Minister Albrecht von Roon, and Field Marshal Helmut von Moltke set the stage for the unification of Germany.

In 1863-64, disputes between Prussia and Denmark grew over Schleswig, which - unlike Holstein - was not part of the German Confederation, and which Danish nationalists wanted to incorporate into the Danish kingdom. The dispute led to the Second War of Schleswig, which lasted from February–October 1864. Prussia, joined by Austria, defeated Denmark easily and occupied Jutland. The Danes were forced to cede both the duchy of Schleswig and the duchy of Holstein to Austria and Prussia. In the aftermath, the management of the two duchies caused growing tensions between Austria and Prussia. The former wanted the duchies to become an independent entity within the German Confederation, while the latter wanted to annex them. The Seven Weeks War broke out in June 1866. There was widespread opposition to the war in Prussia, as few believed that Austria could be defeated. On 3 July, the two armies clashed at Sadowa-Koniggratz in Bohemia in an enormous battle involving half a million men. The Prussian breech-loading needle guns carried the day over the Austrians with their slow muzzle-loading rifles, who lost a quarter of their army in the battle. Austria ceded Venice to Italy, but did not lose any other territory and had to only pay a modest war indemnity. The defeat came as a great shock to the rest of Europe, especially France, who's leader Napoleon III had hoped the two countries would exhaust themselves in a long war, after which France would step in and help itself to pieces of German territory. Now the French faced an increasingly strong Prussia.

North German Federation

Main article: North German Federation

In 1866, the German Confederation was dissolved. In its place the North German Federation (German *Norddeutscher Bund*) was established, under the leadership of Prussia. Austria was excluded from it. The Austrian hegemony in Germany that had begun in the 15th century finally came to an end.

The North German Federation was a transitional organisation that existed from 1867 to 1871, between the dissolution of the German Confederation and the founding of the German Empire. The unification of the German states into a single economic, political and administrative unit excluded the Austrian territories and the Habsburgs.

Railways

Main article: History of rail transport in Germany

Political disunity of three dozen states and a pervasive conservatism made it difficult to build railways in the 1830s. However, by the 1840s, trunk lines did link the major cities; each German state was responsible for the lines within its own borders. Economist Friedrich List summed up the advantages to be derived from the development of the railway system in 1841:

1/ as a means of national defence, it facilitates the concentration, distribution and direction of the army.

2/ It is a means to the improvement of the culture of the nation.... It brings talent, knowledge and skill of every kind readily to market.

3/ It secures the community against dearth and famine, and against excessive fluctuation in the prices of the necessaries of life.

4/ It promotes the spirit of the nation, as it has a tendency to destroy the Philistine spirit arising from isolation and provincial prejudice and vanity. It binds nations by ligaments, and promotes an interchange of food and of commodities, thus making it feel to be a unit. The iron rails become a nerve system, which, on the one hand, strengthens public opinion, and, on the other hand, strengthens the power of the state for police and governmental purposes.

Lacking a technological base at first, the Germans imported their engineering and hardware from Britain, but quickly learned the skills needed to operate and expand the railways. In many cities, the new railway shops were the centres of technological awareness and training, so that by 1850, Germany was self sufficient in meeting the demands of railroad construction, and the railways were a major impetus for the growth of the new steel industry. Observers found that even as late as 1890, their engineering was inferior to Britain's. However, German unification in 1870 stimulated consolidation, nationalisation into state-owned companies, and further rapid growth. Unlike the situation in France, the goal was support of industrialisation, and so heavy lines crisscrossed the Ruhr and other industrial districts, and provided good connections to the major ports of Hamburg and Bremen. By 1880, Germany had 9,400 locomotives pulling 43,000 passengers and 30,000 tons of freight, and forged ahead of France

German Empire

Main article: German Empire

After Germany was united by Bismarck into the **Second German Reich,** Bismarck determined German politics until 1890. Bismarck tried to foster alliances in Europe, on one hand to contain France, and on the other hand to consolidate Germany's influence in Europe. On the domestic front Bismarck tried to stem the rise of socialism by anti-socialist laws, combined with an introduction of health care and social security. At the same time Bismarck tried to reduce the political influence of the emancipated Catholic minority in the Kulturkampf, literally "culture struggle". The Catholics only grew stronger, forming the Center (Zentrum) Party. Germany grew rapidly in industrial and economic power, matching Britain by 1900. Its highly professional army was the best in the world, but the navy could never catch up with Britain's Royal Navy.

In 1888, the young and ambitious Kaiser Wilhelm II became emperor. He could not abide advice, least of all from the most experienced politician and diplomat in Europe, so he fired Bismarck. The Kaiser opposed Bismarck's careful foreign policy and wanted Germany to pursue colonialist policies, as Britain and France had been doing for decades, as well as build a navy that could match the British. The Kaiser promoted active colonization of Africa and Asia for those areas that were not already colonies of other European powers; his record was notoriously brutal and set the stage for genocide. The Kaiser took a mostly unilateral approach in Europe with as main ally the Austro-Hungarian Empire, and an arms race with Britain, which eventually led to the situation in which the assassination of the Austrian-Hungarian crown price could spark off World War I.

Age of Bismarck

On 18 January 1871, the German Empire is proclaimed in the Hall of Mirrors of the Palace of Versailles. Bismarck appears in white.

Disputes between France and Prussia increased. In 1868, the Spanish queen Isabella II was expelled by a revolution, leaving that country's throne vacant. When Prussia tried to put a Hohenzollern candidate, Prince Leopold, on the Spanish throne, the French angrily protested. In July 1870, France declared war on Prussia (the Franco-Prussian War). The debacle was swift. A succession of German victories in northeastern France followed, and one French army was besieged at Metz. After a few weeks, the main army was finally forced to capitulate in the fortress of Sedan. French Emperor Napoleon III was taken prisoner and a republic hastily proclaimed in Paris. The new government, realising that a victorious Germany would demand territorial acquisitions, resolved to fight on. They began to muster new armies, and the Germans settled down to a grim siege of Paris. The starving city surrendered in January 1871, and the Prussian army staged a victory parade in it. France was forced to pay indemnities of 5 billion francs and cede Alsace-Lorraine. It was a bitter peace that would leave the French thirsting for revenge.

During the Siege of Paris, the German princes assembled in the Hall of Mirrors of the Palace of Versailles and proclaimed the Prussian King Wilhelm I as the "German Emperor" on 18 January 1871. The German Empire was thus founded, with 25 states, three of which were Hanseatic free cities, and Bismarck, again, served as Chancellor. It was dubbed the "Little German" solution, since Austria was not included. The new empire was characterised by a great enthusiasm and vigor. There was a rash of heroic artwork in imitation of Greek and Roman styles, and the nation possessed a vigorous, growing industrial economy, while it had always been rather poor in the past. The change from the slower, more tranquil order of the old Germany was very sudden, and many, especially the nobility, resented being displaced by the new rich. And yet, the nobles clung stubbornly to power, and they, not the bourgeois, continued to be the model that everyone wanted to imitate. In imperial Germany, possessing a collection of medals or wearing a uniform was valued more than the size of one's bank account, and Berlin never became a great cultural center as London, Paris, or Vienna were. The empire was distinctly authoritarian in tone, as the 1871 constitution gave the emperor exclusive power to appoint or dismiss the chancellor. He also was supreme commander-in-chief of the armed forces and final arbiter of foreign policy. But freedom of speech, association, and religion were nonetheless guaranteed by the constitution.

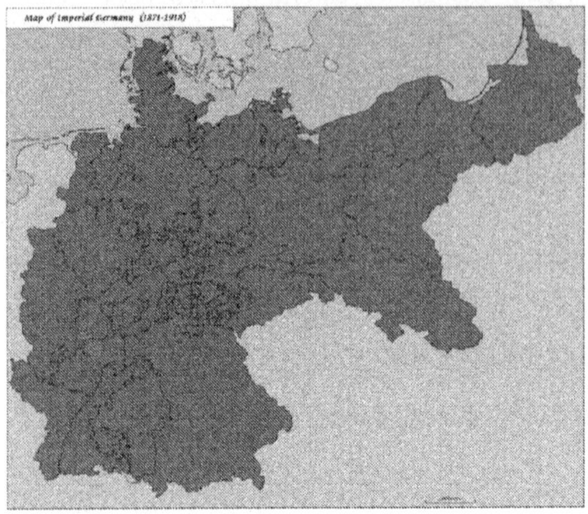

The German Empire of 1871. By excluding Austria, Bismarck chose a "little German" solution.

Otto von Bismarck

Bismarck's domestic policies as Chancellor of Germany were characterised by his fight against perceived enemies of the Protestant Prussian state. In the so-called Kulturkampf (1872–1878), he tried to limit the influence of the Roman Catholic Church and of its political arm, the Catholic Centre Party, through various measures—like the introduction of civil marriage—but without much success. The Kulturkampf antagonised many Protestants as well as Catholics, and was eventually abandoned. Millions of non-Germans subjects in the German Empire, like the Polish, Danish and French minorities, were discriminated against [1][2] and a policy of Germanisation was implemented.

The other perceived threat was the rise of the Socialist Workers' Party (later known as the Social Democratic Party of Germany), whose declared aim was the establishment of a new socialist order through the transformation of existing political and social conditions. From 1878, Bismarck tried to repress the social democratic movement by outlawing the party's organisation, its assemblies and most of its newspapers. Through the introduction of a social insurance system, on the other hand, he hoped to win the support of the working classes for the Empire.

Bismarck's post-1871 foreign policy was conservative and basically aimed at security and preventing the dreaded scenario of a Franco-Russian alliance, which would trap Germany between the two in a war.

The Three Emperor's League (*Dreikaisersbund*) was signed in 1872 by Russia, Austria and Germany. It stated that republicanism and socialism were common enemies and that the three powers would discuss any matters concerning foreign policy. Bismarck needed good relations with Russia in order to keep France isolated. In 1877-1878, Russia fought a victorious war with the Ottoman Empire and attempted to impose the Treaty of San Stefano on it. This upset the British in particular, as they were long concerned with preserving the Ottoman Empire and preventing a Russian takeover of the Bosporous Straits. Germany hosted the Congress of Berlin, whereby a more moderate peace settlement was agreed to. Afterwards, Russia turned its attention eastward to Asia and remained largely inactive in European politics for the next 25 years. Germany had no direct interest in the Balkans however, which was largely an Austrian and Russian sphere of influence, although King Carol of Romania was a German prince.

In 1879, Bismarck formed a Dual Alliance of Germany and Austria-Hungary, with the aim of mutual military assistance in the case of an attack from Russia, which was not satisfied with the agreement reached at the Congress of Berlin.

The establishment of the Dual Alliance led Russia to take a more conciliatory stance, and in 1887, the so-called Reinsurance Treaty was signed between Germany and Russia: in it, the two powers agreed on mutual military support in the case that France attacked Germany, or in case of an Austrian attack on Russia.

In 1882, Italy joined the Dual Alliance to form a Triple Alliance. Italy wanted to defend its interests in North Africa against France's colonial policy. In return for German and Austrian support, Italy committed itself to assisting Germany in the case of a French military attack.

For a long time, Bismarck had refused to give in to Crown Prince Wilhelm II's aspirations of making Germany a world power through the acquisition of German colonies ("a place in the sun", originally a statement of Bernhard von Bülow). Bismarck wanted to avoid tensions between the European great powers that would threaten the security of Germany at all cost. But when, between 1880 and 1885, the foreign situation proved auspicious, Bismarck gave way, and a number of colonies were established overseas: in Africa, these were Togo, the Cameroons, German South-West Africa and German East Africa; in Oceania, they were German New Guinea, the Bismarck Archipelago and the Marshall Islands. In fact, it was Bismarck himself who helped initiate the Berlin Conference of 1885. He did it "establish international guidelines for the acquisition of African territory," (see Colonisation of Africa). This conference was an impetus for the "Scramble for Africa" and "New Imperialism".

In 1888, the old emperor William I died at the age of 90. His son Frederick III, the hope of German liberals, succeeded him, but was already stricken with throat cancer and died three months later. Frederick's son William II then became emperor at the age of 29. He was the antithesis of old, conservative Germans like Bismarck, addicted to the new imperialism that was taking place in Asia and Africa. He sought to make Germany a great world power with a navy to rival Britain's. Bismarck hoped to marginalise him just as he had marginalised his grandfather, but William II was on to Bismarck's tricks, and desired to be his own master. Having a left arm withered by childhood polio, he was painfully insecure and desired above all to be loved by the people. Bismarck's schemes to dominate the emperor and hold onto his own power failed, and he was forced to resign in March 1890. He died in 1898, spending his last years writing his memoirs and attacking William II (despite the latter's attempts at reconciliation).

Wilhelminian Era

Alliances and colonies

Main articles: Triple Alliance (1882) and German colonial empire

When Bismarck resigned, Wilhelm II had declared that he would continue the foreign policy of the old chancellor. But soon, a new course was taken, with the aim of increasing Germany's influence in the world (*Weltpolitik*). The Reinsurance Treaty with Russia was not renewed. Instead, France formed an alliance with Russia, against the Triple Alliance of Germany, Austria-Hungary and Italy. The Triple Alliance itself was undermined by differences between Austria and Italy.

A postage stamp from the Carolines, dating back to the time when the islands were ruled by the German Empire. The new *Weltpolitik* of Kaiser Wilhelm II led to frictions with other imperialist powers.

From 1898, German colonial expansion in East Asia (Jiaozhou Bay, the Marianas, the Caroline Islands, Samoa) led to frictions with the United Kingdom, Russia, Japan and the United States. The construction of the Baghdad Railway, financed by German banks and heavy industry, and aimed at connecting the North Sea with the Persian Gulf via the Bosporus, also collided with British and Russian geopolitical and economic interests.

To protect Germany's overseas trade and colonies, Admiral von Tirpitz started a programme of warship construction in 1898. In 1890, Germany had purchased the island of Heligoland in the North Sea from Britain in exchange for the African island of Zanzibar and proceeded to construct a great naval base there. This posed a direct threat to British hegemony on the seas, with the result that negotiations for an alliance between Germany and Britain broke down. Germany was increasingly isolated. Otto von Bismarck's son Herbert, a member of the Reichstag since 1893, was one of the loudest anti-British voices in Germany until his death in 1904.

In 1905, Germany nearly came to blows with Britain and France when the latter attempted to establish a protectorate over Morocco. The Germans were upset at having not been informed about French intentions, and declared their support for Moroccan independence. William II made a highly provocative speech regarding this. The following year, a conference was held in which all of the European powers except Austria-Hungary (by now little more than a German satellite) sided with France. A compromise was agreed to where the French relinquished some, but not all, control over Morocco.

1911 saw another dispute over Morocco erupt when France tried to suppress a revolt there. Germany, still smarting from the previous quarrel, agreed to a settlement whereby the French ceded some territory in central Africa in exchange for Germany renouncing any right to intervene in Moroccan affairs. This confirmed French control over Morocco, which became a full protectorate of that country in 1912.

World War I and revolution

Main articles: History of Germany during World War I and German Revolution of 1918–19

Imperialist power politics and the determined pursuit of national interests ultimately led to the outbreak in 1914 of the First World War, sparked by the assassination, on 28 June 1914, of the Austrian heir-apparent Franz Ferdinand and his wife at Sarajevo, in the capital of Bosnia and Herzegovina by a Serbian nationalist. The theorised underlying causes have included the opposing policies of the European states, the armaments race, German-British rivalry, the difficulties of the Austro-Hungarian multinational state, Russia's Balkan policy and overhasty mobilisations and ultimatums (the underlying belief being that the war would be short). Germany fought on the side of Austria-Hungary, Bulgaria and the Ottoman Empire against Russia, France, Great Britain, Italy, Japan and several other smaller states. Fighting also spread to the Near East and the German colonies.

In the west, Germany fought a war of attrition with bloody battles. After a quick march through Belgium, German troops were halted on the Marne, north of Paris. The frontlines in France changed little until the end of the war. In the east there were decisive victories against the Russian army, the trapping and defeat of large parts of the Russian contingent at the Battle of Tannenberg, followed by huge Austrian and German successes led to a breakdown of Russian forces and an imposed peace on the newly created USSR under Lenin. Churchill ordered a naval blockade in the North Sea which lasted until 1919, crippling Germany's supplies of raw materials and foodstuffs. The entry of the United States into the war in 1917 following Germany's declaration of *unrestricted submarine warfare* marked a decisive turning-point against Germany.

The end of October 1918, in Kiel, in northern Germany, saw the beginning of the German Revolution of 1918–19. Units of the German Navy refused to set sail for a last, large-scale operation in a war which they saw as good as lost, initiating the uprising. On 3 November, the revolt spread to other cities and states of the country, in many of which so-called workers' and soldiers' councils were established.

Kaiser Wilhelm II and all German ruling princes abdicated. On 9 November 1918, the Social Democrat Philipp Scheidemann proclaimed a Republic. On 11 November, the Compiègne armistice ending the war was signed. In accordance with the Social Democratic government by early 1919 the revolution was violently put down with the aid of the nascent Reichswehr and the Freikorps.

Weimar Republic

Main article: Weimar Republic

States of Germany at the time of the Weimar Republic, with Prussia in blue

On 28 June 1919 the Treaty of Versailles was signed. Germany was to cede Alsace-Lorraine, Eupen-Malmédy, North Schleswig, and the Memel area. All German colonies were to be handed over to the British and French. Poland was restored and most of the provinces of Posen and West Prussia, and some areas of Upper Silesia were reincorporated into the reformed country after plebiscites and independence uprisings. The left and right banks of the Rhine were to be permanently demilitarised. The industrially important Saarland was to be governed by the League of Nations for 15 years and its coalfields administered by France. At the end of that time a plebiscite was to determine the Saar's future status. To ensure execution of the treaty's terms, Allied troops would occupy the left (German) bank of the Rhine for a period of 5–15 years. The German army was to be limited to 100,000 officers and men; the general staff was to be dissolved; vast quantities of war material were to be handed over and the manufacture of munitions rigidly curtailed. The navy was to be similarly reduced, and no military aircraft were allowed. Germany and its allies were to accept the sole responsibility of the war, in accordance with the War Guilt Clause, and were to pay financial reparations for all loss and damage suffered by the Allies.

The humiliating peace terms provoked bitter indignation throughout Germany, and seriously weakened the new democratic regime.

On 11 August 1919 the Weimar constitution came into effect, with Friedrich Ebert as first President.

The two biggest enemies of the new democratic order, however, had already been constituted. In December 1918, the Communist Party of Germany (KPD) was founded, followed in January 1919 by the establishment of the German Workers' Party, later known as the National Socialist German Workers' Party (NSDAP). Both parties would make reckless use of the freedoms guaranteed by the new constitution in their fight against the Weimar Republic.

In the first months of 1920, the Reichswehr was to be reduced to 100,000 men, in accordance with the Treaty of Versailles. This included the dissolution of many Freikorps - units made up of volunteers. Some of them made difficulties.Wikipedia:Please clarify The discontent was exploited by the extreme right-wing politician Wolfgang Kapp. He let the rebelling Freikorps march on Berlin and proclaimed himself *Reich* Chancellor (Kapp Putsch). After only four days the coup d'état collapsed, due to lack of support by the civil servants and the officers. Other cities were shaken by strikes and rebellions, which were bloodily suppressed.

Faced with animosity from Britain and France and the retreat of American power from Europe, in 1922 Germany was the first state to establish diplomatic relations with the new Soviet Union. Under the Treaty of Rapallo, Germany accorded the Soviet Union *de jure* recognition, and the two signatories mutually cancelled all pre-war debts and renounced war claims.

When Germany defaulted on its reparation payments, French and Belgian troops occupied the heavily industrialised Ruhr district (January 1923). The German government encouraged the population of the Ruhr to passive resistance: shops would not sell goods to the foreign soldiers, coal-mines would not dig for the foreign troops, trams in which members of the occupation army had taken seat would be left abandoned in the middle of the street. The passive resistance proved effective, insofar as the occupation became a loss-making deal for the French government. But the Ruhr fight also led to hyperinflation, and many who lost all their fortune would become bitter enemies of the Weimar Republic, and voters of the anti-democratic right. See 1920s German inflation.

In September 1923, the deteriorating economic conditions led Chancellor Gustav Stresemann to call an end to the passive resistance in the Ruhr. In November, his government introduced a new currency, the Rentenmark (later: Reichsmark), together with other measures to stop the hyperinflation. In the following six years the economic situation improved. In 1928, Germany's industrial production even regained the pre-war levels of 1913.

On the evening of 8 November 1923, six hundred armed SA men surrounded a beer hall in Munich, where the heads of the Bavarian state and the local *Reichswehr* had gathered for a rally. The storm troopers were led by Adolf Hitler. Born in 1889 in Austria, a former volunteer in the German army during WWI, now a member of a new party called NSDAP, he was largely unknown until then. Hitler tried to force those present to join him and to march on to Berlin to seize power (Beer Hall Putsch). Hitler was later arrested and condemned to five years in prison, but was released at the end of 1924 after less than one year of detention.

The national elections of 1924 led to a swing to the right (*Ruck nach rechts*). Field Marshal Hindenburg, a supporter of the monarchy, was elected President in 1925.

In October 1925 the Treaty of Locarno was signed between Germany, France, Belgium, the United Kingdom and Italy, which recognised Germany's borders with France and Belgium. Moreover, Britain, Italy and Belgium undertook to assist France in the case that German troops marched into the demilitarised Rheinland. The Treaty of Locarno paved the way for Germany's admission to the League of Nations in 1926.

The stock market crash of 1929 on Wall Street marked the beginning of the Great Depression. The effects of the ensuing world economic crisis were also felt in Germany, where the economic situation rapidly deteriorated. In July 1931, the *Darmstätter und Nationalbank* - one of the biggest German banks - failed, and, in early 1932, the number of unemployed rose to more than 6,000,000.

In addition to the flagging economy came political problems, due to the inability by the political parties represented in the Reichstag to build a governing majority. In March 1930, President Hindenburg appointed Heinrich Brüning Chancellor. To push through his package of austerity measures against a majority of Social Democrats, Communists and the NSDAP, Brüning made use of emergency decrees, and even dissolved Parliament. In March and April 1932, Hindenburg was re-elected in the German presidential election of 1932.

Of the many splinter parties the NSDAP was the largest in the national elections of 1932. The Prussian government had been ousted by a coup (Preussenschlag) in 1932. On 31 July 1932 the NSDAP had received 37.3% of the votes, and in the election on 6 November 1932 it received less, but still the largest share, 33.1, making it the biggest party in the Reichstag. The Communist KPD came third, with 15%. Together, the anti-democratic parties of right and left were now able to hold the majority of seats in Parliament. The NSDAP was particularly successful among young voters, who were unable to find a place in vocational training, with little hope for a future job; among the *petite bourgeoisie* (lower middle class) which had lost its assets in the hyperinflation of 1923; among the rural population; and among the army of unemployed.

On 30 January 1933, pressured by former Chancellor Franz von Papen and other conservatives, President Hindenburg finally appointed Hitler Chancellor.

Weimar Republic Results of Elections 1919-1933 [3], Electiontions 1932, 1933 [4]

Third Reich

Main articles: Nazi Germany, The Holocaust, and Military history of Germany during World War II

Nazi revolution or "Seizure of Power"

In order to secure a majority for his NSDAP in the Reichstag, Hitler called for new elections. On the evening of 27 February 1933, a fire was set in the Reichstag building. Hitler swiftly blamed an alleged Communist uprising, and convinced President Hindenburg to sign the Reichstag Fire Decree. This decree, which would remain in force until 1945, repealed important political and human rights of the Weimar constitution. Communist agitation was banned, but at this time not the Communist Party itself.

Eleven thousand Communists and Socialists were arrested and brought into concentration camps, where they were at the mercy of the Gestapo, the newly established secret police force (9,000 were found guilty and most executed). Communist Reichstag deputies were taken into *protective custody* (despite their constitutional privileges).

Despite the terror and unprecedented propaganda, the last free General Elections of 5 March 1933, while resulting in 43.9% failed to bring the majority for the NSDAP that Hitler had hoped for. Together with the German National People's Party (DNVP), however, he was able to form a slim majority government. With accommodations to the Catholic Centre Party, Hitler succeeded in convincing a required two-thirds of a rigged Parliament to pass the Enabling act of 1933 which gave his government full legislative power. Only the Social Democrats voted against the Act. The Enabling Act formed the basis for the dictatorship, dissolution of the Länder; the trade unions and all political parties other than the National Socialist (Nazi) Party were suppressed. A centralised totalitarian state was established, no longer based on the liberal Weimar constitution. Germany left the League of Nations. The coalition parliament was rigged on this fateful 23 March 1933 by defining the absence of arrested and murdered deputies as voluntary and therefore cause for their exclusion as wilful absentees. Subsequently in July the Centre Party was voluntarily dissolved in a *quid pro quo* with the Holy See under the *anti-communist* Pope Pius XI for the Reichskonkordat; and by these manoeuvres Hitler achieved movement of these Catholic voters into the Nazi party, and a long-awaited international diplomatic acceptance of his regime. It is interesting to note however that according to Professor Dick Geary the Nazis gained a larger share of their vote in Protestant than in Catholic areas of Germany in elections held between 1928 to November 1932 The Communist Party was proscribed in April 1933 . On the weekend of 30 June 1934, he gave order to the SS to seize Röhm and his lieutenants, and to execute them without trial (known as the Night of the Long Knives). Upon Hindenburg's death on 2 August 1934, Hitler's cabinet passed a law proclaiming the presidency vacant and transferred the role and powers of the head of state to Hitler as Führer und Reichskanzler (leader and chancellor).

However, many leaders of the Nazi SA were disappointed. The Chief of Staff of the SA, Ernst Röhm, was pressing for the SA to be incorporated into the Wehrmacht under his supreme command. Hitler felt threatened by these plans.

The SS became an independent organisation under the command of the *Reichsführer SS* Heinrich Himmler. He would become the supervisor of the *Gestapo* and of the concentration camps, soon also of the ordinary police. Hitler also established the Waffen-SS as a separate troop.

The regime showed particular hostility towards the Jews. In September 1935, the Reichstag passed the so-called Nuremberg race laws directed against Jewish citizens. Jews lost their German citizenship, and were banned from marrying non-Jewish Germans. About 500,000 individuals were affected by the new rules.

Hitler re-established the German air force and reintroduced universal military service. The open rearmament was in flagrant breach of the Treaty of Versailles, but neither the United Kingdom, France or Italy went beyond issuing notes of protest.

In 1936 German troops marched into the demilitarised Rhineland. In this case, the Treaty of Locarno would have obliged the United Kingdom to intervene in favour of France. But despite protests by the French government, Britain chose to do nothing about it. The coup strengthened Hitler's standing in Germany. His reputation was going to increase further with the 1936 Summer Olympics, which were held in the same year in Berlin and in Garmisch-Partenkirchen, and which proved another great propaganda success for the regime.

Expansion and defeat

After establishing the "Rome-Berlin axis" with Mussolini, and signing the Anti-Comintern Pact with Japan - which was joined by Italy a year later in 1937 - Hitler felt able to take the offensive in foreign policy. On 12 March 1938, German troops marched into Austria, where an attempted Nazi coup had been unsuccessful in 1934. When Hitler entered Vienna, he was greeted by loud cheers. Four weeks later, 99% of Austrians voted in favour of the annexation (Anschluss) of their country to the German Reich. Hitler thereby fulfilled the old idea of an all encompassing German Reich with the inclusion of Austria - the "greater Germany" solution that Bismarck had shunned when, in 1871, he united the German-speaking lands under Prussian leadership. Although the annexation denounced the Treaty of Saint-Germain, which expressedly forbade the unification of Austria with Germany, the western powers once again merely protested.

After Austria, Hitler turned to Czechoslovakia, where the 3.5 million-strong Sudeten German minority was demanding equal rights and self-government. At the Munich Conference of September 1938, Hitler, the Italian leader Benito Mussolini, British Prime Minister Neville Chamberlain and French Prime Minister Édouard Daladier agreed upon the cession of Sudeten territory to the German Reich by Czechoslovakia. Hitler thereupon declared that all of German Reich's territorial claims had been fulfilled. However, hardly six months after the Munich Agreement, in March 1939, Hitler used the smoldering quarrel between Slovaks and Czechs as a pretext for taking over the rest of Czechoslovakia as the Protectorate of Bohemia and Moravia. In the same month, he secured the return of Memel from Lithuania to Germany. British Prime Minister Neville Chamberlain was forced to acknowledge that his policy of appeasement towards Hitler had failed.

In six years, the Nazi regime prepared the country for World War II. The Nazi leadership attempted to remove or subjugate the Jewish population of Nazi Germany and later in the occupied countries through forced deportation and, ultimately, genocide now known as the Holocaust. A similar policy applied to the various ethnic and national groups considered subhuman such as Poles , Roma or Russians. These groups were seen as threats to the purity of Germany's Aryan race. There were also many groups, such as homosexuals, the mentally handicapped and those who were physically challenged from birth, which were singled out as being detrimental to Aryan purity. After annexing the Sudetenland border country of Czechoslovakia (October 1938), and taking over the rest of the Czech lands as a protectorate (March 1939), the German Reich and the Soviet Union invaded Poland on first September 1939 predominantly as part of the Wehrmacht operation codenamed *Fall Weiss*. The invasion of Poland began World War II.

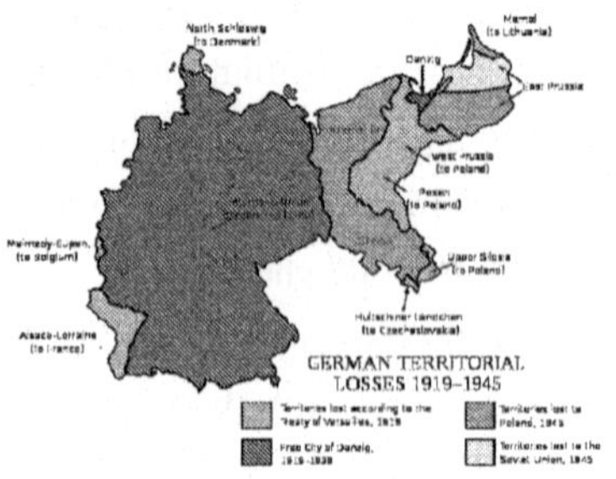

Territorial losses of modern Germany 1919-1945.

By 1941, the Germans had the upper hand, but the tide turned in December 1941 when the invasion of the Soviet Union stalled in front of Moscow and the United States joined the war. Because of the invasion (see Operation Barbarossa), the Soviets joined the Allies. The tide turned further after the Battle of Stalingrad. By late 1944, the United States and Great Britain were closing in on Germany in the West, while the Soviets were closing from the East. In May 1945, Nazi Germany collapsed when Berlin was taken by the Red Army in May, 1945, after a fight to the death in the city streets. Hitler committed suicide.

By September 1945, the German Reich (which lasted only 13 years) and its Axis partners (Italy and Japan) had been defeated, chiefly by the forces of the Soviet Union, the United States, and the United Kingdom. Much of Europe lay in ruins, over sixty million people had been killed (most of them civilians), including approximately six million Jews and five million non-Jews in what became known as the Holocaust. World War II resulted in the destruction of Germany's political and economic infrastructure and led directly to its partition, considerable loss of territory (especially in the east), and historical legacy of guilt and shame.

Germany since 1945

Main article: History of Germany since 1945

Post-war state

Main articles: Partitions of Germany, Potsdam Agreement, and Expulsion of Germans

Germans frequently refer to 1945 as the *Stunde Null* (zero hour) to describe the near-total collapse of their country. At the Potsdam Conference, Germany was divided into four military occupation zones by the Allies. Also in Potsdam, the allies agreed that the provinces east of the Oder and Neisse rivers (the Oder-Neisse line) were transferred to Poland and Russia (Kaliningrad oblast). The agreement also set forth the abolition of Prussia and the expulsion of Germans living in those territories, and formalised the German exodus from Eastern Europe. In the process of the expulsions, millions died, and many suffered from exhaustion and dehydration.

In the immediate post-war years the German population lived on near starvation levels, and the Allied economic policy was one of de-industrialisation (Morgenthau Plan) in order to preclude any future German war-making capability. U.S. policy began to change at the end of 1946 (Restatement of Policy on Germany), and by mid 1947, after lobbying by the Joint Chiefs of Staff, and Generals Clay and Marshall, the Truman administration finally realised that economic recovery in Europe could not go forward without the reconstruction of the German industrial base on which it had previously been dependent. In July, Truman rescinded on "national security grounds" the punitive JCS 1067, which had directed the U.S. forces of occupation in Germany to "take no steps looking toward the economic rehabilitation of Germany." It was replaced by JCS 1779, which instead stressed that "[a]n orderly, prosperous Europe requires the economic contributions of a stable and productive Germany."

Division into East and West Germany

Main articles: East Germany, History of East Germany, and West Germany

Further information: Inner German border and Berlin Wall

The three western occupation zones (U.S., UK and French zone) would later form the **Federal Republic of Germany** (commonly known as West Germany), while the Soviet zone became the **German Democratic Republic** (commonly known as East Germany), both founded in 1949. West Germany was established as a federal democratic republic while East Germany became a communist state under the influence of the Soviet Union.

West Germany eventually came to enjoy prolonged economic growth beginning in the early 1950s (*Wirtschaftswunder*). The recovery occurred largely because of the previously forbidden currency reform of June 1948 and to a minor degree by U.S. assistance through Marshall Plan loans. West Germany joined NATO in 1955 and was a founding member of the European Economic Community in 1958 .

East Germany was an Eastern bloc state under political and military control of the USSR through her occupation forces and the Warsaw Treaty. While claiming to be a democracy, the political power was solely executed by leading members (*Politburo*) of the communist-controlled SED (*Socialist Unity Party of Germany*). Their power was ensured by the Stasi, a secret service of immense size, and a variety of SED-suborganizations controlling every aspect of society. In turn, the basic needs of the population were satisfied at low costs by the state. A Soviet-style command economy was set up, later the GDR became the most advanced Comecon state. While East German propaganda was based on the benefits of the GDR's social programs and the alleged constant threat of a West German invasion, many of her citizens looked to the West for political freedoms and economic prosperity. The Berlin Wall, built in 1961 to stop East Germans from escaping to West Germany, became a symbol of the Cold War.

Reunification

Main article: German Reunification

Demolition of Berlin Wall, January 1990

Relations between the two post-war German states remained icy until the West German Chancellor Willy Brandt launched a highly controversial rapprochement with the East European communist states (*Ostpolitik*) in the 1970s, culminating in the Warschauer Kniefall on 7 December 1970. Although anxious to relieve serious hardships for divided families and to reduce friction, West Germany under Brandt's *Ostpolitik* was intent on holding to its concept of "two German states in one German nation." Relations improved, however, and in September 1973, East Germany and West Germany were admitted to the United Nations.

During the summer of 1989, rapid changes known as *peaceful revolution* or *Die Wende* took place in East Germany, which ultimately led to German reunification. Growing numbers of East Germans emigrated to West Germany, many via Hungary after Hungary's reformist government opened its borders. Thousands of East Germans also tried to reach the West by staging sit-ins at West German diplomatic facilities in other East European capitals, most notably in Prague. The exodus generated demands within East Germany for political change, and mass demonstrations in several cities continued to grow.

Faced with civil unrest, East German leader Erich Honecker was forced to resign in October, and on 9 November, East German authorities unexpectedly allowed East German citizens to enter West Berlin and West Germany. Hundreds of thousands of people took advantage of the opportunity; new crossing points were opened in the Berlin Wall and along the border with West Germany. This led to the acceleration of the process of reforms in East Germany that ended with the German reunification that came into force on 3 October 1990.

Recent history (1990 to present)

Further information: politics of Germany and New states of Germany

After 16 years of the Christian liberal coalition of Helmut Kohl, the Social Democrats together with the Greens won the elections of 1998. SPD leader Gerhard Schröder positioned himself as a centrist "Third Way" candidate in the mold of Britain's Tony Blair and America's Bill Clinton. In 2003, Schröder announced massive labor market reforms, called Agenda 2010, that among other measures include a shakeup of the system of German job offices, commonly known by the name of the chairman of the commission which conceived them as Hartz. From 2005 to 2009, Germany was ruled by a grand coalition led by Angela Merkel as chancellor. Since the 2009 elections, Merkel has headed a centre-right government of the Christian Social Union and the Free Democratic Party.

German chancellor Angela Merkel (with José Barroso in front of the Brandenburg Gate in 2007) was pivotal in drafting and promoting the Treaty of Lisbon to reform the EU.

Together with France and other EU states, the new Germany has played the leading role in the European Union. Germany (especially under Chancellor Helmut Kohl) was one of the main supporters of the wish of many East European countries to join the EU. Germany is at the forefront of European states seeking to exploit the momentum of monetary union to advance the creation of a more unified and capable European political, defence and security apparatus. The German chancellor Schröder expressed an interest in a permanent seat for Germany in the UN Security Council, identifying France, Russia and Japan as countries that explicitly backed Germany's bid.

The German Bundeswehr since 1990 has participated in a number of peacekeeping and disaster relief operations abroad. Since 2002, German troops formed part of the International Security Assistance Force in the war in Afghanistan, resulting in the first German casualties in combat missions since World War II.

Sonderweg debate

Main article: Sonderweg

A major historiographical debate about the German history concerns the *Sonderweg*, the alleged "special path" that separated German history from the normal course of historical development, and whether or not Nazi Germany was the inevitable result of the *Sonderweg*. Proponents of the *Sonderweg* theory such as Fritz Fischer point to such events of the Revolution of 1848, the authoritarian of the Second Empire and the continuation of the Imperial elite into the Weimar and Nazi periods. Opponents such as Gerhard Ritter of the *Sonderweg* theory argue that proponents of the theory are guilty of seeking selective examples, and there was much contingency and chance in German history. In addition, there was much debate within the supporters of the *Sonderweg* concept as for the reasons for the *Sonderweg*, and whether or not the *Sonderweg* ended in 1945.

Terminology related to Germany

The **terminology** for **Germany**, the German states and Germans is complicated due to the complicated history of Germany. This can cause confusions, in German, English as well in other languages. While the notion of *Germans* and *Germany* is older, only since 1871 there is a nation state called Germany. Later political quarrels and the partition of Germany (1945-1990) made it difficult to use the proper term.

Stamp in occupied Germany, 1946: the neutral expression *Deutsche Post* instead of *Deutsche Reichspost*, but still the old currency RM (Reichsmark).

Pre-modern Germany

Further information: Germania and Theodiscus

Roman authors registered a number of tribes they called *Germani*; it is not certain what this word means or where it comes from. Originally it may not even have something to do with ethnics, and these *Germanic* tribes did not call themselves *Germani*. Later these tribes where identified by linguists as belonging to a group of languages, the Germanic languages which include modern languages like German, English and Dutch.

Germani (for the people) and *Germania* (for the area where they lived) became the common Latin words for Germans and Germany.

Germans call themselves *Deutsche* living in *Deutschland. Deutsch* is an adjective (Proto-Germanic *theudisk-) derived from Old High German *thiota, diota* (Proto-Germanic *theudō) meaning "people", "nation", "folk". The word *theudō was distantly related to Celtic *teutā, whence the Celtic tribal name Teuton, later anachronistically applied to the Germans.

In the Late Medieval and Early Modern period, Germany and Germans were kown as *Almany* and *Almains* in English, via Old French *alemaigne, alemans* derived from the name of the Alamanni and Alemannia. These English terms were obsolete by the 18th century.

Germany until 1871

A modern German nation state exists only since 1871 (see Unification of Germany), before that *Germany* referred to a geographical entity.

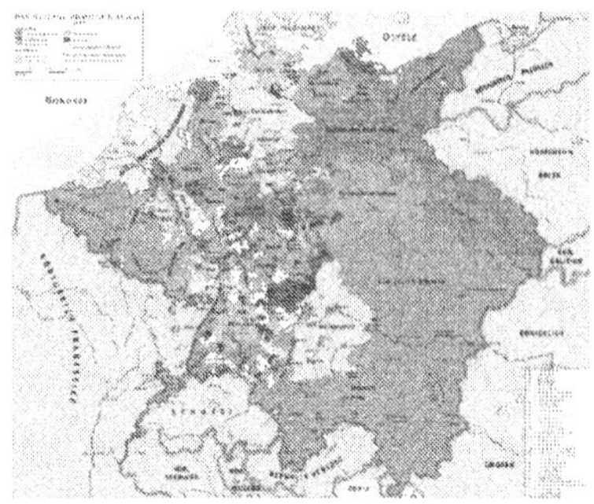

The Holy Roman Empire in 1789

In the Middle Ages, the territory of modern Germany belonged to the realm of the Holy Roman Empire, the Roman Empire restored by the Christian king of Francony, Charlemagne. This feudal state became a union of relatively independent rulers who developed their own territories; modernisation took place on the level of these territories like Austria, Prussia and Bremen, not on the level of the Empire.

This Empire was called in German *Heiliges Römisches Reich*, since the late Middle Ages with the addition *Deutscher Nation* (of German nation), showing that in the meanwhile the former idea of a universal realm has given place to a concentration on the German territories. The last Emperor lay off the crown in 1806 under pressure of Napoléon.

In the 19th and 20th century historiography, this Empire has been often referred to as *Deutsches Reich*, creating a link to the later nation state of 1871. Besides the official *Heiliges Römisches Reich Deutscher Nation*, common expressions are *Altes Reich* (the old Reich) and *Römisch-Deutsches Kaiserreich* (Roman-German Empire of the Emperor).

Reich and Bund

Further information: Reich

In German constitutional history, the expressions *Reich* (reign, realm, empire) and *Bund* (federation, confederation) are quite exchangeable. Sometimes they even existed in the same constitution, like when in the German Empire (1871–1919) the parliament had the name *Reichstag*, the council of the representatives of the German states *Bundesrath*. When in 1871 the North German Confederation was transformed into the German Empire, the preamble said that the participating monarchs are creating *einen ewigen Bund* (an eternal confederation).

Due to the history of Germany, the principle of federalism is strong. Only the state of Hitler (1933–1945) and the state of the communists (East Germany, 1949–1990) were centralist states. This makes the words *Reich* and *Bund* used more frequently than in other countries, because politicians and citizens had and have to differentiate between an imperial or federal level on the one hand and the subnational territorial level on the other. For example, a modern day German minister is called in German *Bundesminister*, in contrary to a *Landesminister* in e.g. Rhineland-Palatinate or Lower Saxony.

Because of the Hitler regime, partially also because of the Imperial Germany until 1919, many Germans - especially on the left - have negative feelings about the word *Reich*. However, it remains a common word such as in *Römisches Reich* (Roman Empire), *Königreich* (Kingdom) or *Tierreich* (animal kingdom).

Also *Bund* is a general word used for contexts other than politics. Many associations in Germany are federations or have a federalised structure and differentiate between a *Bundesebene* (federal / national level) and a *Landesebene* (level of the regional states), similar to the political bodies. An example is the German Football Association *Deutscher Fußballbund*. (Its *Bundestrainer*, the national coach, does not refer to the Federal Republic, but to the Fußball*bund* itself.)

In other German speaking countries, the words *Reich* (Austria before 1918) and *Bund* (Austria since 1918, Switzerland) are used too. An organ called *Bundesrat* exists in all three of them, in Switzerland it is the government and in Germany and Austria the house of regional representatives.

Name of the state	National Diet	House of regional representatives
Heiliges Deutsches Reich Deutscher Nation (-1806)	(did not exist)	(Immerwährender) Reichstag
Deutscher Bund (1815-1848/1866)	(did not exist)	Bundestag (officially Bundesversammlung)
Deutsches Reich (Paulskirchenverfassung, 1849)	Reichstag (Volkshaus)	Reichstag (Staatenhaus)
Norddeutscher Bund (1866/1867-1871)	Reichstag	Bundesrat
Deutsches Reich (1871–1919)	Reichstag	Bundesrat
Deutsches Reich (1919–1933/1945)	Reichstag	Reichsrat
Bundesrepublik Deutschland (1949-)	Bundestag	Bundesrat

19th century until 1871

The French emperor Napoleon made the Emperor of Austria step down as Emperor of the Holy Roman Empire. Some of the German countries were collected in the Confederation of the Rhine, which remained a military alliance under the "protection" of Napoleon rather than transforming into a confederation. In 1815, after the fall of Napoleon, the German states created a German Confederation with the Emperor of Austria as president. Some member states like Prussia and Austria had only a part of their territories inside the Confederation. Within the Confederation and in other territories belonging to member states lived some people who did not have German as their native tongue, for example Poles and Czechs. On the other hand, some German speaking populations lived outside the confederation.

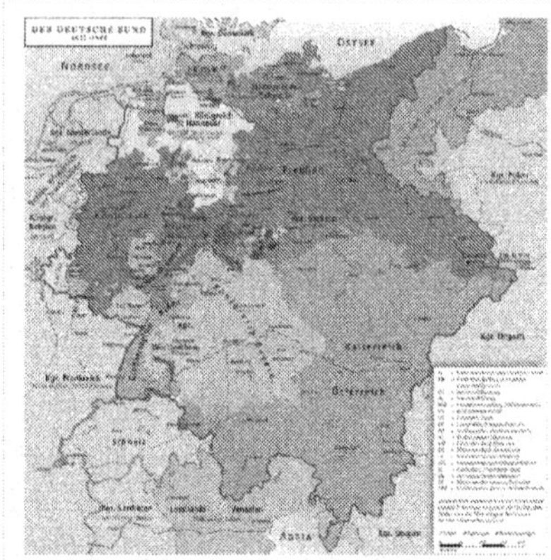

German Confederation, 1815-1866

When Hoffmann von Fallersleben in 1841 wrote the song *Das Lied der Deutschen*, he dreamt of a unified Germany (*Deutschland über Alles*) instead of the single states. Germany was still merely a geographical term.

In 1866/1867 Prussia and her allies left the confederation, made the confederation dissolute and created a state called North German Confederation. The remaining South German countries joined the new confederation in 1870, with the exception of Austria and Liechtenstein. Since then exists a state that is called the German nation state or simply *Germany*, although huge German speaking populations remained outside Germany.

German nation state 1871-1945

The official name of the German state became *Deutsches Reich*, linking itself to the former *Reich* before 1806. This expression was commonly used in official papers and also on maps, while in other contexts *Deutschland* was more frequently used.

Germany (Deutsches Reich) 1871-1918.

The creation of a German nation state had as a consequence that some Germans lived inside of it and were called *Reichsdeutsche*, and others lived outside and were called *Volksdeutsche* (ethnical Germans). The latter expression referred mainly to the German speaking minorities in Eastern Europe. Germans living abroad (for example in America) were and are called *Auslandsdeutsche*.

After the forced abdication of the Emperor in 1918, Germany became the Weimar Republic, named after the city where the National Assembly gathered. The official name of the state remained the same. It became necessary to find a proper term for the Germany between 1871 and 1919: *Kaiserliches Deutschland* (Imperial Germany) or *Deutsches Kaiserreich*. English speaking people feel an unease to use the title *German Empire* for a republic, that made them call the republic *German Reich*.

Germany (Deutsches Reich) 1919-1937.

Nazi Germany

German stamp of 1941

When Hitler was elected into power in 1933, the name of the state was still the same. For a couple of years Hitler used the expression *Drittes Reich* (Third Reich), which was introduced by conservative antidemocratic writers in the last years of the republic. In fact this was only a propaganda term and did not constitute a new state. Another propaganda term was *Tausendjähriges Reich* (Reich of thousand years). Later Hitler renounced the term *Drittes Reich* (officially in June 1939), but it already had become popular among supporters and opponents and is still used in historiography (sometimes in quotation marks). It led later to the name *Zweites Reich* (Second Empire) for Germany of 1871-1919.

The reign of Hitler is most commonly called in English *Nazi Germany*.

There are cases in which an uncertainty comes up whether to use *German* or *Nazi*. In the discussions a major role have arguments dealing with the question of the position of national socialism in Germany of the era 1933-1945. Talking about World War II, some find it unappropriate to say that *the Germans decided to invade Yugoslavia* or *Germany murdered the Jews of Poland*, as Germany was no democracy. The use of *Nazi*, such as in *Nazi troops*, can be confusing or incorrect considering that the German army itself was not national socialist, and that there were indeed troops of the party, especially the *Waffen-SS*. A wording considered by others as improper can cause the accusation of being apologetic.

Greater Germany and "Großdeutsches Reich"

In the 19th century the German politicians, for example in the Frankfurt Parliament of 1848/49, argued about the question what should become of Austria. In the Austrian Empire then lived not only German speaking people, but also Czechs (even on the territory considered part of the German Confederation), Hungarians and others. Including Austria (at least the German speaking parts) was called the *Greater German Solution*, a Germany without Austria the *Smaller German Solution*.

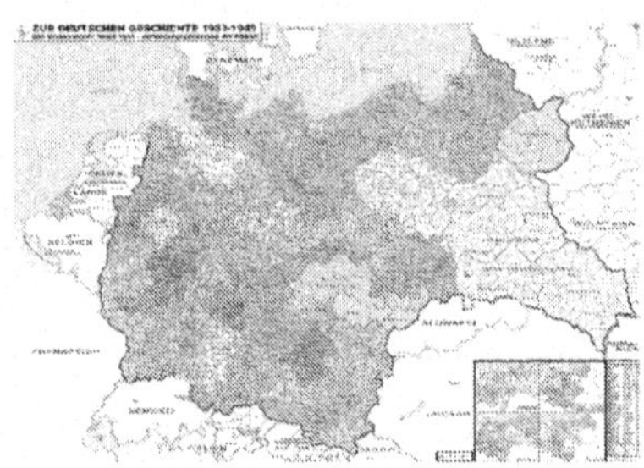
Nazi Germany in 1944

After 1871, the notion *Germany* did no longer include automatically Austria. In 1919 the Weimar Constitution postulated the inclusion of *Deutsch-Österreich* (the German speaking parts of Austria), but the Western Allies objected to this. This was granted only in 1938 to Hitler (*Anschluss*). The national socialist propaganda stated the realisation of Großdeutschland, and in 1943 the German Reich was renamed officially *Großdeutsches Reich*. However, these expressions never became common and popular.

In national socialist propaganda Austria has been called also *Ostmark*. After the *Anschluss* the previous parts of Germany were called *Altreich* (old Reich).

Germany divided 1945-1990

After the defeat in World War II, Germany was occupied by the troops of Britain, France, the United States and Soviet Union.

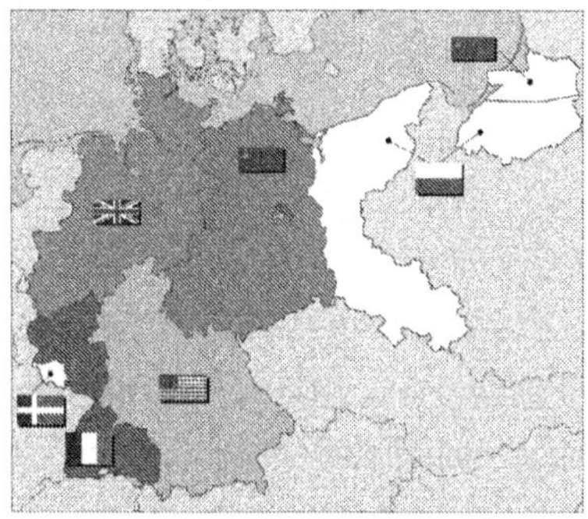

Occupied Germany in 1947, with western (green, blue and yellow) and eastern (red) occupation zones.

Berlin was a case of its own, as it was situated on the territory of the Soviet zone but divided into four sectors. The western sectors were later called West Berlin, the other one East Berlin. The communists tended to consider the Soviet sector of Berlin as a part of GDR; West Berlin was according to them an independent political unit.

The name *Deutsches Reich* was still in use for a couple of years; when in 1947 the Social Democrats gathered in Nuremberg, they called their rally *Reichsparteitag*. In many contexts people still called their country *Germany*, even after two German states were founded in 1949, for example when someone emigrated from Germany to Canada or a bicycle race went through Germany, Poland and Czechoslovakia.

Federal Republic of Germany

The Federal Republic of Germany, *Bundesrepublik Deutschland*, established in 1949, saw itself as the same state founded in 1867/1871, only under a new name and with a new constitution. The expression *Reich* gave place to *Bund*, for example the *Reichskanzler* became the *Bundeskanzler*, *reichsdeutsch* became *bundesdeutsch*, *Reichsbürger* (citizen of the *Reich*) became *Bundesbürger*.

Germany as a whole was called *Gesamtdeutschland*, referring to Germany in the international borders of 1937 (before Hitler started to annex other countries). This could cause confusions internationally (*all German*, *pan germanique*, a chauvinist concept), and in 1969 the Federal Ministry for All German Affairs was renamed into Federal Ministry for Intra-German Relations.

Until for about 1970, the other German state - communist German Democratic Republic - was called *Sowjetische Besatzungszone* (SBZ, Soviet Zone of Occupation), *Sowjetzone*, *Ostzone*, *Mitteldeutschland* or *Pankow* (the GDR government was in Berlin-Pankow).

The term *Westdeutschland* was relatively unusual, because it could mean not only the Federal Republic, but also specific regions in the West of the Federal Republic of Germany.

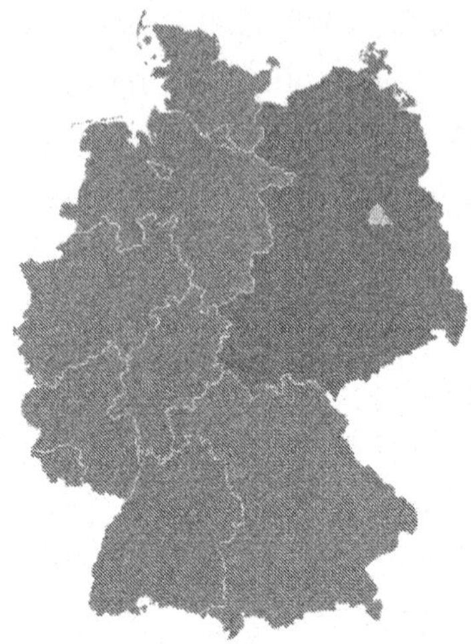

The Federal Republic in blue, GDR in red and West Berlin in yellow, 1949-1990

German Democratic Republic

The communists, protected by Soviet Union, established in 1949 a *Deutsche Demokratische Republik* (DDR, German Democratic Republic, GDR). This state was not considered to be a successor of the Reich, but, nevertheless, to represent all *good Germans*. Rulers and inhabitants of GDR called their state simply DDR or *unsere Republik* (our republic).

Until for about 1970, the GDR still supported the idea a German nation and the need of reunification. The Federal Republic was often called *Westdeutschland* or BRD. After 1970 the GDR called itself a *socialist state of German nation.*

Reunified Germany since 1990

In 1990 the re-established regional states of GDR joined the Federal Republic, and Germany was reunified. Keeping the official name of the *Federal Republic of Germany*, i.e. "Bundesrepublik Deutschland", the country was now being referred to more often simply as "Germany". "Westdeutschland" and "Ostdeutschland" are used more frequently to denote the western and the eastern part of the German territory:

- *Westdeutschland* is also called "alte Bundesrepublik", or "alte Bundesländer" (old regional states)
- *Ostdeutschland* is also called "neue Bundesländer" (new regional states) or "ehemalige DDR" (former GDR)

Although the formal reunification was officially completed on 3 October 1990, the "inner reunification" of the formerly divided country is still an ongoing process to this very day.

Historians

- Johann Gustav Droysen (1808–1884)
- Johann Gottlieb Fichte (1762–1814)
- Johann Gottfried Herder (1744–1803)
- Karl Lamprecht (1856–1945)
- Gottfried Leibniz (1646–1716)
- Karl Marx (1818–1883)
- Samuel von Pufendorf (1632–1694)
- Leopold von Ranke (1795–1886)
- Friedrich Carl von Savigny (1779–1861)
    - German Historical School
- Beatus Rhenanus (also known as Beatus Bild) (1485–1547)
- Heinrich von Treitschke (1834–1896)

20th century scholars in Germany

- Martin Broszat, Nazi era
- Werner Conze
- Fritz Fischer - World War I
- Klaus Hildebrand
- Andreas Hillgruber
- Eberhard Jäckel -Nazi era
- Jürgen Kocka - Bielefeld school; scoial history
- Hartmut Kaelble
- Friedrich Meinecke (1862–1954)
- Hans Mommsen
- Wolfgang Mommsen
- Ernst Nolte
- Detlev Peukert
- Gerhard Ritter
- Oswald Spengler - world history
- Michael Sturmer -20c; geography
- Klemens von Klemperer - Nazi era
- Hans-Ulrich Wehler Bielefeld School; new social history; 19c
- Michael Wolffsohn
- Rainer Zitelmann - Nazi era

outside Germany

- Thomas Carlyle (1795–1881) Frederick the Great
- Alan Bullock - Hitler
- Gordon A. Craig - Army
- Richard J. Evans - Nazi era
- Ian Kershaw, Hitler
- Claudia Koonz - Women in Nazi era
- Timothy Mason -Nazis
- George Mosse --19c-20c culture
- Steven Ozment Reformation
- Hans Rothfels - military
- Fritz Stern - cultural
- Henry Ashby Turner - 20c esp business

Holocaust

- Yehuda Bauer
- Martin Broszat
- Christopher Browning
- Lucy Dawidowicz
- Norman Finkelstein
- Henry Friedlander
- Saul Friedländer
- Daniel Goldhagen
- Raul Hilberg
- Michael Marrus
- Hans Mommsen
- R. J. Rummel

See also

- Medieval East Colonisation by German noblemen and farmers
- German exodus from Eastern Europe
- History of German settlement in Eastern Europe
- Territorial changes of Germany
- Military history of Germany

Bibliography

Surveys and historiography

- Bithell, Jethro, ed. *Germany: A Companion to German Studies* (5th ed. 1955), 578pp; essays on German literature, music, philosophy, art and, especially, history. online edition [5]
- Buse, Dieter K. ed. *Modern Germany: An Encyclopedia of History, People, and Culture 1871-1990* (2 vol 1998)
- Clark, Christopher. *Iron Kingdom: The Rise and Downfall of Prussia, 1600-1947* (2006)
- Detwiler, Donald S. *Germany: A Short History* (3rd ed. 1999) 341pp; online edition [6]
- Evans, Richard J. *Rereading German History: From Unification to Reunification, 1800-1996* (1997) online edition [7]
- Fulbrook, Mary. *A Concise History of Germany* (2004)
- Holborn, Hajo. *A History of Modern Germany* (3 vol 1959-64); vol 1: The Reformation; vol 2: 1648-1840; vol 3. 1840-1945
- Maehl, William Harvey. *Germany in Western Civilization* (1979), 833pp
- Ozment, Steven. *A Mighty Fortress: A New History of the German People* (2005)
- Reinhardt, Kurt F. *Germany: 2000 Years* (2 vols., 1961), stress on cultural topics
- Schulze, Hagen, and Deborah Lucas Schneider. *Germany: A New History* (2001)
- Taylor, A. J. P. *The Course of German History: A Survey of the Development of German History since 1815.* (2001). 280pp; online edition [8]; also

Medieval

- Arnold, Benjamin. *Medieval Germany, 500-1300: A Political Interpretation* (1998)
- Barraclough, Geoffrey. *The Origins of Modern Germany* (2d ed., 1947)
- Fuhrmann, Horst, and Timothy Reuter. *Germany in the High Middle Ages: c.1050-1200* (1986)
- Haverkamp, Alfred, Helga Braun, and Richard Mortimer. *Medieval Germany 1056-1273* (1992)
- Jeep, John M. *Medieval Germany: An Encyclopedia* (2001), 928pp, 650 articles by 200 scholars cover A.D. 500 to 1500
- Reuter, Timothy. *Germany in the Early Middle Ages, C. 800-1056* (1991)

Reformation

see also Martin Luther

- Bainton, Roland H. *Here I Stand: A Life of Martin Luther* (1978; reprinted 1995)
- Dickens, A. G. *Martin Luther and the Reformation* (1969), basic introduction
- Holborn, Hajo. *A History of Modern Germany: vol 1: The Reformation* (1959)
- Junghans, Helmar. *Martin Luther: Exploring His Life and Times, 1483–1546.* (book plus CD ROM) (1998)
- MacCulloch, Diarmaid. *The Reformation* (2005), influential recent survey
- Ranke, Leopold von. *History of the Reformation in Germany* (1905) 792 pp; by Germany's foremost scholar complete text online free [9]
- Smith, Preserved. *The Age of the Reformation* (1920) 861 pages; complete text online free [10]

Early Modern to 1815

- Asprey, Robert B. *Frederick the Great: The Magnificent Enigma* (2007)
- Clark, Christopher. *Iron Kingdom: The Rise and Downfall of Prussia, 1600-1947* (2006)
- Heal, Bridget. *The Cult of the Virgin Mary in Early Modern Germany: Protestant and Catholic Piety, 1500-1648* (2007)
- Hughes, Michael. *Early Modern Germany, 1477-1806* (1992)
- Ozment, Steven. *Flesh and Spirit: Private Life in Early Modern Germany* (2001)

1815-1918

- Berghahn, Volker Rolf. *Modern Germany: society, economy, and politics in the twentieth century* (1987) ACLS E-book [11]
- Blackbourn, David, and Geoff Eley. *The Peculiarities of German History: Bourgeois Society and Politics in Nineteenth-Century Germany* (1984) online edition [12]
- Brose, Eric Dorn. *German History, 1789-1871: From the Holy Roman Empire to the Bismarckian Reich.* (1997) online edition [13]
- Craig, Gordon A. *Germany, 1866-1945* (1978) online edition [14]
- Mann, Golo. *History of Germany since 1789* (1968), very well written
- Mommsen, Wolfgang J. *Imperial Germany 1867-1918: Politics, Culture and Society in an Authoritarian State* (1995)
- Retallack, James. *Germany in the Age of Kaiser Wilhelm II* (1996)
- Scheck, Raffael. "Lecture Notes, Germany and Europe, 1871-1945" (2008) full text online [15], a brief textbook by a leading scholar
- Sheehan, James J. *German History, 1770-1866* (1993), the major survey in English
- Sheehan, James J. *German Liberalism in the Nineteenth Century* (1978, 1995)
- Wehler, Hans-Ulrich. *The German Empire 1871-1918* (1984)

Nazi era

see also Nazi Party for more books

- Bracher, Karl D. *The German Dictatorship: The Origins, Structure and Consequences of National Socialism* (1973). Influential analysis by political scientist
- Burleigh, Michael. *The Third Reich: A New History.* (2000). 864 pp. Stress on antisemitism;
- Evans, Richard J. *The Coming of the Third Reich: A History.* 2004. 622 pp., a major scholarly survey
- Evans, Richard J. *The Third Reich in Power: 1933-1939.* (2005). 800 pp. The major scholarly study
- Evans, Richard J. *The Third Reich at war 1939-1945* (2009)
- Mommsen, Hans. *The Third Reich between Vision and Reality: New Perspectives on German History, 1918-1945* (2001) online edition [16]
- Overy, Richard. *The Dictators: Hitler's Germany and Stalin's Russia* (2004)
- Roderick, Stacke. *Hitler's Germany: Origins, Interpretations, Legacies* (1999)
- Scheck, Raffael. "Lecture Notes, Germany and Europe, 1871-1945" (2008) full text online [15], a brief textbook by a leading scholar
- Zentner, Christian and Bedürftig, Friedemann, eds. *The Encyclopedia of the Third Reich.* 2 vol. Macmillan, 1991. 1120 pp.

Nazi Leaders

see Adolf Hitler for more books

- Breitman, Richard. *The Architect of Genocide: Himmler and the Final Solution* (1992)
- Bullock, Alan. *Hitler: A Study in Tyranny,* (1962) online edition [17]
- Geary, Dick. *Hitler and Nazism,* (2000) 97 pages
- Kershaw, Ian. *Hitler, 1889-1936: Hubris.* vol. 1. 1999. 700 pp. ; vol 2: *Hitler, 1936-1945: Nemesis.* 2000. 832 pp.; the leading scholarly biography.
- Kershaw, Ian. *The "Hitler Myth": Image and Reality in the Third Reich.* (1987). 297 pp.
- Nicholls, David. *Adolf Hitler: A Biographical Companion.* ABC-CLIO, 2000. 344 pp.
- Overy, Richard. *Goering* (2000).
- Speer, Albert. *Inside the Third Reich: Memoirs* 1970.
- Welch, David. *Hitler* UCL Press 1998. 123pp online edition [18]
- Williamson, David. "Was Hitler a Weak Dictator?," *History Review.* 2002. pp 9+. online version [19]

Holocaust

- Dawidowicz, Lucy. *The War against the Jews, 1933–45,* (1977).
- Friedlander, Saul. *Nazi Germany and the Jews: Volume 1: The Years of Persecution 1933-1939* (1998)
- Friedlander, Saul. *The Years of Extermination: Nazi Germany and the Jews, 1939-1945* (2007), the standard history
- Gilbert, Martin. *The Holocaust: A History of the Jews of Europe During the Second World War* (1987)
- Gilbert, Martin. *The Routledge Atlas of the Holocaust* (2002)
- Landau, Ronnie. *The Nazi Holocaust* (2002)
- Niewyk, Donald, and Francis Nicosia. *The Columbia Guide to the Holocaust.* (2000) online edition [20]
- Wistrich, Robert S. *Hitler and the Holocaust.* 2001. 295 pp.

Economics and Labor

- Baranowsky, Shelley. *Strength Through Joy: Consumerism and Mass Tourism in the Third Reich* (2004)
- Overy, R. J. *The Nazi Economic Recovery 1932-1938* (1996)
- Tooze, Adam. *The Wages of Destruction: The Making and Breaking of the Nazi Economy* (2007), highly influential new study

Resistance

- Benz, Wolfgang, and Walter H. Pehle, eds. *Encyclopedia of German Resistance to the Nazi Movement.* (1997). 354 pages
- Hamerow, Theodore S. *On the Road to the Wolf's Lair: German Resistance to Hitler* (1997) 454 pages
- R. P. Heller. *The Flame of Freedom: The German Struggle against Hitler.* (1994) focus on Army online edition [21]
- Thomsett, Michael C. *The German Opposition to Hitler: The Resistance, the Underground, and Assassination Plots, 1938-1945* (2nd ed 2007) 278 pages

Women, children, youth

- Bridenthal, Renate, Atina Grossmann, and Marion Kaplan. *When Biology Became Destiny: Women in Weimar and Nazi Germany* (1984).
- Cosner, Shaaron and Cosner, Victoria. *Women under the Third Reich: A Biographical Dictionary.* Greenwood, 1998. 203 pp.
- Koonz, Claudia. *Mothers in the Fatherland: Women, Family Life, and Nazi Ideology, 1919-1945.* (1986). 640 pp. The major study
- Rempel, Gerhard. *Hitler's Children: The Hitler Youth and the SS,* (1989) online edition [22]
- Stephenson, Jill. *The Nazi Organisation of Women.* (1981). 246 pp.
- Stibbe, Matthew. *Women in the Third Reich,* 2003, 208 pp.

1945-1990

- Berghahn, Volker Rolf. *Modern Germany: society, economy, and politics in the twentieth century* (1987) ACLS E-book [11]
- Granieri, Ronald J. *The Ambivalent Alliance: Konrad Adenauer, the CDU/CSU, and the West, 1949-1966* (2004) 250 pages excerpt and text search [23]
- Jarausch, Konrad H.*After Hitler: Recivilizing Germans, 1945-1995* (2008)
- Schwarz, Hans-Peter. *Konrad Adenauer: A German Politician and Statesman in a Period of War, Revolution and Reconstruction. Vol. 1: From the German Empire to the Federal Republic, 1876-1952.*
  - Schwarz, Hans-Peter. *vol 2: Konrad Adenauer a German politician and statesman in a period of war, revolution and reconstruction* (1995) 759 pp. excerpt and text search vol 2 [24]; also full text online [25]
- Williams, Charles. *Konrad Adenauer: The Father of the New Germany* (2001), 624pp

Primary sources

- Adenauer, Konrad. *Memoirs,* (4 vols. English edition 1966-70)
- Jarausch, Konrad H., and Volker Gransow, eds. *Uniting Germany: Documents and Debates, 1944-1993* (1994)

GDR

- Fulbrook, Mary. *Anatomy of a Dictatorship: Inside the GDR, 1949-1989* (1998)
- Klessmann, Christoph. *The Divided Past: Rewriting Post-War German History* (2001) online edition [26]
- Jarausch, Konrad H.. and Eve Duffy. *Dictatorship As Experience: Towards a Socio-Cultural History of the GDR* (1999)
- Pritchard, Gareth. *The Making of the GDR, 1945-53* (2004)

- Ross, Corey. *The East German Dictatorship: Problems and Perspectives in the Interpretation of the GDR* (2002)
- Steiner, André. *The Plans That Failed: An Economic History of East Germany, 1945-1989* (2010)

Historiography

- Berghahn, Volker R., and Simone Lassig, eds. *Biography between Structure and Agency: Central European Lives in International Historiography* (2008)
- Hagemann, Karen, and Jean H. Quataert, eds. *Gendering Modern German History: Rewriting Historiography* (2008)
- Jarausch, Konrad H., and Michael Geyer, eds. *Shattered Past: Reconstructing German Histories* (2003)
- Lehmann, Hartmut, and James Van Horn Melton, eds. *Paths of Continuity: Central European Historiography from the 1930s to the 1950s* (2003)
- Stuchtey, Benedikt, and Peter Wende, eds. *British and German Historiography, 1750-1950: Traditions, Perceptions, and Transfers* (2000)

External links

- History of Germany - World History Database [27]
- The full text of the "Reichsdeputationshauptschluss" of 25 February 1803 [28]
- Constitution of the German Empire [29] ("Constitution of Paulskirche") of 28 March 1849, in full text
- Constitutional charter [30] for the Prussian State (Imposed Constitution of 5 December 1848, in full text)
- Kingdom of Prussia: Constitutional charter [31] for the Prussian State (Revised Constitution of 31 January 1850, in full text)
- History of Germany: Primary Documents [32]
- Pessimistic Germans Losing Faith in Democracy, Study Shows [33]

Geography of Germany

Germany is a country in Central Europe, stretching from the Alps, across the North European Plain to the North Sea and the Baltic Sea. Germany has the second largest population in Europe (after the European part of Russia) and is seventh largest in area. The territory of Germany covers 357021 km^2 (137847 sq mi), consisting of 349223 km^2 (134836 sq mi) of land and 7798 km^2 (3011 sq mi) of water. Elevation ranges from the mountains of the Alps (highest point: the Zugspitze at 2962 metres (9718 ft) in the south to the shores of the North Sea (Nordsee) in the northwest and the Baltic Sea (Ostsee) in the northeast. Between lie the forested uplands of central Germany and the low-lying lands of northern Germany (lowest point: Neuendorf-Sachsenbande at 3.54 metres (11.6 ft) below sea level), traversed by some of Europe's major rivers such as the Rhine, Danube and Elbe. Because of its central location, Germany shares borders with nine European countries, second only to Russia: Denmark in the north, Poland and the Czech Republic in the east, Austria and Switzerland in the south, France in the southwest and Belgium, Luxembourg and the Netherlands in the west. German Unity Day is celebrated on October 3 every year.

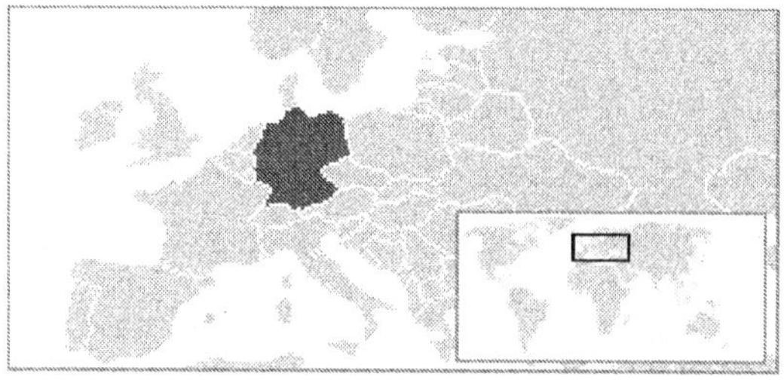

The location of Germany

General map of Germany

The current, post-1990 territory of the Federal Republic of Germany is 30.3% bigger than the Cold-War era West Germany and 23.8% and 33.9% smaller than the former territories of Weimar and Imperial Germany, respectively.

Terrain

Physical map of Germany

The northern third of the country lies in the North European Plain, with flat terrain crossed by northward-flowing watercourses (Elbe, Ems, Weser, Oder). Wetlands and marshy conditions are found close to the Dutch border and along the Frisian coast. Sandy Mecklenburg in the northeast has many glacier-formed lakes dating to the last glacial period.

Moving south, central Germany features rough and somewhat patternless hilly and mountainous countryside, some of it formed by ancient volcanic activity. The Rhine valley cuts through the western part of this region. The central uplands continue east and north as far as the Saale and merge with the Ore Mountains on the border with the Czech Republic. Upland regions include the Eifel, Hunsrück and Palatine Forest west of the Rhine, the Taunus hills north of Frankfurt, the Vogelsberg massif, the Rhön, and the Thüringer Wald. South of Berlin, the east-central part of the country is more like the low northern areas, with sandy soil and river wetlands such as the Spreewald region.

Southern Germany's landforms are defined by various linear hill and mountain ranges like the two adjacent ranges of the Swabian and Franconian Alb (reaching approximately from the source of the Danube in the southwest of Baden-Württemberg, south of Stuttgart, across Swabia into Central Franconia and to the valley of the river Main) and the Bavarian Forest along the border between Bavaria and the Czech Republic. The Alps on the southern border are the highest mountains, but relatively little Alpine terrain lies within Germany (in southeastern Swabia and Upper Bavaria) compared to Switzerland and Austria. The Black Forest, on the southwestern border with France, separates the Rhine from the headwaters of the Danube on its eastern slopes.

Climate

Alpine scenery in Bavaria

See also: Climate of Germany

Germany's climate is temperate and marine, with cool, cloudy, wet winters and summers and in the south occasional warm föhn wind. The greater part of Germany lies in the cool/temperate climatic zone in which humid westerly winds predominate. In the northwest and the north the climate is extremely oceanic and rain falls all the year round. Winters there are relatively mild and summers comparatively cool. In the east the climate shows clear continental features; winters can be very cold for long periods, and summers can become very warm. Here too, long dry periods are often recorded. In the centre and the south there is a transitional climate which may be predominantly oceanic or continental, according to the general weather situation. Winters are mild and summers tend to be cool, though maximum temperatures can exceed 30 °C (86 °F) for several days in a row during heat waves. The warmest regions of Germany can be found in the south-west (see rhine rift, German Wine Route and Palatinate). Here summers can be hot with a high number of days exceeding 30 °C (86 °F). Sometimes minimum temperatures don't drop under 20 °C (68 °F), which is relatively rare in other regions.

Land use

Germany covers a total of 357,021 km², of which 4,750 km² is irrigated land and 7,798 km² is covered by water, the largest lakes being Lake Constance (total area of 536 km², with 62% of the shore being German; international borders are not defined on the lake itself), Müritz (117 km²) and Chiemsee (80 km²). The majority of Germany is covered by either arable land (33%) or forestry and woodland (31%). Only 15% is covered by permanent pastures.

Germany has a total of 2,389 km of coastline, and borders totalling 3,621 km (clockwise from north: Denmark 68 km, Poland 456 km, Czech Republic 646 km, Austria 784 km, Switzerland 334 km, France 451 km, Luxembourg 138 km, Belgium 167 km, Netherlands 577 km). The German-Austrian border crosses itself near Jungholz. The border with Belgium includes 5 German exclaves because the Vennbahn railway is on Belgian territory crossing in and out of Germany.

Caves

Throughout the Karst rocks many caves were formed especially in the valley of the Hönne. The biggest culture cave of Europe is located in Balve.

Rivers

The three main rivers in Germany are:

- the Rhine (*Rhein* in German) with a German part of 865 km (main tributaries including the Neckar, the Main and the Moselle (*Mosel*));
- the Elbe with a German part of 727 km (also drains into the North Sea); and,
- the Danube (*Donau*) with a German part of 687 km.

Further important rivers include the Isar in the southeast, the Main in central Germany, the Neckar in the southwest, and the Weser in the North. See also the list of rivers in Germany.

The major German rivers

Maritime claims

- Continental shelf: 200 m depth or to the depth of exploitation
- Exclusive economic zone: 200 nmi (370.4 km; 230.2 mi). The exact EEZ is due to conventions with neighbouring states.
- Territorial sea: 12 nmi (22.2 km; 13.8 mi)

Natural resources

- Iron ore, coal, potash, timber, lignite, uranium, copper, natural gas, salt, nickel, arable land, water

Environment

Current issues

- Emissions from coal-burning utilities and industries contribute to air pollution; acid rain, resulting from sulphur dioxide emissions, is damaging forests; pollution in the Baltic Sea from raw sewage and industrial effluents from rivers in eastern Germany; hazardous waste disposal; government (under Chancellor Schröder, SPD) announced intent to end the use of nuclear power for producing electricity; government working to meet EU commitment to identify nature preservation areas in line with the EU's Flora, Fauna, and Habitat directive. Germany's last glacier is disappearing. [1]

International agreements

- Party to: Air Pollution, Air Pollution-Nitrogen oxides, Air Pollution-Sulphur 85, Air Pollution-Sulphur 94, Air Pollution-Volatile Organic Compounds, Antarctic-Environmental Protocol, Antarctic Treaty, Biodiversity, Climate Change, Climate Change-Kyoto Protocol, Desertification, Endangered Species, Environmental Modification, Hazardous Wastes, Law of the Sea, Marine Dumping, Nuclear Test Ban, Ozone Layer Protection, Ship Pollution, Tropical Timber 83, Tropical Timber 94, Wetlands, Whaling
- Signed, but not ratified: Air Pollution-Persistent Organic Pollutants

Natural hazards

- Flooding through rivers after heavy rainfall, such as during the 2002 European floods, or Storm surge, such as the North Sea flood of 1962 or the historic floods of 1634 and 1362 that changed the coastline of what is now the west coast of Schleswig-Holstein.

hey:D

Extreme points

Latitude and longitude

This is a list of the **extreme points of Germany**, the points that are farther north, south, east or west than any other location.

- northernmost point: List, Sylt, Schleswig-Holstein 55°03′N 8°24′E
- southernmost point: Haldenwanger Eck, Oberstdorf, Bavaria 47°16′12.39″N 10°10′41.95″E
- westernmost point: Isenbruch, Selfkant, North Rhine-Westphalia 51°1′N 5°53′E
- easternmost point: Deschka, Neißeaue, Saxony 51°16′N 15°2′E

The northernmost point in mainland Germany lies near Aventoft, Schleswig-Holstein at 54°54′N 8°49′E

The extreme points of the German Confederation are mentioned in the first stanza of *Das Lied der Deutschen*, of which the third stanza is today the national anthem of Germany. They were accurate when the song was penned in 1841, but are no longer accurate today. The limits mentioned are the following rivers:

- Meuse River which crosses France, Belgium and the Netherlands and formed the border of the Duchy of Limburg, then part of the German Confederation and today the Dutch Province of Limburg.
- Memel, which runs through Belarus and Lithuania but previously formed part of the border of East Prussia
- Adige (*Etsch*), beginning in the province of Bolzano-Bozen (then in Austria) which was transferred from the Habsburg Empire to Italy after World War I

- Belt which is a part of the Baltic Sea between Germany and Denmark.

Elevation

- lowest point: Wilstermarsch at Neuendorf-Sachsenbande (near Itzehoe) 3.53 m below sea level 53°57′48″N 9°19′05″E
- highest point: Zugspitze (in the Bavarian Alps, on the Austrian border) 2,962 m 47°25′N 10°59′E

See also

- Geography of Europe
- Germany
- List of administrative divisions of Germany
- National parks (Germany)

Politics of Germany

Germany

This article is part of the series:
Politics and government of Germany

Other countries · Atlas
Politics portal

Germany is a federal parliamentary republic, based on representative democracy. The Chancellor is the head of government, and federal legislative power is vested in the Bundestag (the parliament of Germany) and the Bundesrat (the representative body of the regional states). There is a multi-party system that, since 1949, has been dominated by the Christian Democratic Union (CDU) and the Social Democratic Party of Germany (SPD).

The judiciary of Germany is independent of the executive and the legislature. The political system is laid out in the 1949 constitution, the *Grundgesetz* (Basic Law), which remained in effect with minor amendments after 1990's German reunification.

The constitution emphasizes the protection of individual liberty in an extensive catalogue of human rights and also divides powers both between the federal and state levels and between the legislative, executive, and judicial branches. In many ways, the 1949 Basic Law is a response to the perceived flaws of the 1919 Weimar Constitution, which may have had its share in the decline of the republic and the subsequent rise of the Nazi party in 1933.

Federal executive branch

Main article: Chancellor of Germany (Federal Republic of Germany)

The *Bundeskanzler* (Federal Chancellor) heads the *Bundesregierung* (Federal Government) and thus the executive branch of the federal government. He or she is elected by and responsible to the *Bundestag*, Germany's parliament. Germany, like the United Kingdom, can thus be classified as a parliamentary system.

Chancellery in Berlin, since 2001

The Chancellor cannot be removed from office during a four year term unless the *Bundestag* has agreed on a successor. This Constructive Vote of No Confidence is intended to avoid the situation of the Weimar Republic in which the executive did not have enough support in the legislature to govern effectively, but the legislature was too divided to name a successor.

Except in the periods 1969–72 and 1976–82, when the Social Democratic party of Chancellor Brandt and Schmidt came in second in the elections, the Chancellor has always been the candidate of the largest party, usually supported by a coalition of two parties with a majority in the parliament. One of the ministers the Chancellor appoints Vice-Chancellor (Vizekanzler). The office itself is hardly important but often indicates who is the main cabinet member of the smaller coalition partner.

By contrast, the duties of the *Bundespräsident* (Federal President) are largely representative and ceremonial. The President is elected every five years on May 23 by the Federal Assembly (*Bundesversammlung*), a special body convened only for this purpose, comprising the entire *Bundestag* and an equal number of state delegates selected especially for this purpose in proportion to election results for the state diets.

Horst Köhler of the CDU was first elected in May 2004 and was reelected five years later, in May 2009. As this party has usually the biggest support in national elections but also in the *Länder*, it is quite common that the Federal President is a Christian Democrat. Horst Köhler resigned on May 31st, 2010, due to remarks he made concerning the military while speaking before the troops in Afghanistan.

Main office holders

Office	Name	Party	Since
President	Christian Wulff	Christian Democratic Union	30 June 2010
Chancellor	Angela Merkel	Christian Democratic Union	22 November 2005
Other government parties		Free Democratic Party	
		Christian Social Union	

Although Mr. Köhler has been a member of the CDU the German Basic Law requests in Article 55 that the Federal President not hold another office, practice a profession or hold a membership in any corporation. Accordingly, every Federal President has let his party membership lie dormant and has not belonged to a political party during his term of office.

Federal legislature

Main articles: Bundestag and Bundesrat of Germany

Federal legislative power is divided between the *Bundestag* and the *Bundesrat*. The *Bundestag* is directly elected by the German people, whilst the *Bundesrat* represents the regional states (*Länder*). The federal legislature has powers of exclusive jurisdiction and concurrent jurisdiction with the states in areas specifically enumerated by the constitution.

The Reichstag building, seat of the Bundestag

The *Bundestag* is more powerful than the *Bundesrat* and only need the latter's consent for proposed legislation related to revenue shared by the federal and state governments, and the imposition of responsibilities on the states. In practice, this means that the agreement of the *Bundesrat* in the legislative process is very often required, as federal legislation often has to be executed by state or local agencies. In the event of disagreement between the *Bundestag* and the *Bundesrat* a conciliation committee is formed to find a compromise.

Bundestag

The *Bundestag* (Federal Diet) is elected for a four year term and consists of 598 or more members elected by a means of mixed member proportional representation, which Germans call "personalized proportional representation." 299 members represent single-seat constituencies and are elected by a First Past the Post electoral system. Parties that obtain fewer constituency seats than their national share of the vote indicates they ought to have are allotted seats from party lists to make up the difference. In contrast parties that obtain more constituency seats than their national share of the vote indicates they ought to have are allowed to keep these so-called overhang seats. In the current parliament elected in 2009 there are 24 overhang seats, giving the *Bundestag* a total of 622 members.

A party must receive either five percent of the national vote or win at least three directly elected seats to be represented in the *Bundestag*. This rule, often called the "five percent hurdle", was incorporated into Germany's election law to prevent political fragmentation and strong minor parties. The first *Bundestag* elections were held in the Federal Republic of Germany ("West Germany") on August 14, 1949. Following reunification, elections for the first all-German *Bundestag* were held on December 2, 1990. The last election was held on 18 September 2005, the 16th Bundestag convened on 18 October 2005. The number of Bundestag Deputies was reduced from 656 to 598 beginning in 2002, although under the additional member system, more deputies may be admitted if a party wins more directly elected seats than it would be entitled to under proportional representation.

Judicial branch

The independence of the judiciary of Germany is historically older than democracy in Germany, the organization of courts is traditionally strong, and almost all state actions are subject to judicial review. Besides a so-called "ordinary" judicial branch that handles civil and criminal cases, which is in turn composed of four levels of courts up to the *Bundesgerichtshof* in a fairly complex appeals system, there are separate branches for administrative, tax, labour, and social security issues, each with their own hierarchies. Courts are generally in the hands of the states, except for the highest courts of each branch, which are federal, respectively, to maintain a certain degree of unity in jurisdiction.

In addition, Germany has a powerful Constitutional Court, the *Bundesverfassungsgericht*. This is somewhat unique since the Basic Law stipulates that every person may file a complaint to that court when his or her constitutional rights, especially the human rights, have been violated by the state and when he or she has exhausted all stages of appeal in the regular court system.

Such actions can include laws passed by the legislative branch, court decisions, or acts of the administration. While in practice, only a small percentage of these constitutional complaints are successful, the Constitutional Court is known to frequently antagonise both the executive and the legislative branches with far-reaching decisions. This has even gone so far as judges openly stating that they are indifferent to the reactions of the government, the *Bundestag*, public opinion or any financial consequences arising from a decision with the only relevant point being the constitution. It should also be mentioned that the Bundesverfassungsgericht has very high approval rates throughout the general population.

The Constitutional Court also handles several other procedures such as disputes between state institutions over their constitutional powers. It has also the power to outlaw political parties when their goals contravene the principles of the constitution. However so far the Constitutional court has only used this power twice, outlawing the SRP (Socialist Reichs Party, a successor to the NSDAP) in 1952, and the KPD (Communist Party of Germany) in 1956.

Recent politics

"Red-Green" coalition of 1998-2002

After 16 years of the Christian liberal coalition of Helmut Kohl, the Social Democrats together with the Greens won the elections of 1998. SPD leader Gerhard Schröder positioned himself as a centrist "Third Way" candidate in the mold of Britain's Tony Blair and America's Bill Clinton. The Kohl government was hurt at the polls by slower growth in the east in the past two years, widening the economic gap between east and west, and constantly high unemployment.

The final margin of victory was sufficiently high to permit a "red-green" coalition of the SPD with Alliance '90/The Greens (*Bündnis '90/Die Grünen*), bringing the Greens into a national government for the first time.

Initial problems of the new government, marked by policy disputes between the moderate and traditional left wings of the SPD, resulting in some voter disaffection. CDU won in the first state election after the federal election held in Hesse in February 1999, but in other state elections of this time, the respective SPD- or CDU-led coalition governments were re-elected into power. The popularity of the CDU dropped severely when in 2000 it became public that Kohl had accepted high party donations not reporting them to the authorities as required by law. As a result of this CDU crisis, Angela Merkel became chair.

The next election for the *Bundestag* was September 22, 2002. Gerhard Schröder led the coalition of SPD and Greens to an eleven seat victory over the Christian democrat challengers headed by Edmund Stoiber (CSU). Three factors are generally cited that enabled Schröder to win the elections despite poor approval ratings a few months before and a weaker economy: good handling of the 100-year-flood, firm opposition to the USA's 2003 invasion of Iraq, and Stoiber's unpopularity in the east that cost the CDU crucial seats there.

Christian Democrat comeback

In its second term, the red green coalition lost several very important state elections, for example in Lower Saxony where Schröder was the prime minister from 1990 to 1998. The liberal FDP, weakened by the loss of power in 1998 and not quite recovering in 2002, became again more successful on state level. On the other hand, some far right wing parties had their moments in state elections, too.

In April 20, 2003, chancellor Schröder announced massive labor market reforms, called Agenda 2010, that among other measures include a shakeup of the system of German job offices, cuts in unemployment benefits and subsidies for unemployed persons who start their own businesses. These changes are commonly known by the name of the chairman of the commission which conceived them as Hartz I - Hartz IV. Although these reforms have sparked massive protests they are now credited with being in part responsible for the economic downswing and the rise of unemployment in Germany in the years 2006/7.

The European elections on June 13, 2004 brought a staggering defeat for the Social Democrats, who polled only slightly more than 21%, the lowest election result for the SPD in a nationwide election since the Second World War. Many observers believe that this election marked the beginning of the end of the Schröder government and indicates a process in which the SPD party seems to shrink and/or fall apart.

Grand coalition 2005-2009

On May 22, 2005, as predicted, the SPD received a devastating defeat in its former heartland, North Rhine-Westphalia. Half an hour after the election results, the SPD chairman Franz Müntefering announced that the chancellor would clear the way for special federal elections by the means of a purposely lost vote of confidence in the Bundestag.

This took the republic by surprise, especially because the SPD was below 25% in polls at the time. On the following Monday the CDU announced Angela Merkel as Christian Democrat candidate for chancellor, aspiring to be the first female chancellor in German history.

New for the 2005 election was the alliance between the newly formed Electoral Alternative for Labor and Social Justice (WASG) and the PDS, planning to fuse into a common party (see Left Party.PDS). With the former SPD chairman, Oskar Lafontaine for the WASG and Gregor Gysi for the PDS as prominent figures, this alliance soon found interest in the media and in the population. Polls in July saw them as high as 12%.

Whereas in May and June 2005 victory of the Christian Democrats seemed highly likely, with some polls giving them an absolute majority, this picture changed shortly before the election at September 18, 2005, especially after the Christian Democrats introduced Paul Kirchhof as potential minister of the treasury, and after a TV duel between Merkel and Schröder where many considered Schröder to have performed better.

The election results of September 18, 2005 were surprising insofar as they differed widely from the polls of the previous weeks. The Christian Democrats lost votes compared to 2002, reaching only 35.2%, and failed to get a majority for a "black-yellow" government of CDU/CSU and liberal FDP. The FDP polled a stunning 9.8% of the votes, one of their best results ever. But the red-green coalition also failed to get a majority, with the SPD losing votes, but polling 34.2% and the greens staying at 8.1%. The left party alliance reached 8.7% and entered the German Parliament, whereas the NPD only got 1.6%.

The most likely outcome of coalition talks was a so-called "grand coalition" between the Christian Democrats (CDU/CSU) and the Social Democrats (SPD), with the three smaller parties (liberals, greens and the left) in the opposition. Other possible coalitions include a "traffic light coalition" between SPD, FDP and Greens and a "Jamaica coalition" between CDU/CSU, FDP and Greens.

Coalitions involving the Left Party have been ruled out by all parties (including the Left Party itself).

On November 22, 2005, Angela Merkel was sworn in by president Horst Köhler for the office of Bundeskanzlerin. Merkel is the first woman, the first East German and the first scientist to be chancellor as well as the youngest post-war German chancellor. The existence of the grand coalition on federal level helps smaller parties' electoral prospects in state elections.

Since in 2008, the CSU lost its absolute majority in Bavaria and formed a coalition with the FDP, the grand coalition had no majority in the *Bundesrat* and depended on FDP votes on important issues. In November 2008, the SPD re-elected Franz Müntefering as its chairman and made Frank-Walter Steinmeier its leading candidate for the federal election in September 2009.

As a result of the that federal election, the grand coalition came to an end. The SPD suffered the heaviest losses in its history and was unable to form a coalition government. Consequently, the SPD's status as a Volkspartei has come into question (a Volkspartei is a party in the German system that has traditionally drawn votes from a broad group of supporters and claims to represent the interests of all German citizens, as opposed to special interest parties that focus most of their energy around a single issue, such as the Pirate Party or the RRP). Many political commentators speculated in televised interviews on election night that Müntefering would most likely resign as party leader, and that Steinmeier would eventually step down from the ranks of the party's leadership sometime thereafter. Many voters who had traditionally been supporters of the SPD split their votes in the 2009 election between the FDP, the Left Party or the CDU, as the SPD had lost much of its former vitality and direction as a result of its secondary role in the grand coalition and its subsequently weak campaign efforts against the CDU before the 2009 election.

The three smaller parties thus have more seats in the German Bundestag than ever before, for example the liberal party FDP won 14,6% of votes. Each one of them had its best result ever. The profound crisis within the SPD will likely continue as the party struggles to unify its base and refine its ideology and platform. Foremost among its concerns will likely be a redefinition of its relationship to the Left Party (which profited greatly in the election from voters who had traditionally supported the more left-wing elements of the SPD), which the SPD had refused to govern with prior to the election for a number of reasons.

See also

- Political culture of Germany
- German federal election, 2005
- German federal election, 2009
- List of political parties in Germany
- States of Germany

External links

- Official Site of the Bundesregierung [1], in English
- Official source of election results [2]
- Official source from the German Embassy in Washington, DC [3]
- distribution of power [4]

Economy of Germany

Economy of Germany	
Rank	4th (nominal) / 5th (PPP)
Currency	Euro (EUR)
Fiscal year	calendar year
Trade organisations	EU, WTO (via EU membership) and OECD
Statistics	
GDP	$3.673 trillion (2008)
GDP growth	-4.9%(2009)
GDP per capita	Nominal: $44,729 (2008)
GDP by sector	agriculture: 0.9%; industry: 27.1%; services: 72% (2009 est.)
Inflation (CPI)	1.2% (March 2010)
Population below poverty line	11% (2001)
Gini index	27 (2006)
Labour force	43.51 million (2009 est.)
Labour force by occupation	agriculture (2,4%), industry (29,7%), services (67,5%) (2005)
Unemployment	7% (June 2010)
Main industries	iron, steel, coal, cement, chemicals, machinery, vehicles, machine tools, electronics, food and beverages, shipbuilding, textiles
Ease of Doing Business Rank	25th
External	
Exports	$1.121 trillion (2009 est.)
Export goods	machinery, vehicles, chemicals, metals and manufactures, foodstuffs, textiles
Main export partners	France 10.2%, U.S. 6.7%, Netherlands 6.7%, U.K. 6.6%, Italy 6.3%, Austria 6%, China 4.5%, Switzerland 4.4% (2009 est.)
Imports	$931.3 billion (2009 est.)
Import goods	machinery, vehicles, chemicals, foodstuffs, textiles, metals

Main import partners	Netherlands 8.5%, China 8.2%, France 8.2%, U.S. 5.9%, Italy 5.9%, U.K. 4.9%, Belgium 4.3%, Austria 4.3%, Switzerland 4.2% (2009 est.)
FDI stock	$1.021 trillion (31 December 2009 est.)
Gross external debt	$5.208 trillion (30 June 2009)
Public finances	
Public debt	77.2% of GDP (2009 est.)
Revenues	$1.398 trillion (2009 est.)
Expenses	$1.54 trillion (2009 est.)
Economic aid	*donor*: $7.5 billion, 0.28% of GDP GDP Germany is ranked on the CPI [1] 2009 as 14th for the perceived level of public sector corruption, with a confidence range between 7.7-8.3. (2004)
Foreign reserves	$138 billion (31 December 2008 est.)
Main data source: CIA World Fact Book [2] *All values, unless otherwise stated, are in US dollars*	

Germany is the largest national economy in Europe, the fourth-largest by nominal GDP in the world, and fifth by GDP (PPP) in 2008. Since the age of industrialisation, the country has been a driver, innovator, and beneficiary of an ever more globalised economy. Germany is the world's second largest exporter with $1.120 trillion exported in 2009 (Eurozone countries are included). Exports account for more than one-third of national output.

Germany is relatively poor in raw materials. Only lignite and potash salt are available in economically significant quantities. Power plants burning lignite are one of the main sources of electricity in Germany. Oil, natural gas and other resources are, for the most part, imported from other countries. Germany imports about two thirds of its energy.

The service sector contributes around 70% of the total GDP, industry 29.1%, and agriculture 0.9%. Most of the country's products are in engineering, especially in automobiles, machinery, metals, and chemical goods. Germany is the leading producer of wind turbines and solar power technology in the world. The largest annual international trade fairs and congresses are held in several German cities such as Hanover, Frankfurt, and Berlin.

Of the world's 500 largest stock market listed companies measured by revenue, the Fortune Global 500, 37 are headquartered in Germany. In 2010 the ten largest were Volkswagen, Allianz, E.ON, Daimler, Siemens, Metro, Deutsche Telekom, Munich Re, BASF, and BMW. Other large German companies include: Robert Bosch, Thyssen Krupp, and MAN (diversified industrials); Bayer and Merck (pharmaceuticals); Adidas and Puma (clothing and footwear); Commerzbank and Deutsche Bank (banking and finance); Aldi, Lidl and Edeka (retail); SAP (computer software); Infineon (semiconductors); Henkel (household and personal consumer products); Deutsche Post (logistics); and

Hugo Boss (luxury goods). Well known global brands are Mercedes Benz, BMW, Adidas, Audi, Porsche, Volkswagen, DHL, T-Mobile, Lufthansa, SAP, and Nivea.

As of September 2008, as measured by ILO standards the German unemployment rate was 6.2 percent (compared with 7.4 percent as measured by German standards).

History

Main article: Economic history of Germany

Nazi Era

Main article: Economy of Nazi Germany

The economy of Germany during the Hitler era (1933 – 1945) developed a hothouse prosperity, supported with high government subsidies to those sectors that Hitler favored because they gave Nazi Germany military power and economic autarky, that is, economic independence from the global economy.

Adolf Hitler, believing that "the economy is something of secondary importance", left the details of the economic National Socialist Programme out of *Mein Kampf*. The Nazis rose to power while unemployment was very high, but achieved full employment later thanks to massive rearmament. Their pre-war economic policies, resembling Keynesianism, were in the beginning the brainchildren of their non-Nazi Minister of Economics, Hjalmar Schacht, who was later made to focus more on war production (cf: Military Keynesianism), and was eventually replaced by a Nazi, Hermann Göring.

The trading policies of the Third Reich aimed at discouraging trade with countries outside the German sphere of influence, while making southern Europe largely dependent on Germany. Eventually, the Nazi party developed strong relationships with big business and abolished trade unions while real wages dropped by a fourth, and employees could not easily change employer. Taxes, though, were still low well into the war. Already before the war, people undesirable to the regime were used as slave labour, and in 1944 they reached one quarter of the workers. Some have argued that the Second World War was a direct effect of the German economic system, which made expansionism necessary for domestic prosperity, indeed, survival; and which made Jingoism necessary for the quelling of class conflicts.

Wirtschaftswunder of the West

See also: Wirtschaftswunder

Beginning with the replacement of the Reichsmark with the Deutsche Mark as legal tender, a lasting period of low inflation and rapid industrial growth was overseen by the government led by German Chancellor Konrad Adenauer and his minister of economics, Ludwig Erhard, raising West Germany from total wartime devastation to one of the most developed nations in modern Europe.

Contrary to popular belief, the Marshall Plan, which was extended to also include Western Germany after it was realized that the suppression of the Western German economy was holding back the recovery of the rest of Europe, was not the main force behind the *Wirtschaftswunder*. The amount of monetary aid (which was in the form of loans) received by Germany through the Marshall Plan (about \$1.65 billion in total) was far overshadowed by the amount the Germans had to pay back as war reparations and by the charges the Allies made on the Germans for the ongoing cost of occupation (about \$2.4 billion per year). In 1953 it was decided that Germany was to repay \$1.1 billion of the aid it had received. The last repayment was made in June 1971.

Apart from these factors, hard work and long hours at full capacity among the population in the 1950s, 1960s and early 1970s and extra labour supplied by thousands of Gastarbeiter ("guest workers") provided a vital base for the economic upturn.

East Germany

Main article: Economy of the German Democratic Republic

By the early 1950s the Soviet Union had seized reparations in form of agricultural and industrial products and demanded further heavy reparation payments. Lower Silesia, which contained coal mines, and Stettin, a prominent natural port, were lost to Poland.

The Trabant was the most common car manufactured in the GDR.

Exports from West Germany exceeded \$323 billion in 1988. In the same year, East Germany exported \$30.7 billion of goods; 65% to other communist states. East Germany had zero unemployment.

In 1976 average annual GDP growth was roughly 5.9%.

Post-reunification

The German economy practically stagnated in the beginning of the 2000s. The worst growth figures were achieved in 2002 (+1.4%), in 2003 (+1.0%) and in 2005 (+1.4%). Unemployment was also chronically high. Due to these problems, together with Germany's aging population, the welfare system came under a lot of strain. This led the government to push through a wide-ranging programme of belt-tightening reforms, Agenda 2010, including the labour market reforms known as Hartz I - IV. In the latter part of the first decade of 2000 the world economy experienced high growth, from which Germany as a leading exporter also profited. Some attribute the Hartz reforms to the high German growth and declining unemployment, while others contend that it resulted in a massive decrease in standards of living, and that its effects are limited and temporary. This prediction appeared to have come true with the onset of the late 2000s recession, which hit Germany especially hard.

2008–2009 recession

The nominal GDP of Germany contracted in the second and third quarters of 2008, putting the country in a technical recession following a global and European recession cycle. German industrial output dropped to 3.6% in September vis-a-vis August. In January 2009 the German government under Angela Merkel approved a €50 billion ($70 billion) economic stimulus plan to protect several sectors from a downturn and a subsequent rise in unemployment rates.

Germany exited the recession in the second and third quarters of 2009, mostly due to rebounding manufacturing orders and exports - primarily from outside the Euro Zone - and relatively steady consumer demand.

GDP growth in 1992-2009

The following table lists the non-seasonally adjusted GDP growth in 1992-2009.

	1992	1993	1994	1995	1996	1997	1998	1999
GDP	€1646.62 bn	€1694.37 bn	€1780.78 bn	€1848.45 bn	€1878.18 bn	€1915.58 bn	€1965.38 bn	€2012.00 bn
Change	+7.3%	+2.9%	+5.1%	+3.8%	+1.5%	+2.1%	+2.6%	+2.4%

	2000	2001	2002	2003	2004	2005	2006	2007	2008	2009
GDP	€2062.50 bn	€2113.16 bn	€2143.18 bn	€2163.80 bn	€2210.90 bn	€2242.20 bn	€2325.10 bn	€2428.20 bn	€2495.80 bn	€2409.10 bn
Change	+2.5%	+2.5%	+1.4%	+1.0%	+2.2%	+1.4%	+3.7%	+4.4%	+2.8%	-3.5%

Economic regions

In several unitary European countries, such as United Kingdom and France, the capital city dominates the national economy. Germany - a federation -, on the other hand, does not have a single economic center: it is a polycentric country. Only 3 of Germany's 100 largest companies are headquartered in the capital Berlin. For example, the stock exchange is located in Frankfurt am Main, the largest Media company (Bertelsmann AG) is headquartered in Gütersloh; the most important car manufacturers are in Wolfsburg, Stuttgart and München.

Old Bundesländer

One of Germany's strongest (and at the same time oldest) economic regions is the Ruhr area in the west, between Bonn and Dortmund. 27 of the country's 100 largest companies are located there. The region also has one of the highest GDP per capita figures in Germany. In recent years, however, the area, whose economy is based on natural resources and heavy industry, has seen a substantial rise in unemployment. The economy of Bayern, the state with the lowest number of unemployed people, on the other hand, is based on high-value products. Important sectors are electronics, aerospace and biomedicine, among others. The reason for the low unemployment is that Bayern started its economic rise later, after the Second World War, and does not have as many traditional industries, which are presently encountering problems due to competition from countries such as China and India, as well as the exhaustion of natural resources.

New Bundesländer

Main article: New federal states

With unification on October 3, 1990, Germany began the major task of reconciling the economic systems of the two former republics. Its task was complicated by the dismantling of the extensive welfare system of the former German Democratic Republic, which resulted in a temporary but significant drop of the standard of living of its citizens; interventionist economic planning ensured a quick return of the standard of living and a gradual increase up to the level of that of western Germany. Since reunification, hundreds of thousands of former East Germans have migrated into western Germany to find work. Drastic changes in the socioeconomic landscape brought about by reunification have resulted in troubling social problems. Economic uncertainty in eastern Germany is often cited as one factor contributing to extremist violence, primarily from the political right. Confusion about the causes of the current hardships and a need to place blame have found expression in harassment and violence by some Germans directed toward foreigners, particularly non-Europeans.

Even after the German reunification in 1990, the standard of living and annual income remains significantly higher in the former West German states. The modernisation and integration of the eastern German economy continues to be a long-term process scheduled to last until the year 2019, with annual transfers from west to east amounting to roughly $80 billion. The overall unemployment rate has consistently fallen since 2005 and reached a 15-year low in June 2008 with 7.5%. The percentage ranges from 6.2% in former West Germany to 12.7% in former East Germany.

Natural resources

The German soil is relatively poor in raw materials. Only lignite (brown coal) and potash salt (Kalisalz) are available in significant quantities. Oil, natural gas and other resources are, for the most part, imported from other countries.

The potash salt deposits are a result of the drying up of the Zechstein sea, which 250 million years ago covered large parts of North and Central Europe. Potash salt is mined in the center of the country (Niedersachsen, Sachsen-Anhalt and Thüringen). The most important producer is K+S AG (formerly Kali und Salz AG).

Germany's bituminous coal deposits were created more than 300 million years ago from swamps which extended from the present-day South England, over the Ruhr area to Poland. Lignite deposits developed in a similar way, but during a later period, about 65 million years ago. Due to the fact that the wood is not yet completely transformed into coal, brown coal contains less energy than bituminous coal.

Lignite is extracted in the extreme western and eastern pars of the country, mainly in Nordrhein-Westfalen, Sachsen and Brandenburg. Considerable amounts are burned in coal plants near to the mining areas, to produce electricity. Transporting lignite over far distances is not economically feasible, therefore the plants are located practically next to the extraction sites. Bituminous coal is mined in Nordrhein-Westfalen and Saarland. Most power plants burning bituminous coal operate on imported material, therefore the plants are located not only near to the mining sites, but throughout the country.

Sectors

Primary

In 2008 agriculture, forestry, and mining accounted for only 0.9% of Germany's gross domestic product (GDP) and employed only 2.4% of the population, down from 4% in 1991.[citation needed] Much of the reduction in employment occurred in the eastern states, where the number of agricultural workers declined by as much as 75% following reunification.[citation needed] However, agriculture is extremely productive, and Germany is able to cover 90% of its nutritional needs with domestic production.[citation needed] In fact, Germany is the third largest agricultural producer in the European Union after France and Italy.[citation needed] Germany's principal agricultural products are potatoes, wheat, barley, sugar beets, fruit, and cabbages.[citation needed] Despite Germany's high level of industrialization, almost one-third of its territory is covered by forest. The forestry industry provides for about two-thirds of domestic consumption of wood and wood products, so Germany is a net importer of these items.[citation needed]

Industry

See also: Mittelstand

The world's largest coherent chemistry plant BASF near Ludwigshafen

Industry and construction accounted for 29% of gross domestic product in 2008, and employed 29.7% of the workforce. Germany excels in the production of automobiles, machinery, electrical equipment and chemicals. With the manufacture of 5.5 million vehicles in 2003, Germany was the world's third largest producer of automobiles after the United States and Japan, although the People's Republic of China was threatening to displace Germany in the world rankings as early as 2005.[citation needed] In 2004 Germany enjoyed the largest world market share in machine tools (19.3%).[citation needed] Of vital importance is the role of small- to medium-sized manufacturing firms, which specialize in niche products and often are owned by management.

Tertiary sector

In 2008 services constituted 69% of gross domestic product (GDP), and the sector employed 67.5% of the workforce. The subcomponents of services are financial, renting, and business activities (30.5%); trade, hotels and restaurants, and transport (18%); and other service activities (21.7%).[citation needed]

Energy

Main articles: Energy in Germany and Transport in Germany

Germany is the world's fifth largest consumer of energy, and two-thirds of its primary energy was imported in 2002. In the same year, Germany was Europe's largest consumer of electricity, totaling 512.9 terawatt-hours. Government policy promotes energy conservation and the development of renewable energy sources, such as solar, wind, biomass, hydroelectric, and geothermal energy. As a result of energy-saving measures, energy efficiency has been improving since the beginning of the 1970s. The government has set the goal of meeting half the country's energy demands from renewable sources by 2050.

In 2000, the government and the German nuclear power industry agreed to phase out all nuclear power plants by 2021. The government reversed this decision in January 2010, electing to keep plants open. Renewable energy still plays a more modest role in energy consumption.

In 2009, Germany consumed energy from the following sources:

- Oil 34.6%
- Natural gas 21.7%
- Lignite 11.4%
- Bituminous coal 11.1%
- Nuclear power 11.0%
- Hydro and wind power 1.5%
- Others 9.0%

Renewable energy is far more present in the domestically *produced* energy, since Germany imports about two thirds of its energy.

Oil and gas transport

There are 3 major entry points for oil pipelines: in the northeast (the Druzhba pipeline, coming from Gdańsk), west (coming from Rotterdam) and southeast (coming from Nelahozeves). The oil pipelines of Germany do not constitute a proper network, and sometimes only connect two different locations. Major oil refineries are located in or near the following cities: Schwedt, Spergau, Vohburg, Burghausen, Karlsruhe, Köln, Gelsenkirchen, Lingen, Wilhelmshafen, Hamburg and Heide.

Germany's network of natural gas pipelines, on the other hand, is dense and well-connected. Imported pipeline gas comes mostly from Russia, the Netherlands and the United Kingdom. Although gas imports from Russia have been historically reliable, even during the cold war, recent price disputes between Gazprom and the former Soviet states, such as Ukraine, have also affected Germany. As a result, high political importance is placed on the construction of the Nord Stream pipeline, running from Vyborg in Russia along the Baltic sea to Greifswald in Germany. This direct connection avoids third-party transit countries.

Infrastructure

With its central position in Europe, Germany is an important transportation hub. This is reflected in its dense and modern transportation networks. The extensive motorway (Autobahn) network that ranks worldwide third largest in its total length and features a lack of blanket speed limits on the majority of routes.

Germany has established a polycentric network of high-speed trains. The InterCityExpress or *ICE* is the most advanced service category of the Deutsche Bahn and serves major German cities as well as destinations in neighbouring countries. The train maximum speed varies between 160 km/h and 300 km/h (100-185 mph). Connections are offered at either 30-minute, hourly, or two-hourly intervals.

The ICE 3 trainset

Problems

A problem, pointed out by Gabor Steingart, is that the country's investment ratio (investment/GDP) has sunken from 18% in 1970 to 3%, and is now only a third of that of the United States. In Western Europe (including Germany) no new company has made it to the top 100 in the last 20 years - some consider this an problematic issue, while others cite it as an indicator of fair competition and lack of monopolization. This is in stark contrast to the United States, where newly founded high-tech companies have experienced significant increases.

See also

- Deutsche Bundesbank
- German model
- List of German states by GDP per capita
- Metropolitan regions in Germany
- Taxation in Germany
- Trade unions in Germany

External links

- OECD's Germany country Web site [3] and OECD Economic Survey of Germany [4]
- Federal Statistical Office Germany [5]
- Archive copy [6] at the Wayback Machine. Germany's growth performance in the 1990s - Published by the European Commission

Foreign relations of Germany

Germany

This article is part of the series:
Politics and government of Germany

Other countries · Atlas
Politics portal

The **Federal Republic of Germany** is a Central European country and member of the European Union, Group of 8 and NATO (among others). Germany is one of the world's leading industrialized countries and biggest market economy in Europe, with "windows to the East and West".

Since reunification in 1990, Germany has further extended its commitments and central position in European and global affairs.

History since 1945

Main article: History of Germany since 1945

Since 1951, Germany has been at the heart of European Integration and after German reunification in 1990 further promoted peaceful integration with its neighbors. Strong ties with the United States remain central to German foreign policy.

Within the framework of NATO and an integrated European Union Military Staff, the Federal Republic has resumed the deployment of military units to mediate in conflict regions worldwide.

Germany is one of the world's strongest supporters for ecological awareness in response to climate change and global warming.

Centerpieces of German foreign policy since 1945

Franco-German cooperation

Main article: Franco-German cooperation

Being the historic core of Europe and the "twin engine for European integration", the cooperation with France is one of the most central elements of German foreign policy. The Elysée Treaty from 1963 set the foundation for a collaboration that - next to the European project - also repeatedly called for a "Core Union" with maximum integration 1 [1].

European integration

European integration has gone a long way since the European Coal and Steel Community (ECSC) and the Elysée Treaty. Peaceful collaborations with its neighbors remain one of Germany's biggest political objectives, and Germany has been on the forefront of most achievements made in European integration:

- Maastricht Treaty

Most of the social issues facing European countries in general: immigration, aging populations, straining social-welfare and pension systems - are all important in Germany. Germany seeks to maintain peace through the "deepening" of integration among current members of the European Union member states

- European Defence Force
- Introduction of the single currency € Euro

Germany has been the largest net contributor to EU budgets for decades (in absolute terms - given Germany's comparatively large population - not per capita) and seeks to limit the growth of these net payments in the enlarged union.

- European Constitution

Westbindung

"Bindung" is the German word for *fixation* or *bond*; "Westbindung" is Germany's implant into Western Europe and the Western World.

In particular during the Cold War - but continuous into the 21st century - (West-) German foreign policy pursues the country's integration into NATO and a strong co-operation and collective security with its Western partners.

As a free democracy and market economy, the world's largest exporting nation and the world's third-richest economy (nominal GDP) (behind the U.S. and Japan), Germany shares the interest and institutions of a free and secure world trade.

Israel and the Near East

Main articles: Germany-Israel relations, Jews in Germany, Iran-Germany relations, and German-Iraqi relations

Following German history during the Holocaust, one of Postwar Germany's aims were to establish and maintain relations of Wiedergutmachung with the State of Israel. Starting with the Reparations Agreement in 1952, support for the national security of the State of Israel is central to German foreign policy.

Germany has been actively involved in the Israel-Egypt Peace Treaty in 1979, the Oslo Accords (1993) which led to the Israel-Jordan Peace Treaty in 1994 and the continuous Peace process in the Israeli-Palestinian conflict which make Germany arguably (next to the United States) Israel's closest ally.

Germany also holds a special relationship with Turkey and is active in maintaining diplomatic relationships with Iran.

Ostpolitik

Main article: Ostpolitik

Under the Hallstein Doctrine, the FRG did not have any diplomatic relations with countries in Eastern Europe until the early 1970s, when Willy Brandt's *Ostpolitik* led to increased dialogue and treaties like the Treaty of Warsaw, where West Germany accepted the Oder-Neisse line as German-Polish border, and the Basic Treaty, where West and East Germany accepted each other as sovereign entities. Both Germany states were admitted to the United Nations on 18 September 1973.

Development aid

Germany is one of the largest net contributors of the United Nations and has several development agencies working in Africa and the Middle East.

German reunification

Main article: German reunification

After the Fall of the Berlin Wall and the Treaty on the Final Settlement With Respect to Germany, German reunification took effect on 3 October 1990.

On 14 November 1990, Germany and Poland signed a treaty confirming the Oder-Neisse line. They also concluded a cooperation treaty on 17 June 1991. Germany concluded four treaties with the Soviet Union covering the overall bilateral relationship, economic relations, the withdrawal of Soviet troops from the territory of the former GDR, and German support for those troops.

Russia accepted obligations under these treaties as successor to the Soviet Union.

Centerpieces of German Foreign Policy since 1990

Central & Eastern Europe

- OSCE
- NATO enlargement

The German government was a strong supporter of the enlargement of NATO.

- Balkan Crisis

Germany was one of the first nations to recognize Croatia and Slovenia as independent nations, rejecting the concept of Yugoslavia as the only legitimate political order of the Balkan (unlike other European powers, who first proposed a pro-Belgrad policy). This is why Serb authorities sometimes referred to "new German imperialism" as one of the main reasons of Yugoslavia's collapse. German troops participate in the multinational efforts to bring peace and stability to the Balkans.

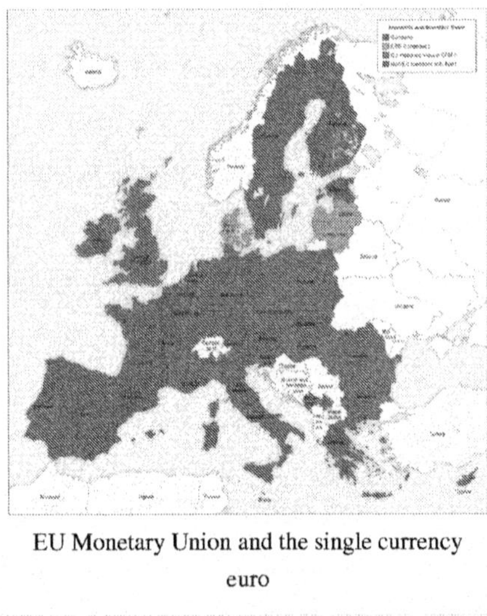

EU Monetary Union and the single currency euro

- European Union enlargement

Weimar triangle; Germany continues to be active economically in the states of central and eastern Europe, and to actively support the development of democratic institutions. In the 2000s Germany has been arguably the centerpiece of the European Union (though the importance of France cannot be overlooked in this connection).

(*see also* Foreign relations of the European Union)

Ecological involvement

see also Intergovernmental Panel on Climate Change

Kyoto protocol

Initiative for a permanent seat in the UNSC

The German Federal Government began an initiative to obtain a permanent seat in the United Nations Security Council, as part of the Reform of the United Nations. This would require approval of a two-thirds majority of the member states and approval of all five Security Council veto powers.

This aspiration could be successful due to Germany's good relations with the People's Republic of China and the Russian Federation. Germany is a stable and democratic republic and a G7 country which are also favourable attributes. The United Kingdom and France support German ascension to the supreme body. [2] The U.S. is sending mixed signals.

War on terror

In 2001, the discovery that the terrorist cell which carried out the attacks against the United States on September 11, 2001, was based in Hamburg, sent shock waves through the country.

The government of Chancellor Gerhard Schröder backed the following U.S. military actions, sending Bundeswehr troops to Afghanistan to lead a joint NATO program to provide security in the country after the ousting of the Taliban.

Nearly all of the public was strongly against America's 2003 invasion of Iraq, and any deployment of troops. This position was shared by the SPD/Green government, which led to some friction with the United States.

In August 2006, the German government disclosed a botched plot to bomb two German trains. The attack was to occur in July 2006 and involved a 21-year-old Lebanese man, identified only as Youssef Mohammed E. H. Prosecutors said Youssef and another man left suitcases stuffed with crude propane-gas bombs on the trains.

As of February 2007, Germany had about 3,000 NATO-led ISAF force in Afghanistan as part of the War on Terrorism, the third largest contingent after the United States (14,000) and the United Kingdom (5,200). [3] German forces are mostly in the more secure north of the country.

However, Germany, along with some other larger European countries (with the exception of the UK and the Netherlands), have been criticised by the British and Canadians for not sharing the burden of the more intensive combat operations in southern Afghanistan. [4] [5]

Foreign military relations

Under the doctrine introduced by the 2003 Defense Policy Guidelines, Germany continues to give priority to the transatlantic partnership with the United States through the North Atlantic Treaty Organization. However, Germany is giving increasing attention to coordinating its policies with the European Union through the Common European Security and Defence Policy.

Membership in international institutions

Council of Europe, European Union, European Space Agency, G4, G8, IMF, NATO, OECD, OSCE, UNO, World Bank Group, WTO

Bilateral relations

Europe

Country	Formal Relations Began	Notes
Austria		See Austria–Germany relations Due to German being the common language of the two European countries relations between them are close.
Belarus	1999	• Belarus has an embassy in Berlin and a Branch office in Bonn. • Germany has an embassy in Minsk. • German Federal Foreign Office about relations with Belarus [6]
Belgium		See Foreign relations of Belgium
Bulgaria		See Bulgarian-German relations • Bulgaria has an embassy in Berlin, a general-consulate in Munich and an office in Bonn. • Germany has an embassy in Sofia. • German Foreign Ministry about relations with Bulgaria [7] • German embassy in Sofia (in German and Bulgarian only) [8]
Croatia	1992-01-15	See Croatian-German relations • Croatia has an embassy in Berlin and 5 general consulates (in Düsseldorf, Frankfurt, Hamburg, Munich, and Stuttgart). • Germany has an embassy in Zagreb and an honorary consulate in Split. • There are more than 200,000 Croats who live in Germany.Historically Germany has had a close collaboration with Croatia. • Croatian Ministry of Foreign Affairs and European Integration: list of bilateral treaties signed with Germany [9] • German Federal Foreign Office about relations with Croatia [10]

<table>
<tr><td>Cyprus</td><td></td><td>See Foreign relations of Cyprus</td></tr>
<tr><td>Czech Republic</td><td></td><td>See Czech–German relations

Today, both countries share 815 km of common borders. The Czech Republic has an embassy in Berlin, 3 general consulates (in Bonn, Dresden and Munich), and 6 honorary consulates (in Dortmund, Frankfurt, Hamburg, Nürnberg, Rostock and Stuttgart). Germany has an embassy in Prague.</td></tr>
<tr><td>Denmark</td><td></td><td>See Danish-German relations

Denmark has an embassy in Berlin and 3 General Consulates in Flensburg, Hamburg and Munich. Both countries closely border each other.</td></tr>
<tr><td>UK</td><td></td><td>See Anglo-German relations

The two countries fought against each other in World War I and World War II.</td></tr>
<tr><td>France</td><td></td><td>See France – Germany relations

In recent times, France and Germany are among the most enthusiastic proponents of the further integration of the EU. They are sometimes described as the "twin engine" or "core countries" pushing for moves.

The two countries were arch enemies for centuries and fought against each other in World War I and World War II.</td></tr>
<tr><td>Greece</td><td>1834 (Prussia)</td><td>• The first Greek Embassy in Berlin was established in 1834, when Berlin was the capital of the Kingdom of Prussia.
• Greece has an embassy in Berlin and eight General Consulates in (Hamburg, Hannover, Cologne, Leipzig, Munich, Düsseldorf, Stuttgart, and Frankfurt).
• Germany has an embassy in Athens and a General Consulate in Thessaloniki.
• German Ministry of Foreign Affairs about relations with Greece [11]
• Greek Ministry of Foreign Affairs about relations with Germany [12]</td></tr>
<tr><td>Hungary</td><td>1973-12-21</td><td>See Germany-Hungary relations

• Germany has an embassy in Budapest.
• Hungary has an embassy in Berlin, 2 general consulates (in Düsseldorf and Münich) and 9 honorary consulates (in Bremerhaven, Erfurt, Hamburg, Nürnberg, Schwerin, Dresden, Essen, Frankfurt and Stuttgart).
• Both countries are full members of NATO and of the European Union.
• German Federal Foreign Office about relations with Hungary [13]
• Germany embassy in Budapest (in German and Hungarian only) [14]</td></tr>
<tr><td>Iceland</td><td></td><td>• Germany has an embassy in Reykjavik.
• Iceland has an embassy in Berlin and 10 honorary consulates in Bremerhaven, Cuxhaven, Düsseldorf, Frankfurt am Main, Hamburg, Köln, München, Rostock, Stuttgart, and Wissen.
• German-Icelandic cultural relations go back more than a thousand years, both country share Germanic cultural background.
• Both countries are NATO members.
• Germany Federal Foreign Office about relations with Iceland [15]</td></tr>
</table>

Ireland	1922	• Germany has an embassy in Dublin and 2 honorary consulates (in Cork and Galway). • Ireland has an embassy in Berlin and 4 honorary consulates (in Bergisch-Gladbach, Frankfurt am Main, Hamburg and Munich). • Both countries are full members of the European Union. • German Ministry of Foreign Affairs about relations with Ireland [16]
Italy		• Relations were established after the Unification of Italy. • Both countries enjoy friendly relations and were members of the Axis during World War Two, formed an alliance during the Cold War (West Germany), and are full members of the European Union. • Italy also has embassies in the following cities, Berlin, Frankfurt, Freiburg, Hamburg, Hanover, Munich, Nuremberg, Saarbrücken, and Stuttgart. • Germany has embassies in Rome, Milan and Naples.
Netherlands		• Relations were established following the unification of Germany in 1871. • During the First World War, the German army refrained from attacking the Netherlands, and thus relations between the two states were preserved. At war's end in 1918, the former Kaiser Wilhelm II fled to the Netherlands, where he lived till his death in 1941. • The German army occupied the Netherlands during the Second World War and kept the country under occupation in 1940-1945.
Kosovo		See German–Kosovan relations • Germany recognized Kosovo on 20 February 2008. • Germany has an embassy in Pristina since 27 February 2008. • Kosovo will open an embassy in Berlin. • Germany is the second-largest donor to Kosovo behind the US.
Latvia	1920 and again 1991-08-28	• Diplomatic relations were first established following Latvia's independence from Russian rule, under agreement signed in Berlin on July 15, 1920. These relation lasted until the Soviet take over of Latvia in 1940. • Relations were reestablished in 1991, following the collapse of the Soviet Union. • Germany has an embassy in Riga. • Latvia has an embassy in Berlin, a general consulate in Bonn and 7 honorary consulates (in Düsseldorf, Frankfurt, Hamburg, Köln, Künzelsau, Lübeck and München). • Both countries are full members of the Council of the Baltic Sea States, of NATO and of the European Union. • German Federal Foreign Office about relations with Latvia [17]
Malta	1965	• The German embassy opened in Valletta in 1965. • Malta has an embassy in Berlin. • Both countries are members of the European Union. • German Foreign Ministry about relations with Malta [18]
Moldova	1992-04-30	See Germany–Moldova relations • The Federal Republic of Germany recognised independence of Moldova on 14 December 1991. • Germany opened its embassy in Chişinău on 2 November 1992. • Moldovan Embassy, Berlin; Moldova opened its own embassy in Bonn on 28 March 1995.

Lithuania		• Germany has an embassy in Vilnius. • Lithuania has an embassy in Berlin, an office in Bonn and 7 honorary consulates (in Dresden, Düsseldorf, Erfurt, Frankfurt, Hamburg, Künzelsau and München). • Both countries are full members of the Council of the Baltic Sea States, of NATO and of the European Union. • German Federal Foreign Office about relations with Lithuania [19]
Poland		See German–Polish relations During the Cold War, communist Poland had good relations with East Germany, but had strained relations with West Germany. After the fall of communism, Poland and the reunited Germany have had a mostly positive but occasionally strained relationship due to some political issues. After the collapse of the Soviet Union, Germany has been a proponent of Poland's participation in NATO and the European Union. The Polish-German border is 467 km long.
Romania	1872	• Both countries have - due to a formerly significant number of Germans of Romania - also cultural relations. • Germany has an embassy in Bucharest and 2 consulates (in Sibiu and Timişoara). • Romania has an embassy in Berlin and 2 consulates-general (in Bonn and Munich). • German Federal Foreign Office about relation with Romania [20] • Romanian Ministry of Foreign Affairs about relations with Germany [21]
Russia		See Germany–Russia relations Germany tries to keep Russia engaged with the Western world. The future aim is to promote a stable market-economy liberal democracy in Russia, which is part of the Western world.
Serbia	1951	• Germany has an embassy in Belgrade. • Serbia has an embassy in Berlin and 5 general consulates (in Frankfurt, Hamburg, Munich, Stuttgart and Düsseldorf). • There are around 505,000 people of Serbian descent living in Germany. (See also Germans of Serbia, Serbs in Germany) • German Federal Foreign Office about relations with Serbie [22] • German embassy Belgrade(in German and Serbian only) [23] • Serbian Ministry of Foreign Affairs about relations with Germany [24]
Slovakia	1993	• Germany has an embassy in Bratislava. • Slovakia has an embassy in Berlin, an embassy branch in Bonn, a general consulate in Munich and 6 honorary consulates (in Bad Homburg vor der Höhe, Hamburg, Langenhagen, Leipzig, Stuttgart and Wuppertal). • Both countries are full members of NATO and of the European Union. • There are around 20,000 people of Slovak descent living in Germany. • German Foreign Office about the relation with Slovakia [25]
Sweden		• Relations have been strong with cultural and economic cooperation. • Germany has an embassy in Stockholm. • Sweden has an embassy in Berlin. • Sweden also has 12 honorary consulates in Germany.

Turkey		See German–Turkish relations Based on good Turkish-German relations from the 19th century onwards, Germany promoted a Turkish immigration to Germany. However, large scale didn't occur until the 20th century. Germany suffered an acute labor shortage after World War II and, in 1961, the Federal Republic of Germany (West Germany) officially invited Turkish workers to Germany to fill in this void, particularly to work in the factories that helped fuel Germany's economic miracle. The German authorities named these people *Gastarbeiter* (German for *guest workers*). Most Turks in Germany trace their ancestry to Central and Eastern Anatolia. Today, Turks are Germany's largest ethnic minority and form most of Germany's Muslim minority. Berlin is home to about 250,000 Turks, making it the largest Turkish community outside of Turkey.
Ukraine		See Germany–Ukraine relations • Germany has an embassy in Kiev. • Ukraine has an embassy in Berlin and 3 Consulates-General (in Frankfurt, Hamburg and Munich).

Americas

Country	Formal Relations Began	Notes
Barbados	1967-03-14	See Barbados–Germany relations • Barbados is represented in Germany through its embassy in Brussels, (Belgium). • Germany is represented in to Barbados from its embassy in Port of Spain, (Trinidad and Tobago).
Bolivia		• Diplomatic relations between the two states were broken during the First World War. • Relations were restored after the war under the agreement concluded on July 20, 1921.
Canada		See Canada–Germany relations Until 2005 Canada's embassy was in Bonn, but in April 2005 a new embassy opened in Berlin. Canada also operates consulates in Munich, Düsseldorf and Hamburg. The provinces of Ontario and Alberta have representatives in Germany, co-located in the consulates. Quebec runs a stand-alone bureau in Munich, with an "antenne culturelle" office in Berlin. In addition to its embassy in Ottawa, Germany maintains consulates in Toronto, Montreal and Vancouver. Additional diplomats responsible for specialized files are also accredited from Washington.
Paraguay	1860-08-01	• Germany has an embassy in Asuncion. • Paraguay has an embassy in Berlin. • German Federal Foreign Office about relations with Paraguay [26] • Paraguayan Ministry of Foreign Relations about relations with Germany [27]
United States		See Germany – United States relations Since 2006, the current chancellor Angela Merkel has sought warmer relations with the United States and to rebuild political ties on common values and beliefs.

Uruguay		See Germany–Uruguay relations Germany has an embassy in Montevideo. Uruguay has an embassy in Berlin, a general consulate in Hamburg and 6 honorary consulate (in Bremen, Düsseldorf, Frankfurt am Main, Munich, Potsdam and Stuttgart). Germany is the Uruguay's principal trading partner in the European Union.

Asia

Country	Formal Relations Began	Notes
Armenia		See Armenia–Germany relations Armenian-German relations have always been stable and solid, with both countries continuing to work together and advance through the years with in cooperation. Both countries' leaders have discussed bilateral relations and noted that they have considerably improved over the last few years.
Azerbaijan		• Azerbaijan has an embassy in Berlin. • Germany has an embassy in Baku. • Both countries are full members of the Council of Europe and the Organization for Security and Co-operation in Europe (OSCE).
Georgia		See Foreign relations of Georgia
India		See Germany–India relations Germany and India have great military and trade relations with each other. Germany being one of the first countries to agree with the Indo-US Nuclear deal.
Iraq		See Germany–Iraq relations • Iraq has an embassy in Berlin. • Germany has an embassy in Baghdad. • There are currently some 84,000-150,000 Iraqis living in Germany.
Israel		See Germany–Israel relations Germany-Israel relations refers to the special relationship between Israel and Germany based on shared beliefs, Western values and a combination of historical perspectives. Among the most important factors in their relations is Nazi Germany's role in the genocide of European Jews during the Holocaust.
Japan		See Germany–Japan relations Regular meetings between the two countries have led to several cooperations. In 2004 German Chancellor Gerhard Schröder and Prime Minister Junichiro Koizumi agreed upon cooperations in the assistance for reconstruction of Iraq and Afghanistan, the promotion of economic exchange activities, youth and sports exchanges as well as exchanges and cooperation in science, technology and academic fields. After China, Japan is Germany's principal trading partner in Asia in 2006:

Malaysia		See Germany–Malaysia relations • Germany has an embassy in Kuala Lumpur. • Malaysia has an embassy in Berlin.
Pakistan		Pakistan and Germany enjoy closely cordial relations. Germany has taken extreme measures to aid the South Asian country in its' economic and governmental hardship. Commercial trade between Islamabad and Berlin has also been very essential in recent years seeing as Germany is Pakistan's fourth largest trade partner. Also, Germany is home to 35,081 Pakistani immigrants. • See also Pakistanis in Germany
People's Republic of China		See People's Republic of China – Germany relations Germany has traditionally good relationships with the People's Republic of China, even though Angela Merkel and large parts of Germany's political class have recently criticised the People's Republic for holding back reforms in the field of democracy and human rights. In recent years trade between both countries has reached high volumes, both in import and exports.

Africa

Country	Formal Relations Began	Notes
Egypt	1957-12	See Egypt–Germany relations Egypt has an embassy in Berlin, as well as consulates in Frankfurt and Hamburg. Germany has an embassy in Cairo.
Libya		See Germany–Libya relations Germany is represented in Libya with an embassy in Tripolis, while Libya has an embassy in Berlin. The relationship between these countries was tense in the late 1980s following a bombing incident, but has improved since with increasingly close co-operation especially on economic matters.
Namibia		See Germany–Namibia relations Peter Katjavivi, a founder of the University of Namibia and longtime South West Africa People's Organization member, has been the Namibian ambassador in Berlin since 2006.

See also

- Security issues in Germany
- Human rights in Germany
- List of diplomatic missions in Germany
- List of diplomatic missions of Germany
- Sino-German cooperation (1911–1941)
- Visa requirements for German citizens

Further reading

- Germany in Europe [28]
- German -Bashing and the Breakup of Yugoslavia, ("The Donald W. Treadgold Papers in Russian, East European and Central Asian Studies, n° 16, March 1998). University of Washington: HMJ School of International Studies [29]
- The German Economy in the New Europe [30]
- EU Enlargement and Transatlantic Relations [31]
- Bierling, Stephan. *Die Außenpolitik der Bundesrepublik Deutschland: Normen, Akteure, Entscheidungen. 2. Auflage*. München: Oldenbourg, 2005 ISBN 3-486-57766-2.
- von Bredow, Wilfried. *Die Außenpolitik der Bundesrepublik Deutschland: Eine Einführung*. Wiesbaden: VS Verlag für Sozialwissenschaften, 2006 ISBN 3-531-13618-6.

External links

- Permanent Mission of Germany to the United Nations [32]
- Auswärtiges Amt [33]
- AICGS American Institute for Contemporary German Studies [34]
- SWP German Institute for International and Security Affairs [35]

Culture of Germany

This article deals with the Culture of Germany as a political state *within Europe; for a review of the culture of the* German-speaking world, *see Culture of German-speaking Europe.*

Johann Wolfgang von Goethe was a significant German poet

German culture began long before the rise of Germany as a nation state. Due to its rich cultural history, Germany is often known as *das Land der Dichter und Denker* (the land of poets and thinkers).

Germany, over the centuries, has produced a great number of polymaths, geniuses and notable people, such as Albert Einstein, Ludwig van Beethoven, Johannes Kepler, Johann Wolfgang von Goethe, Immanuel Kant, Johann Sebastian Bach, Karl Marx, Richard Wagner, Martin Luther, Friedrich Nietzsche, Karl Benz, Georg Ohm, Rudolf Diesel, Gottfried Leibniz, Johannes Gutenberg and Richard Strauss among others.

Literature

Main article: German literature

Walk of Ideas, Berlin, a sculpture honoring Johannes Gutenberg and some of Germany's most influential writers

German literature can be traced back to the Middle Ages, with the most notable authors of the period being Walther von der Vogelweide and Wolfram von Eschenbach. The *Nibelungenlied*, whose author remains unknown, is also an important work of the epoch, as is the *Thidrekssaga*. The fairy tales collections collected and published by Jacob and Wilhelm Grimm in the 19th century became famous throughout the world.

Theologian Luther, who translated the Bible into German, is widely credited for having set the basis for the modern "High German" language. Among the most admired German poets and authors are Lessing, Goethe, Schiller, Kleist, Hoffmann, Brecht, Heine and Schmidt. Nine Germans have won the Nobel Prize in literature:

Theodor Mommsen, Paul von Heyse, Gerhart Hauptmann, Thomas Mann, Nelly Sachs, Hermann Hesse, Heinrich Böll, Günter Grass, and Herta Müller.

Philosophy and the history of ideas

Main article: German philosophy

German philosopher Immanuel Kant

Germany's influence on philosophy is historically significant and many German philosophers have helped shape western philosophy from as early as the Middle Ages (Albertus Magnus). Later, Leibniz (17th century) and most importantly Kant played central roles in the history of philosophy. Kantianism inspired the work of Schopenhauer and Nietzsche as well as German idealism defended by Fichte and Hegel. Marx and Engels developed communist theory in the second half of the 19th century while Heidegger and Gadamer pursued the tradition of German philosophy in the 20th century. A number of German intellectuals were also influential in sociology, most notably Adorno, Habermas, Horkheimer, Luhmann, Simmel, Tönnies, and Weber. The University of Berlin founded in 1810 by linguist and philosopher Wilhelm von Humboldt served as an influential model for a number of modern western universities.

Science

Main article: Science and technology in Germany

Main article: German inventors and discoverers

Germany has been the home of many famous inventors and engineers, such as Johannes Gutenberg, who is credited with the invention of movable type printing in Europe; Hans Geiger, the creator of the Geiger counter; and Konrad Zuse, who built the first computer. German inventors, engineers and industrialists such as Zeppelin, Daimler, Diesel, Otto, Wankel, Von Braun and Benz helped shape modern automotive and air transportation technology including the beginnings of space travel.

The work of Albert Einstein and Max Planck was crucial to the foundation of modern physics, which Werner Heisenberg and Erwin Schrödinger developed further. They were preceded by such key physicists as Hermann von Helmholtz, Joseph von Fraunhofer, and Gabriel Daniel Fahrenheit, among others. Wilhelm Conrad Röntgen discovered X-rays, an accomplishment that made him the first winner of the Nobel Prize in Physics in 1901. The Walhalla temple for "laudable and distinguished Germans", features a number of scientists, and is located east of Regensburg, in Bavaria.

Music

Main article: Music of Germany

In the field of music, Germany claims some of the most renowned classical composers of the world including Bach, Mozart and Beethoven, who marked the transition between the Classical and Romantic eras in Western classical music. Other composers of the Austro-German tradition who achieved international fame include Brahms, Wagner, Haydn, Schubert, Händel, Schumann, Liszt, Mendelssohn Bartholdy, Johann Strauss II, Bruckner, Mahler, Telemann, Richard Strauss, Schoenberg, Orff, and most recently, Henze, Lachenmann, and Stockhausen.

As of 2006, Germany is the fifth largest music market in the world and has exerted a strong influence on Dance and Rock music, and pioneered trance music. Artists such as Herbert Grönemeyer, Scorpions, Rammstein, Nena, Dieter Bohlen, Tokio Hotel and Modern Talking have enjoyed international fame. German musicians and, particularly, the pioneering bands Tangerine Dream and Kraftwerk have also contributed to the development of electronic music. Germany hosts many large rock music festivals annually. The Rock am Ring festival is the largest music festival in Germany, and among the largest in the world. German artists also make up a large percentage of Industrial music acts, which is called Neue Deutsche Härte. Germany hosts one of the largest Goth rock scenes and festivals in the entire world, with events like Wave-Gotik-Treffen easily attracting up to 30,000 people.

Cinema

Main article: Cinema of Germany

German cinema dates back to the very early years of the medium with the work of Max Skladanowsky. It was particularly influential during the years of the Weimar Republic with German expressionists such as Robert Wiene and Friedrich Wilhelm Murnau. The Nazi era produced mostly propaganda films although the work of Leni Riefenstahl still introduced new aesthetics in film. From the 1960s, New German Cinema directors such as Volker Schlöndorff, Werner Herzog, Wim Wenders, Rainer Werner Fassbinder placed West-German cinema back onto the international stage with their often provocative films, while the *Deutsche Film-Aktiengesellschaft* controlled film production in the GDR. More recently, films such as *Das Boot* (1981), *The Never Ending Story* (1984) *Run Lola Run* (1998), *Das Experiment* (2001), *Good Bye Lenin!* (2003), *Gegen die Wand (Head-on)* (2004) and *Der Untergang (Downfall)* (2004) have enjoyed international success. In 2007 the Academy Award for Best Foreign Language Film went to F.H. von Donnersmarck's The Lives of Others. The Berlin Film Festival, held yearly since 1951, is one of the world's foremost film and cinemas festivals.

Fine arts and decorative arts

Important German Renaissance painters include Albrecht Altdorfer, Lucas Cranach the Elder, Matthias Grünewald, Hans Holbein the Younger and the well-known Albrecht Dürer. The most important Baroque artists from Germany are Cosmas Damian Asam. Further artists are the romantic Caspar David Friedrich, the surrealist Max Ernst, the conceptualist Joseph Beuys or the neo-expressionist Georg Baselitz.

Architecture

Further information: German architecture

Architectural contributions from Germany include the Carolingian and Ottonian styles, important precursors of Romanesque. The region then produced significant works in styles such as the Gothic, Renaissance and Baroque. The nation was particularly important in the early modern movement through the Deutscher Werkbund and the Bauhaus movement identified with Walter Gropius. The Nazis closed these movements and favoured a type of neo-classicism. Since World War II, further important modern and post-modern structures have been built, particularly since the reunification of Berlin.

Religious tradition

Main article: Religion in Germany

The German government has limited responsibilities for culture, which is devolved to the states of Germany, called *Länder*.

Portrait of Martin Luther

64.1 percent of the German population belongs to Christian denominations. 31.4 percent are Roman Catholic, and 32.7 percent are affiliated with Protestantism (the figures are known accurately because Germany imposes a church tax on those who disclose a religious affiliation / but there are many people, who are religious but not registered[citation needed]). The North and East is predominantly Protestant, the South and West rather Catholic. Nowadays there is a non-religious majority in Hamburg and the East German states. Germany formed a substantial part of the Roman Catholic Holy Roman Empire, but was also the source of Protestant reformers such as Martin Luther. Historically, Germany had a substantial Jewish population. Only a few thousand people of Jewish origin remained in Germany after the Holocaust, but the German Jewish community now has approximately 100,000 members, many from the former Soviet Union. Germany also has a substantial Muslim minority, most of whom are from Turkey.

German theologians include Luther, Melanchthon, Schleiermacher, Feuerbach, and Rudolf Otto. Also Germany brought up many mystics including Meister Eckhart, Rudolf Steiner, Jakob Boehme, and some popes (e.g. Benedict XVI).

Academic landmarks

Germany is home to some of the finest academic centers in Europe. Some famous Universities include those of both Munich and Berlin, University of Tübingen, University of Göttingen, University of Marburg, University of Berlin, Heidelberg University, Mining Academy Freiberg and Freiburg University, among many others.

Since about 1970, Germany has once again had a thriving popular culture, now increasingly being led by its new-old capital Berlin and the city of Hamburg, and a self-confident music and art scene. Germany is also very well known for its many renowned opera houses, such as Semperoper, Komische Oper Berlin and Staatstheater am Gärtnerplatz. Richard Wagner has built the Bayreuth Festspielhaus.

Cuisine

Main article: German cuisine

Berliners are a typical German pastry

German cuisine varies from region to region, but concentrates on meat and varieties of sweet desserts and cakes (such as Black Forest gateau *Schwarzwälder Kirschtorte*) and *Stollen* (a fruit cake). Germans also are famous for rye bread. Germany also produces a large quantity of beer, and (mostly white) wine, particularly Riesling, but also Müller-Thurgau and other varieties.

German cuisine is very similar to English and American cuisine and also to the cooking styles of its immediate neighbors (The Netherlands, France, Austria, Poland). Although sausage is the most famous food product from Germany, one could not gain much understanding of German cuisine by reducing it to sausage. In Germany it is mostly consumed as a snack (Landjaeger), at barbecues and it also appears in a few dishes. A stereotypical German dish contains a type of meat (typically pork, beef or poultry), a type of potatoes (mashed, fried, as dumplings or boiled) and a type of vegetable (typically peas, carrots or cabbage) and sauce. The "home cuisine" differs very much from the "restaurant cuisine". More traditional dishes can be found in restaurants. Cuisine differs also greatly according to regions (in the north people eat fish, in the Rhine region beer is replaced with wine, in Bavaria roasted pork is consumed) and season (in spring people eat white asparagus with ham and sauce hollandaise, in fall people eat green cabbage with a special kind of sausage and mustard and in winter/for Christmas people eat duck or goose with red cabbage, dumplings and brown gravy).

Sport

Main article: Sport in Germany

Opened in 2005: the Allianz Arena, one of the world's most modern football stadiums.

Sport forms an integral part of German life, as demonstrated by the fact that 27 million Germans are members of a sports club and an additional twelve million pursue such an activity individually. Football is by far the most popular sport, and the German Football Federation (Deutscher Fußballbund) with more than 6.3 million members is the largest athletic organisation in the country. It also attracts the greatest audience, with hundreds of thousands of spectators attending Bundesliga matches and millions more watching on television. The other two most popular sports in Germany are marksmanship and tennis represented by the German Marksmen's Federation and the German Tennis Federation respectively, both including more than a million members. Other popular sports include handball, volleyball, basketball, and ice hockey. Germany has historically been one of the strongest contenders in the Olympic Games. In the 2008 Summer Olympics, Germany finished fifth overall, whereas in the 2006 Winter Olympics Germany finished first.

See also

- Bundesliga
- German wine
- German literature
- Goethe-Institut
- List of Germans
- Music of Germany
- Prussian virtues
- Public holidays: German Unity Day
- Science and technology in Germany

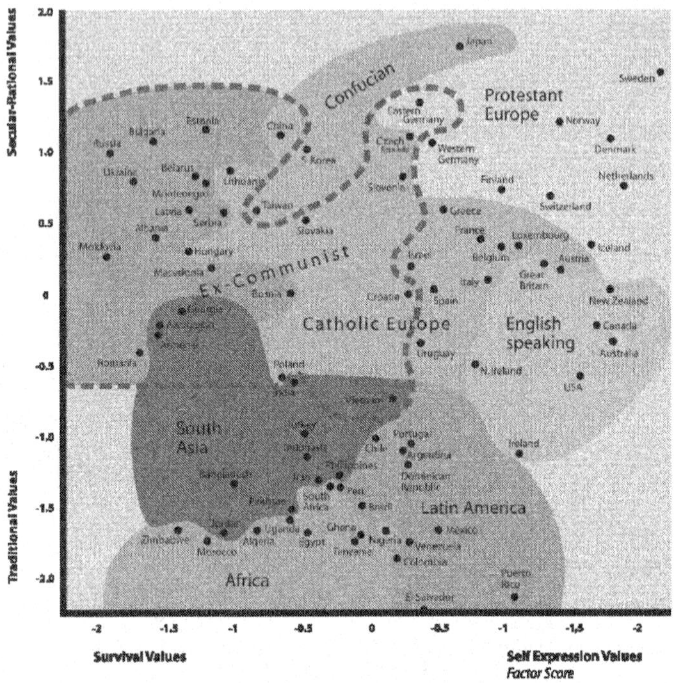

Cultural map of the world according to the World Values Survey, describing Germany as high in "Rational-Secular Values" and average-high in "Self-Expression values".

External links

- Facts about Germany: culture [1]
- German Embassy, Washington, DC: culture [2]
- Goethe Institute [3]
- Thomas Gloning [4]

Neuschwanstein Castle

Geographical coordinates: 47°33′27″N 10°45′00″E

Castle_Neuschwanstein.jpg	
Architectural style	Romanesque Revival
Location	Schwangau, Germany
Owner	Bavarian Palace Department
Started	5 September 1869
Completed	c.1892 (unfinished)
Architect	Eduard Riedel
Civil engineer	Eduard Riedel, Georg von Dollmann, Julius Hofmann thumb|Castillo de Hades de Saint Seiya
Other designers	Ludwig II, Christian Jank

Neuschwanstein Castle (German: ***Schloss Neuschwanstein***, pronounced [nɔʏˈʃvaːnʃtaɪn]) is a 19th-century Romanesque Revival palace on a rugged hill above the village of Hohenschwangau near Füssen in southwest Bavaria, Germany. The palace was commissioned by Ludwig II of Bavaria as a retreat and as a homage to Richard Wagner.

The palace was intended as a personal refuge for the reclusive king, but it was opened to the paying public immediately after his death in 1886. Since then over 60 million people have visited Neuschwanstein Castle. More than 1.3 million people visit annually, with up to 6,000 per day in the summer. The palace has appeared prominently in several movies and was the inspiration for Disneyland's Sleeping Beauty Castle.

Location

The municipality of Schwangau lies at an elevation of 800 m (2620 ft) at the south west border of the German state of Bavaria. Its surroundings are characterized by the transition between the Alpine foothills in the south (towards the nearby Austrian border) and a hilly landscape in the north that appears flat by comparison. In the Middle Ages, three castles overlooked the village.

One was called *Schwanstein Castle*. In 1832 Ludwig's father King Maximilian II of Bavaria bought its ruins to replace them by the comfortable neo-Gothic palace known as Hohenschwangau Castle. Finished in 1837, the palace became his family's summer residence, and his elder son Ludwig (born 1845) spent a large part of his childhood here.[*citation needed*]

Vorderhohenschwangau Castle and *Hinterhohenschwangau Castle* sat on a rugged hill overlooking Schwanstein Castle, two nearby lakes (Alpsee and Schwansee), and the village. Separated only by a moat, they jointly consisted of a hall, a keep, and a fortified tower house. In the 19th century only ruins remained of the medieval twin castles, but those of Hinterhohenschwangau served as a lookout place known as *Sylphenturm*.

Modern panorama from Neuschwanstein (1008 m/3307 ft) showing (left to right): palace access road; Alpsee with locality of Hohenschwangau in front; 19th century Hohenschwangau Castle on a hill with Schwansee behind it on the right (west); locality of Alterschrofen with town of Füssen behind it; core of Schwangau in front of large Forggensee reservoir (1952); Bannwaldsee (north)

The ruins above the family palace were known to the crown prince from his excursions. He first sketched one of them in his diary in 1859. When the young king came to power in 1864, the construction of a new palace in place of the two ruined castles became the first in his series of palace building projects. Ludwig himself called the new palace *New Hohenschwangau Castle* – only after his death was it renamed *Neuschwanstein*. The confusing result is that Hohenschwangau and Schwanstein have effectively swapped names: Hohenschwangau Castle replaced the ruins of Schwanstein Castle, and Neuschwanstein Castle replaced the ruins of the two Hohenschwangau Castles.

Concept and ethos

Neuschwanstein embodies both the contemporaneous architectural fashion known as *castle romanticism* (German: *Burgenromantik*), and Ludwig II's immoderate enthusiasm for the operas of Richard Wagner.

In the 19th century many castles were constructed or reconstructed, often with significant changes to make them more picturesque. Palace-building projects similar to Neuschwanstein had been undertaken earlier in several of the German states and included Hohenschwangau Castle, Lichtenstein Castle, Hohenzollern Castle and numerous buildings on the River Rhine such as Stolzenfels Castle. The inspiration for the construction of Neuschwanstein came from two journeys in 1867: One in May to the reconstructed Wartburg near Eisenach, another in July to the Château de Pierrefonds, which Eugène Viollet-le-Duc was transforming from a ruined castle into a historistic palace.

Examples of 19th century castle romanticism

Hohenschwangau Castle

Hohenzollern Castle

Stolzenfels Castle

Château de Pierrefonds

Wartburg

The king saw both buildings as representatives of a romantic interpretation of the Middle Ages as well as the musical mythology of his friend Richard Wagner. Wagner's operas Tannhäuser and Lohengrin had made a lasting impression on him.

In February 1868 Ludwig's grandfather Ludwig I died, freeing the considerable sums that were previously spent on the abdicated king's appanage. This allowed him to start the architectural project of building a private refuge in the familiar landscape far from the capital Munich, so that he could live his idea of the Middle Ages.

Ludwig II (c.1868)

> It is my intention to rebuild the old castle ruin of Hohenschwangau near the Pöllat Gorge in the authentic style of the old German knights' castles, and I must confess to you that I am looking forward very much to living there one day [...]; you know the revered guest I would like to accommodate there; the location is one of the most beautiful to be found, holy and unapproachable, a worthy temple for the divine friend who has brought salvation and true blessing to the world. It will also remind you of "Tannhäuser" (Singers' Hall with a view of the castle in the background), "Lohengrin'" (castle courtyard, open corridor, path to the chapel) [...].

– Ludwig II, *Letter to Richard Wagner*, May 1868

The building design was drafted by the stage designer Christian Jank and realized by the architect Eduard Riedel. For technical reasons the ruined castles could not be integrated into the plan. Initial ideas for the palace drew stylistically on Nuremberg Castle and envisaged a simple building in place of the old Vorderhohenschwangau Castle, but they were rejected and replaced by increasingly extensive drafts, culminating in a bigger palace modelled on the Wartburg. The king insisted on a detailed plan and on personal approval of each draft. His control went so far that the palace has been regarded as his own creation rather than that of the architects involved.

Whereas contemporary architecture critics flouted Neuschwanstein, one of the last big palace building projects of the 19th century, as kitsch, Neuschwanstein and Ludwig II's other buildings are now counted among the major works of European historicism. For financial reasons a project similar to Neuschwanstein – Falkenstein Castle – never left the planning stages.

The palace can be regarded as typical for 19th century architecture. The shapes of Romanesque (simple geometric figures such as cuboids and semicircular arches), Gothic (upward-pointing lines, slim towers, delicate embellishments) and Byzantine architecture and art (the Throne Hall décor) were mingled in an eclectic fashion and supplemented with 19th century technical achievements. The Patrona Bavariae and Saint George on the court face of the Palas (main building) are depicted in the local Lüftlmalerei style, a fresco technique typical for Allgäu farmers' houses, while the unimplemented drafts for the Knights' House gallery foretell elements of Art Nouveau. Characteristic for Neuschwanstein's design are theater themes: Christian Jank drew on coulisse drafts from his time as a scenic painter.

The basic style was originally planned to be neo-Gothic but was primarily built in Romanesque style in the end. The operatic themes moved gradually from Tannhäuser and Lohengrin to Parcival.

Construction

In 1868 the ruins of the medieval twin castles were demolished completely; the remains of the old keep were blown up. The foundation stone for the Palas was laid on September 5, 1869; in 1872 its cellar was completed and in 1876 everything up to the first floor. But the Gatehouse was finished first. At the end of the year 1874 it was completed and fully furnished, allowing Ludwig to take provisional lodgings there and observe the further construction work. In 1874 direction of the civil works passed from Eduard Riedel to Georg von Dollmann. The topping out ceremony for the Palas was in 1880, and in 1884 the king could move into the new building. In the same year the direction of the project passed to Julius Hofmann, after Dollmann had fallen in disgrace.

Neuschwanstein under construction: Bower still missing, Rectangular Tower under construction (photograph c.1882–85)

The palace was erected as a conventional brick construction and later encased with other types of rock. The white lime stone used for the fronts came from a nearby quarry. The sandstone bricks for the portals and bay windows came from Schlaitdorf in Württemberg. Marble from Untersberg near Salzburg was used for the windows, the arch ribs, the columns and the capitals. The Throne Hall was a later addition to the plans and required a steel framework.

Neuschwanstein under construction: upper courtyard (photograph c.1886)

The transport of building materials was facilitated by a scaffolding and a steam crane that lifted the material to the construction site. Another crane was used at the construction site itself. The recently founded Dampfkessel-Revisionsverein (Steam Boiler Inspection Association) regularly inspected both boilers.

For about two decades the construction site was the principal employer of the region. In 1880 about 200 craftsmen were occupied at the site, not counting suppliers and other persons indirectly involved in the construction. At times when the king insisted on particularly close deadlines and urgent changes, reportedly up to 300 workers per day were active, sometimes at night by the light of oil lamps. Statistics from the years 1879/1880 support an immense amount of building materials: 465 t (513 short tons) of Salzburg marble, 1550 t (1710 short tons) of sandstone, 400,000 bricks and 2050 m^3 (2680 cu yd) of wood for the scaffolding.

In 1870 a society was founded for insuring the workers, for a low monthly fee, augmented by the king. The heirs of construction casualties (30 cases are mentioned in the statistics) received a small pension.

In 1884 the king could move into the (still unfinished) Palas,, and in 1885 he invited his mother Marie to Neuschwanstein on the occasion of her 60th birthday. By 1886 the external structure of the *Palas* (hall) was mostly finished. In the same year, Ludwig had the first, wooden *Marienbrücke* over the Pöllat Gorge replaced by a steel construction.

Despite its size, Neuschwanstein did not have space for the royal court, but contained only the king's private lodging and servants' rooms. The court buildings served decorative, rather than residential purposes: The palace was intended to serve Ludwig II as a kind of inhabitable theatrical setting. As a *temple of friendship* it was also devoted to life and work of Richard Wagner, who died in 1883 before he had set foot in the building. In the end, Ludwig II only lived in the palace for a total of 172 days.

Architecture

The effect of the Neuschwanstein ensemble is highly theatrical, both externally and internally. The king's influence is apparent throughout, and he took a keen personal interest in the design and decoration. An example can be seen in his comments, or commands, regarding a mural depicting Lohengrin in the Palas; "His Majesty wishes that ... the ship be placed further from the shore, that Lohengrin's neck be less tilted, that the chain from the ship to the swan be of gold and not of roses, and finally that the style of the castle shall be kept medieval."[*citation needed*]

The suite of rooms within the Palas contains the Throne Room, Ludwig's suite, the Singers' Hall, and the Grotto. Throughout, the design pays homage to the German legends of Lohengrin, the Swan Knight. Hohenschwangau, where Ludwig spent much of his youth, had decorations of these sagas. These themes were taken up in the operas of Richard Wagner. Many rooms bear a border depicting the various operas written by Wagner, including a theater permanently featuring the set of one such play. Many of the interior rooms remain undecorated, with only 14 rooms finished before Ludwig's death. With the palace under construction at the King's death, one of the major features of the palace remained unbuilt. A massive keep was planned for the middle of the upper courtyard but was never built, at the decision of the King's family. The foundation for the keep is visible in the upper courtyard.

View from south-east, Palas on the left

Neuschwanstein Castle consists of several individual structures which were erected over a length of 150 metres on the top of a cliff ridge. The elongate building is furnished with numerous towers, ornamental turrets, gables, balconies, pinnacles and sculptures. Following Romanesque style, most window openings are fashioned as bi- and triforia. Before the backdrop of the Tegelberg and the Pöllat Gorge in the south and the Alpine foothills with their lakes in the north, the ensemble of individual buildings provides varying picturesque views of the palace from all directions. It was designed as the romantic ideal of a knights' castle. Unlike "real" castles, whose building stock is in most cases the result of centuries of building activity, Neuschwanstein was planned from the inception as an intentionally asymmetric building, and erected in consecutive stages. Typical attributes of a castle were cited, but real fortifications – the most important feature of a medieval aristocratic estate – were dispensed with.

Exterior

The palace complex is entered through the symmetrical Gatehouse flanked by two stair towers. The eastward-pointing gate building is the only structure of the palace whose wall area is fashioned in high-contrast colors; the exterior walls are cased with red bricks, the court fronts with yellow lime stone. The roof cornice is surrounded by pinnacles. The upper floor of the Gatehouse is surmounted by a crow-stepped gable and held Ludwig II's first lodging at Neuschwanstein, from which he occasionally observed the building work before the hall was completed. The ground floors of the Gatehouse were intended to accommodate the stables.

View from location of unrealized chapel along upper courtyard level: Bower (left), Palas front, and Knights' House (right)

The passage through the Gatehouse, crowned with the royal Bavarian coat of arms, leads directly into the courtyard. The courtyard has two levels, the lower one being defined to the east by the Gatehouse and to the north by the foundations of the so-called Rectangular Tower and by the gallery building. The southern end of the courtyard is open, imparting a view of the surrounding mountain scenery. At its western end the courtyard is delimited by a bricked embankment, whose polygonally protracting bulge marks the choir of the originally projected chapel. A flight of steps at the side gives access to the upper level.

The most striking structure of the upper court level is the so-called Rectangular Tower (45 metres). Like most of the court buildings, it mostly serves a decorative purpose as part of the ensemble. Its viewing platform provides a vast view over the Alpine foothills to the north. The northern end of the upper courtyard is defined by the so-called Knights' House. The three-story building is connected to the Rectangular Tower and the Gatehouse by means of a continuous gallery fashioned with a blind arcade. From the point of view of castle romanticism the Knights' House was the abode of a stronghold's menfolk; at Neuschwanstein, estate and service rooms were envisioned here. The Bower, which complements the Knights' House as the "ladies' house" but was never used as such, defines the south side of the court yard. Both structures together form the motif of the *Antwerp Castle* featuring in the first act of *Lohengrin*. Embedded in the pavement is the floor plan of the planned palace chapel.

Gatehouse

The western end of the courtyard is delimited by the *Palas* (hall). It constitutes the real main and residential building of the castle and contains the king's stateroom and the servants' rooms. The Palas is a colossal five-story structure in the shape of two huge cuboids that are connected in a flat angle and covered by two adjacent high gable roofs. The building's shape follows the course of the ridge. In its angles there are two stair towers, the northern one surmounting the palace roof by several stories with its height of 65 metres. With their polymorphic roofs, both towers are reminiscent of the Château de Pierrefonds. The western Palas front supports a two-story balcony with view on the Alpsee, while northwards a low chair tower and the conservatory protract from the main structure. The entire Palas is spangled with numerous decorative chimneys and ornamental turrets, the court front with colorful frescos. The court-side gable is crowned with a copper lion, the western (outward) gable with the likeness of a knight.

Interior

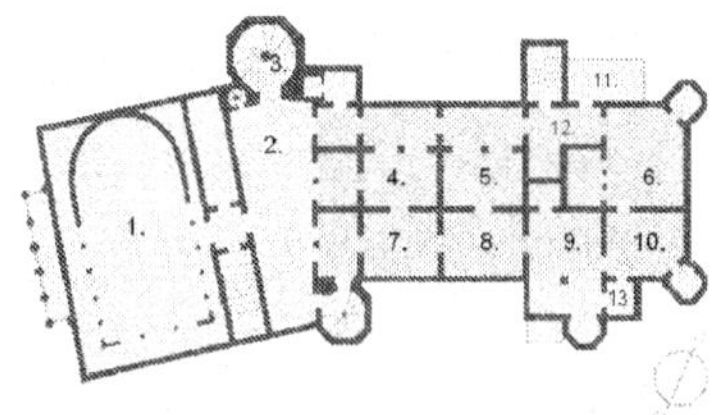

Floor plan of third floor, position of fourth-floor Hall of the Singers marked in red

Had it been completed, the palace would have had more than 200 interior rooms, including premises for guests and servants as well as for service and logistics. Ultimately, no more than about 15 rooms and halls were finished. In its lower stories the Palas accommodates administrative and servants' rooms and the rooms of today's palace administration. The king's staterooms are situated in the upper stories: The anterior structure accommodates the lodgings in the third floor, above them the *Hall of the Singers*. The upper floors of the west-facing posterior structure are filled almost completely by the Throne Hall. The total floor space of all floors amounts to nearly 6000 square metres.

Corridor

Neuschwanstein houses numerous significant interior rooms of German historicism. The palace was fitted with several of the latest technical innovations of the late 19th century. Among other things it had a battery-powered bell system for the servants and telephone lines. The kitchen equipment included a Rumford oven which turned the skewer with its heat and so automatically adjusted the turning speed. The hot air was used for a calorifère central heating system. Further novelties for the era were running warm water and toilets with automatic flushing.

The largest room of the palace is the Hall of the Singers, followed by the Throne Hall. The 27 metres by 10 metres Hall of the Singers is located in the eastern, court-side wing of the Palas, in the fourth floor above the king's lodgings. It is

Throne Hall detail

designed as an amalgamation of two rooms of the Wartburg: The Hall of the Singers and the Ballroom. It was one of the king's favorite projects for his palace. The rectangular room was decorated with themes from Lohengrin and Parzival. Its longer side is terminated by a gallery which is crowned by a tribune, modelled after the Wartburg. The eastern narrow side is terminated by a stage which is structured by arcades and known as the *sängerlaube*. The Hall of the Singers was never designed for court festivities of the reclusive king. Rather, like the Throne Hall it served as a walkable monument in which the culture of knights and courtly love of the Middle Ages was represented. The first performance in this hall took place in 1933: A concert commemorating the 50th anniversary of Richard Wagner's death.

The Throne Hall, 20 metres by 12 metres, is situated in the west wing of the Palas. With its height of 13 metres it occupies the third and fourth floors. Julius Hofmann modelled it after the Allerheiligen-Hofkirche in the Munich Residenz. On three sides it is surrounded by colorful arcades, ending in an apse that was intended to hold Ludwig's throne – which was never completed. The throne dais is surrounded by paintings of Jesus, the Twelve Apostles and six canonized kings. The mural paintings were created by Wilhelm Hauschild. The floor mosaic was completed after the king's death. The chandelier is fashioned after a Byzantine crown. The Throne Hall makes a sacral impression. Following the king's wish, it amalgamated the Grail Hall from Parzival with a symbol of the divine right of kings, an incorporation of unrestricted sovereign power, which Ludwig as the head of a constitutional monarchy no longer held.

Palas rooms (late 19th century Photochrom prints)
Hall of the Singers

Throne Hall

Drawing room

Study room

Dining room

Bedroom

Apart from the large ceremonial rooms several smaller rooms were created for use by Ludwig II. The royal lodging is on the third floor of the palace in the east wing of the Palas. It consists of eight rooms with living space and several smaller rooms. In spite of the gaudy décor, the living space with its moderate room size and its sofas and suites makes a relatively modern impression on today's visitors. Ludwig II did not attach importance on representative requirements of former times, in which the life of a monarch was mostly public. The interior decoration with mural paintings, tapestry, furniture and other handicraft generally refers to the king's favorite themes": the grail legend, the works of Wolfram von Eschenbach, and their interpretation by Richard Wagner.

The eastward drawing room is adorned with themes from the Lohengrin legend. The furniture – sofa, table, armchairs and seats in a northward alcove – is comfortable and homelike. Next to the drawing room is a little artificial grotto that forms the passage to the study. The unusual room, originally equipped with an artificial waterfall and a so-called rainbow machine, is connected to a little conservatory. Depicting the Hörselberg grotto, it relates to Wagner's *Tannhäuser*, as does the décor of the adjacent study. In the park of Linderhof Palace the king had installed a similar grotto of greater dimensions. Opposite the study follows the dining room, adorned with themes of courtly love. Since the kitchen in Neuschwanstein is situated three stories below the dining room, it was impossible to install a wishing table (dining table disappearing by means of a mechanism) as at Linderhof Palace and Herrenchiemsee. Instead, the dining room was connected with the kitchen by means of a service lift.

The bedroom adjacent to the dining room and the subsequent house chapel are the only rooms of the palace that remain in neo-Gothic style. The king's bedroom is dominated by a huge bed adorned with carvings. Fourteen carvers worked more than four years on the bed canopy with its numerous pinnacles and on the oaken panelings. It was in this room that Ludwig was arrested in the night from 11 to 12 June 1886. The adjacent little house chapel is consecrated to Saint Louis, after whom the owner was named.

Kitchen

The servants' rooms in the basement of the Palas are quite scantily equipped with massive oak furniture. Besides one table and one cabinet there are two beds of 1.80 metres length each. Opaque glass windows separated the rooms from the corridor that connects the exterior stairs with the main stairs, so that the king could enter and leave unseen. The servants were not allowed to use the main stairs, but were restricted to the much narrower and steeper servants' stairs.

Funding

The king's wishes and demands expanded during the construction of Neuschwanstein, and so did the expenses. Drafts and estimated costs were revised repeatedly. Initially a modest study was planned instead of the great throne hall, and projected guest rooms were struck from the drafts to make place for a *Moorish Hall*, which could not be realised due to lack of resources. Completion was originally projected for 1872, but deferred repeatedly.

Dark clouds over Neuschwanstein

Neuschwanstein, the symbolic medieval knight's castle, was not Ludwig II's only huge construction project. It was followed by the rococo style Lustschloss of Linderhof Palace and the baroque palace of Herrenchiemsee, a monument for the era of absolutism. Linderhof, the smallest of the projects, was finished in 1886, and the other two remain incomplete. All three projects together drained his resources. The king paid for his construction projects by private means and from his civil list income. Contrary to frequently heard claims, the Bavarian treasury was not directly burdened by his buildings. From 1871 Ludwig had an additional secret income in return for a political favor given to Otto von Bismarck.

Artistic depiction of Ludwig II on his deathbed

The construction costs of Neuschwanstein to the king's lifetime amounted to 6.2 million mark, almost twice the initial cost estimate of 3.2 million mark. As his private means were insufficient for his increasingly escalating construction projects, the king continuously took up new credits. In 1876, a court counselor was replaced after pointing out the danger of insolvency. By 1883 he already owed 7 million mark, and in spring 1884 and August 1885 debt conversions of 7½ million mark and 6½ million mark, respectively, became necessary.

Even after his debts had reached 14 million mark, Ludwig insisted on continuation of his architectural projects; he threatened suicide if his creditors seized his palaces. In early 1886 Ludwig asked his cabinet for a credit of 6 million mark, which was denied. In April he followed Bismarck's advice to apply for the money to his parliament. In June, the Bavarian government decided to depose the king, who was living at Neuschwanstein at the time. On June 9 he was incapacitated, and on June 10 he had the deposition commission arrested in the Gatehouse. In expectation of the commission he had alarmed the gendarmerie and fire brigades of surrounding places for his protection. A second commission headed by Bernhard von Gudden arrived on the next day, and the king was forced to leave the palace in the same night. Ludwig was put under the supervision of von Gudden. On June 13 both died under mysterious circumstances in the shallow shore water of Lake Starnberg near Castle Berg.

After Ludwig's death

At the time of Ludwig's death the palace was far from complete. The external structures of the Gatehouse and the Palas were mostly finished, but the Rectangular Tower was still scaffolded. Work on the Bower had not started but, was completed in simplified form by 1892, without the planned female saints figures. The Knights' House was also simplified. In Ludwig's plans the columns in the Knights' House gallery were held as tree trunks and the capitals as the corresponding crowns. Only the foundations existed for the core piece of the palace complex: a keep of 90 metres height planned in the upper courtyard, resting on a three-nave chapel. This was not realized, and a connection wing between the Gatehouse and the Bower saw the same fate. Plans for a castle garden with terraces and a fountain west of the Palas were also abandoned after the king's death.

The interior of the royal living space in the palace was mostly completed in 1886; the lobbies and corridors were painted in a simpler style by 1888. The *Moorish Hall* desired by the king (and planned below the Throne Hall) was not realized any more than the so-called *Knights' Bath*, which, modeled after the Knights' Bath in the Wartburg, was intended to render homage to the knights' cult as a medieval baptism bath. A *Bride Chamber* in the Bower (after a location in *Lohengrin*), guest rooms in the first and second floor of the Palas and a great banquet hall were further abandoned projects. In fact, a complete development of Neuschwanstein had never even been planned, and at the time of the king's death there was not a utilization concept for numerous rooms .

Neuschwanstein front façade and surroundings (Photochrom print, c.1900)

When Ludwig II died in 1886, Neuschwanstein was still incomplete. The king had never intended to make the palace accessible to the public. But no more than six weeks after the king's death the regent Luitpold ordered the palace opened to paying visitors. The administrators of Ludwig's estate managed to balance the construction debts by 1899. From then until the First World War Neuschwanstein was a stable and lucrative source of revenue for the House of Wittelsbach, indeed Ludwig's castles were probably the single largest income source earned by the Bavarian royal family in the last years prior to 1914. To guarantee a smooth course of visits, some rooms and the court buildings were finished first. Initially the visitors were allowed to move freely in the palace, causing the furniture to wear quickly.

When Bavaria became a republic in 1918, the government socialized the civil list. The resulting dispute with the House of Wittelsbach led to a split in 1923: Ludwig's palaces including Neuschwanstein fell to the state and are now managed by the Bavarian Palace Department, a division of the Bavarian finance ministry. Nearby Hohenschwangau Castle fell to the Wittelsbacher Ausgleichsfonds, whose revenues go to the House of Wittelsbach. The visitor numbers continued to rise, reaching 200,000 in 1939.

Due to its secluded location, the palace survived the two world wars without destruction. Under the Reichsleiter Rosenberg Institute for the Occupied Territories (Einsatzstab Reichsleiter Rosenberg für die Besetzen Gebiete), a suborganization of the Nazi Party, it served until 1944 as a depot for Nazi plunder from France. The works of art were catalogued photographically. (After World War II 39 photo albums were found in the palace, documenting the dimension of the robbery. The albums are now stored in the American National Archives.)

At the end of the war the German Reichsbank deposited gold in the palace, which in the last days of the war was taken to an unknown place.

In April 1945 the SS considered blowing up the palace to prevent the building itself and the artwork it contained from falling to the enemy. However, the plan was not realized by the SS-Gruppenführer who had been consigned the task, and at the end of the war the palace was surrendered undamaged to representatives of the Allied forces. Thereafter the Bavarian archives used some of the rooms as a provisional store for salvaged archivalia, as the premises in Munich had been bombed.

Neuschwanstein is a global symbol of the era of Romanticism. The palace served as a model for the Sleeping Beauty Castle of Disneyland and became a location for films such as Helmut Käutner's Ludwig II (1955) and Luchino Visconti's Ludwig (1972) as well as Chitty Chitty Bang Bang (1968).

West German stamp (1977)

In 1977, Neuschwanstein Castle became the motif of a West German definitive stamp, and it is to appear on a €2 commemorative coin for the German Bundesländer series in 2012. In 2007, it was a finalist in the widely publicized on-line selection of the New Seven Wonders of the World. The palace is not on the list of UNESCO World Heritage Sites. In 2009 a plan was discussed to make it a transnational candidate jointly with Ludwig's Linderhof and Herrenchiemsee palaces and two similar palaces in Romania: Peleş Castle and Pelişor Castle.

Today, with 1.3 million visitors per year Neuschwanstein is one of the most popular tourist destinations in Europe.. For security reasons the palace can only be visited during a 35-minute guided tour. There are also special guided tours that focus on specific topics. In the peak season from June until August, Neuschwanstein has up to 6000 visitors per day, and guests without advance reservation may have to wait several hours. Ticket sales are processed exclusively via the ticket center in Hohenschwangau. As of 2008 the total number of visitors was more than 60 million. In 2004 the revenues were booked as 6.5 million Euros.

A meteorite that reached Earth spectacularly on April 6, 2002 at the Austrian border near Hohenschwangau was named *Neuschwanstein* after the palace. Three fragments were found: *Neuschwanstein I* (1.75 kg, found July 2002) and *Neuschwanstein II* (1.63 kg, found May 2003) on the German side, and *Neuschwanstein III* (2.84 kg, found June 2003) on the Austrian side near Reutte. The meteorite is classified as an enstatite chondrite with unusually large proportions of pure iron (29%), enstatite and the extremely rare mineral sinoite (Si_2N_2O).

Sources

- Ammon, Thomas (2007), *Ludwig II. für Dummies: Der Märchenkönig - Zwischen Wahn, Wagner und Neuschwanstein*, Wiley-VCH, ISBN 978-3527703197
- Bayerisches Staatsministerium der Finanzen, ed. (2005), *Faltlhauser begrüßte 50-millionsten Besucher im Schloss Neuschwanstein* [1], retrieved 2010-03-11
- Bayerisches Staatsministerium der Finanzen, ed. (2008), *Neue Homepage für Schloss Neuschwanstein in fünf Sprachen* [2], retrieved 2010-03-11
- Bayerisches Staatsministerium der Finanzen, ed. (2009), *Pschierer: Schloss Neuschwanstein ist heute eine weltweite Premiummarke* [3], retrieved 2010-03-11
- Bayerische Verwaltung der staatlichen Schlösser, Gärten und Seen, ed. (2004), *Neuschwanstein Castle: Official Guide*, Munich
- Biedermann, Henning (April 2009), *Neuschwanstein auf dem Weg zum Weltkulturerbe? Noch mehr Ruhm - noch mehr Schutz für das Königsschloss* [4], Bayerisches Fernsehen
- Bitterauf, Theodor (1910), "Ludwig II. (König von Baiern)" [5], *Allgemeine Deutsche Biographie*, **55**, pp. 540–555
- Blunt, Wilfried (1970), *Ludwig II.: König von Bayern*, Heyne, ISBN 978-3453550063
- Blunt, Wilfred (1973), *The Dream King: Ludwig II of Bavaria*, Penguin Books, ISBN 978-0140036060
- Buchali, Frank (2009), *Schwangau: Neuschwanstein – Traumschloss als Postkartenmotiv* [6], burgen-web.de [7]
- Desing, Julius (1992), *Royal Castle Neuschwanstein*, Kienberger
- Farmer, Walter I. (2002), *Die Bewahrer des Erbes: Das Schicksal deutscher Kulturgüter am Ende des Zweiten Weltkrieges*, Gruyter, ISBN 978-3899490107
- Hatton, Barry (29 July 2007), "New 7 wonders of the world are named" [8], *Deseret News*
- Heinlein, Dieter (2004), *Die Feuerkugel vom 6. April 2002 und der sensationelle Meteoritenfall "Neuschwanstein"*, Augsburg
- Koch von Berneck, Max (1887), *München und die Königsschlösser Herrenchiemsee, Neuschwanstein, Hohenschwangau, Linderhof und Berg*, Zurich: Caesar Schmidt
- Linnenkamp, Rolf (1986), *Die Schlösser und Projekte Ludwigs II.*, ISBN 978-3453022690
- Merkle, Ludwig (2001), *Ludwig II. und seine Schlösser*, Stiebner, ISBN 978-3830710240
- National Archives, ed. (2007), *National Archives Announces Discovery of "Hitler Albums" Documenting Looted Art* [9]
- Petzet, Michael; Bunz, Achim (1995), *Gebaute Träume: Die Schlösser Ludwigs II. von Bayern*, Hirmer, pp. 46–123, ISBN 978-3777466002

- Parkyn, Neil (2002), *Siebzig Wunderwerke der Architektur*, zweitausendeins, ISBN 978-3861504542
- Petzet, M.; Hojer, G. (1991), *Amtlicher Führer Schloss Neuschwanstein*, Bayerische Verwaltung der staatlichen Schlösser, Gärten und Seen
- Pevsner, Nikolaus; Honour, Hugh; Fleming, John (1992), *Lexikon der Weltarchitektur*, Prestel, ISBN 3-7913-2095-5
- Rauch, Alexander (1991), *Neuschwanstein*, Atlantis Verlag, ISBN 978-3881998741
- Schlim, Jean Louis (2001), *Ludwig II.: Traum und Technik*, Buchendorfer Verlag, ISBN 978-3-934036-52-9
- Schröck, Rudolf (November 2007), "Madness in Bavaria", *The Atlantic Times*
- Spangenberg, Marcus (1999), *The Throne Room in Schloss Neuschwanstein: Ludwig II of Bavaria and his Vision of Divine Right*, ISBN 978-3-7954-1233-3 (Page numbers refer to the German edition, ISBN 978-3-7954-1225-8.)
- Sykora, Katharina (2004), *"Ein Bild von einem Mann"; Ludwig II. von Bayern: Konstruktion und Rezeption eines Mythos*, Campus Verlag, ISBN 978-3593374796

External links

- Official website [10].
- Neuschwanstein Castle [11] on Bavarian Palace Department website.
- Floor Plan [12] All floors.
- Webcam [13].
- Many 360° panoramas, with locations on three floor plans [14] on ZDF site (requires Flash version 9 or higher).
- Several 360º panoramas [15] (requires QuickTime VR).
- A visitors perspective of Neuschwanstein Castle [16]

pnb:نیوشوانس□ائن

Brandenburg Gate

The Brandenburg Gate

The **Brandenburg Gate** (German: *Brandenburger Tor*) is a former city gate and one of the main symbols of Berlin and Germany. It is located west of the city center at the junction of Unter den Linden and Ebertstraße, immediately west of the Pariser Platz. It is the only remaining gate of a series through which Berlin was once entered. One block to the north stands the Reichstag building. The gate is the monumental entry to Unter den Linden, the renowned boulevard of linden trees which formerly led directly to the city palace of the Prussian monarchs. It was commissioned by King Frederick William II of Prussia as a sign of peace and built by Carl Gotthard Langhans from 1788 to 1791. Having suffered considerable damage in World War II, the Brandenburg Gate was fully restored from 2000 to 2002 by the Stiftung Denkmalschutz Berlin [1] (Berlin Monument Conservation Foundation). Today, it is regarded as one of Europe's most famous landmarks.

Design and history

In the time of Frederick William (1688), shortly after the Thirty Years' war and a century before the gate was constructed, Berlin was a small walled city within a star fort with several named gates: Spandauer Thor, St. Georgen Thor, Stralower Thor, Cöpenicker Thor, Neues Thor, and Leipziger Thor *(see map)*. Relative peace, a policy of religious tolerance, and status as capital of the Kingdom of Prussia facilitated the growth of the city.

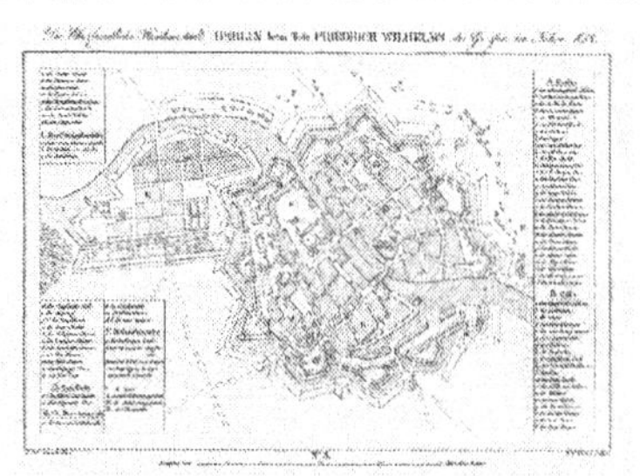

Berlin in 1688. The future site of the Brandenburg gate was near the middle left of the map, separating the Tiergarten from Unter den Linden. Travelers going west from the city toward Brandenburg an der Havel could pass in this direction.

The Brandenburg Gate was not part of the old fortifications but one of 18 gates within the fiscal excise wall (German: *Akzisemauer*), erected in the 1730s, including the old fortified city and many of its then suburbs. Between 1788 and 1791 the prior simple guard houses siding the gate were replaced by the current construction. The Gate consists of twelve Doric columns, six to each side, forming five passageways. Citizens originally were allowed to use only the outermost two. Atop the gate is the Quadriga, a chariot drawn by four horses driven by Victoria, the Roman goddess of victory.

The Gate's design is based upon the Propylaea, the gateway to the Acropolis in Athens, Greece and is consistent with Berlin's history of architectural classicism (first, Baroque, and then neo-Palladian). The Gate was the first "Athens on the River Spree" by architect Carl Gotthard von Langhans. The capital Quadriga was sculpted by Johann Gottfried Schadow.

The Brandenburg Gate's design has remained essentially unchanged since its completion even as it has played different political roles in German history. After the 1806 Prussian defeat at the Battle of Jena-Auerstedt, Napoleon took the Quadriga to Paris.

After Napoleon's defeat in 1814 and the Prussian occupation of Paris by General Ernst von Pfuel, the Quadriga was restored to Berlin and Victoria's wreath of oak leaves was supplemented with a new symbol of Prussian power, the Iron Cross. The Quadriga faces east, as it did when it was originally installed in 1793. At that time, only the royal family was allowed to pass through the central archway, as well as members of the Pfuel family from 1814 to 1919. In addition, the central archway was also used by the coaches of Ambassadors on the single occasion of their presenting their letters of credence to the monarch.

When the Nazis ascended to power they used the Gate as a party symbol. The Gate survived World War II and was one of the damaged structures still standing in the Pariser Platz ruins in 1945 (another being the Academy of Fine Arts). The gate was badly damaged with holes in the columns from bullets and nearby explosions. Following Germany's surrender and the end of the war, the governments of East Berlin and West Berlin restored it in a joint effort. The holes were patched, and were visible for many years following the war.

In 1990, the Quadriga was removed from the gate as part of renovation work carried out by the East German authorities.

On December 21, 2000, the Brandenburg Gate was privately refurbished at a cost of six million dollars (U.S.).

On October 3, 2002, the twelfth anniversary of German Reunification, the Brandenburg Gate was once again reopened following extensive refurbishment.

The Brandenburg Gate is now again closed for vehicle traffic, and much of Pariser Platz has been turned into a cobblestone pedestrian zone.

A Soviet flag flew from a flagpole atop the gate from 1945 until 1957, when it was replaced by an East German flag. Since the reunification of Germany, the flag and the pole have been removed.

Berlin Wall and its fall

East German border guards checking vehicles entering East Berlin the day the Wall went up.

Vehicles and pedestrians could travel freely through the gate, located in East Berlin, until the Berlin Wall was built, 13 August 1961. Then one of altogether eight Berlin Wall crossings was opened on the eastern side of the gate, usually not open for East Berliners and East Germans, who from then on needed a hard-to-obtain exit visa. On 14 August West Berliners gathered on the western side of the gate to demonstrate against the Berlin Wall, among them West Berlin's Governing Mayor Willy Brandt, who had spontaneously returned from a West German federal election campaigning tour in West Germany early the same day.

Under the pretext that Western demonstrations required it, the East closed the checkpoint at the Brandenburg Gate the same day, 'until further notice', a situation that was to last until 22 December 1989. The Wall was erected as an arc just west of the gate, cutting off access from West Berlin. On the eastern side, the "baby Wall", drawn across the eastern end of Pariser Platz rendered it off limits to East Berliners as well.

When the Revolutions of 1989 occurred and the Wall fell, the gate symbolized freedom and the desire to unify the city of Berlin. Thousands of people gathered at the Wall to celebrate its fall on 9 November 1989. On 22 December 1989, the Brandenburg Gate crossing was reopened when Helmut Kohl, the West German chancellor, walked through to be greeted by Hans Modrow, the East German prime minister. Demolition of the rest of the Wall around the area took place the following year.

Newly opened Brandenburg Gate crossing on two sides of the gate.

Twentieth anniversary celebrations of the Fall of the Wall at Brandenburg Gate on 9 November 2009 featuring a performance by Paul van Dyk.

Brandenburg Gate became the main venue for the 20th anniversary celebrations of the fall of the Berlin Wall or "Festival of Freedom" on the evening of 9 November 2009. The high point of the celebrations was when over 1000 colorfully designed foam domino tiles, each over 2.5 meters tall, were lined up along the route of the former wall through the city center. The domino "wall" was then toppled in stages converging here.

Political history at the gate

In 1963, U.S. President John F. Kennedy visited the Brandenburg Gate. The Soviets hung large red banners across it to prevent him looking into the East. In the 1980s, decrying the existence of two German states, West Berlin mayor Richard von Weizsäcker said: *"The German question is open as long as the Brandenburg Gate is closed."*

On June 12, 1987, U.S. President Ronald Reagan spoke to the West Berlin populace at the Brandenburg Gate, demanding the razing of the Berlin Wall. Addressing CPSU General Secretary Mikhail Gorbachev, Reagan said,

> General Secretary Gorbachev, if you seek peace, if you seek prosperity for the Soviet Union and Eastern Europe, if you seek liberalization: Come here to this gate! Mr. Gorbachev, open this gate! Mr. Gorbachev, tear down this wall!

On July 12, 1994, U.S. President Bill Clinton spoke at the Gate about peace in post-Cold War Europe.

On November 9, 2009, Chancellor of Germany, Angela Merkel, walked through Brandenburg Gate with Russia's Mikhail Gorbachev and Poland's Lech Wałęsa as part of the 20-year celebration of tearing down the Berlin Wall.

Gallery

Brandenburg Gate then and now

After the 1870 Battle of Sedan. In English, the sign reads "What a change through God's guidance"

The Brandenburg Gate in 1871

The Gate and surroundings in 2005

The Quadriga atop the Brandenburg Gate

The Berlin Wall goes up

Checks being done by East German guards on those crossing the border from West Berlin to the East just before the construction of the Wall in 1961.

East Germans guarding the Brandenburg Gate with a wire fence marking the border between East and West Berlin in 1961.

Guards line up in front of the Brandenburg Gate, closing of the border between the two parts of Germany.

From the East-Side 1968 the "Baby Wall" with flowers was the nearest point for visitors.

View from the air of the Berlin Wall forming a semicircle west of the Brandenburg Gate (at foreground), Pariser Platz (just behind the gate) which was out-of-bounds to the public, and the Unter den Linden.

Ronald Reagan giving a speech on June 12, 1987

A graffiti mural of The Brandenburg Gate on the East Side Gallery of the Berlin Wall (2008)

And down

Crowds gather after the fall of the Berlin Wall in 1989.

Crowds gather after the fall of the Berlin Wall in December 1989. East Germans have been allowed to cross the "baby wall" and come close to the Outer Wall.

The media gathering to cover the fall of the Wall and anticipated opening of the Brandenberg Gate crossing in November 1989.

A crane removing a section of the Berlin Wall beside the Brandenburg Gate in Dec 1989.

Cranes removing parts of the Wall to create an opening for a new crossing in the early hours of opening day on 22 November 1989.

East German Border Police Pamphlet announcing the opening of Brandenburg Gate as border checkpoint for pedestrians only.

West German chancellor Dr. Helmut Kohl, West Berlin mayor Walter Momper, West German Foreign Minister Hans-Dietrich Genscher and East German president Dr. Hans Modrow at the opening of the Brandenburg Gate crossing on 22 November 1989.

Getting passports stamped at the Brandenburg Gate crossing on opening day.

Police personnel (NCOs and enlisted men) of the East German Volkspolizei wait for the official opening of the Brandenburg Gate 22 December 1989.

Dismantling the Wall at Brandenburg Gate in April 1990.

Passport stamp for the newly opened crossing.

Souvenir hunters chip off parts of the Wall in front of the Reichstag building in December 1989.

Brandenburg Gate and where the Wall used to stand, marked by the row of cobblestones.

See also

- Berlin Wall
- Mitte (locality)

External links

- Stiftung Denkmalschutz Berlin (Berlin Monument Conservation Foundation) [2]
- Brandenburg Gate described in its historic context. [3]
- Panorama Brandenburg Gate [4] - Panoramic view from the Pariser Platz
- Webcam: Live-View of the Street "Unter den Linden" with Brandenburg Gate in Berlin, Germany [5]
- Ronald Reagan's *Tear this Wall* speech [6]
- Complete text, audio and video of Ronald Reagan's Brandenburg Gate Address [7] from AmericanRhetoric.com
- Bill Clinton's *Berlin is free* speech [8]
- Video News report of the Brandenburg Gate re-opening [9] - Real Player needed

- Germany, Berlin, Brandenburger Tor [10] Virtual tour with map and compass effect by Tolomeus
- Panorama Brandenburg Gate 1945 [11] - Panoramic view into the past, 60 years after WWII
- Celebrating 20 years after tearing down the Berlin wall, 1989 [12] - Pictures at Brandenburg Gate on November 9, 2009
- Three-dimensional view [13] of Brandenburger Gate (without plugin English, German, Spanish)

Geographical coordinates: 52°30′58.58″N 13°22′39.80″E

pnb:بران□نبرگ گی□

Black Forest

Geographical coordinates: 48°N 8°E

Black Forest	
range	
Country	Germany
Region	Baden-Württemberg
Part of	Southwest German Uplands/Scarplands
Coordinates	48°N 8°E
Highest point	Feldberg
- elevation	1493 m (4898 ft)
Length	150 km (93 mi)
Geology	Gneiss, Bunter sandstone
Orogeny	Central Uplands
Topography of the Black Forest	

The **Black Forest** (German: *Schwarzwald*) is a wooded mountain range in Baden-Württemberg, southwestern Germany. It is bordered by the Rhine valley to the west and south. The highest peak is the Feldberg with an elevation of 1,493 meters (4,898 ft). The region is almost rectangular with a length of 200 km (120 mi) and breadth of 60 km (37 mi). Hence it has an area of approximately 12000 km^2 (4600 sq mi). The name *Schwarzwald*, i.e. Black Forest, goes back to the Romans who referred to the thickly forested mountains there as *Silva Nigra* , i.e. "Black Forest," because the dense growth of conifers in the forest blocked out most of the light inside the forest.

Geology

The Black Forest consists of a cover of sandstone on top of a core of gneiss and granites. Formerly it shared tectonic evolution with the nearby Vosges Mountains. Later during the Middle Eocene a rifting period affected the area and caused formation of the Rhine graben. During the last glacial period of the Würm glaciation, the Black Forest was covered by glaciers; several tarn lakes such as the Mummelsee are remains of this period.

Rivers

Rivers in the Black Forest include the Danube (which originates in the Black Forest as the confluence of the Brigach and Breg rivers), the Enz, the Kinzig, the Murg, the Nagold, the Neckar, the Rench, and the Wiese. The Black Forest is part of the continental divide between the Atlantic Ocean drainage basin (drained by the Rhine) and the Black Sea drainage basin (drained by the Danube).

List of highest mountains

- Feldberg (1493 m (4898 ft))
- Herzogenhorn (1415 m (4642 ft))
- Belchen (1414 m (4639 ft))
- Spiesshorn (1349 m (4426 ft))
- Schauinsland (1284 m (4213 ft))
- Kandel (1241 m (4072 ft))
- Hochblauen (1165 m (3822 ft))
- Hornisgrinde (1164 m (3819 ft))

Political

Administratively, the Black Forest belongs completely to the state of Baden-Württemberg and comprises the city of Pforzheim as well as the following districts (*Kreise*). In the north: Enz, Rastatt and Calw; in the middle: Freudenstadt, Ortenaukreis and Rottweil; in the south: Emmendingen, Schwarzwald-Baar, Breisgau-Hochschwarzwald, Lörrach and Waldshut.

Ecology and economy

The forest mostly consists of pines and firs, some of which are grown in commercial monoculture. Similar to other forested regions, the Black Forest has had areas that were decimated by mass logging. Due to logging and land use changes the forest proper is only a fraction of its original size. The storm Lothar downed trees on hundreds of acres of mountaintops in 1999. This left some of the high peaks and scenic hills bare, with only primary growth shrubs and young fir trees.

The main industry is tourism. In addition to the towns and monuments noted below, the Black Forest is crossed by numerous long distance footpaths, including some of the first to be established. The European long-distance path E1 crosses the Black Forest following the routes of some of the local long-distance paths. There are numerous shorter paths suitable for day walks, as well as mountain biking and cross-country skiing trails. The total network of tracks amounts to around 23000 kilometres (14000 mi), and is maintained and overseen by a voluntary body, the *Schwarzwaldverein* (Black Forest Society), which has around 90,000 members (figures from Bremke, 1999, p. 9).

Points of interest

There are many old towns in the Black Forest. Popular tourist destinations include Freiburg, Calw (the birth town of Hermann Hesse), Gengenbach, Staufen, Schiltach, Haslach and Altensteig. Other popular destinations include such mountains as the Feldberg, the Belchen, the Kandel, and the Schauinsland; the Titisee and Schluchsee lakes; the All Saints Waterfalls; the Triberg Waterfalls, not the highest, but the most famous waterfalls in Germany; and the gorge of the River Wutach.

Winter on Schauinsland: famous "Windbuchen" Beeches bent by the wind

The Schwarzwälder Freilichtmuseum Vogtsbauernhof is an open-air museum that shows the life of sixteenth or seventeenth century farmers in the region, featuring a number of reconstructed Black Forest farms. The German Clock Museum in Furtwangen shows the history of the clock industry and of watchmakers.

For drivers, the main route through the region is the rapid A5 (E35) motorway, but a variety of sign-posted scenic routes such as the Schwarzwald-Hochstrasse (60 km (37 mi), Baden-Baden to Freudenstadt), Schwarzwald Tälerstrasse (100 km (62 mi), the Murg and Kinzig valleys) or Badische Weinstrasse (Baden Wine Street, 160 km (99 mi), a wine route from Baden-Baden to Weil am Rhein) offers calmer driving along high roads. [1] The last is a picturesque trip starting in the south of the Black Forest going north and includes numerous old wineries and tiny villages. Another, more specialized route is the 'Deutsche Uhrenstraße' ("German Clock Road"), [2] a circular route which traces the horological history of the region.

Due to the rich mining history dating from medieval times (the Black Forest was one of the most important mining regions of Europe circa 1100) there are many mines re-opened to the public. Such mines may be visited in the Kinzig valley, the Suggental, the Muenster valley, and around Todtmoos.

The Black Forest was visited on several occasions by Count Otto von Bismarck during his rule 1873-1890. Allegedly, he especially was interested in the Triberg Waterfalls. [3] There is now a monument in Triberg dedicated to Bismarck, who apparently enjoyed the tranquility of the region, which was lacking at his residence in Berlin.

Fauna

In addition to the expected kinds of wildlife to be found in a European forest area, the following types of animals may be observed in the Black Forest. Some of these animals include

- Cattle: The Black Forest cattle belong to the rare breed of "Hinterwälderberg" cattle
- The giant earthworm *Lumbricus badensis* is found only in the Black Forest region
- *Black Forest Foxes* are a breed of horse, previously indispensable for heavy field work
- Eagles and owls can be seen at close range

Culture

Dialects spoken in the Black Forest area are Alemannic and Swabian.

Fasnet

The German holiday of Fastnacht, or Fasnet, as it is known in the Black Forest region, occurs in the time leading up to Lent. On Rosenmontag, or the Monday before Ash Wednesday, crowds of people line the streets, wearing masks. One prominent style of mask is called the Black Forest Style, originating from the Black Forest Region.

Crafts

Wood-carving is a traditional cottage industry in the region and carved ornaments now are produced in substantial numbers as souvenirs for tourists. Cuckoo clocks are a popular example; they have been made in the region since the early eighteenth century and much of their development occurred there.

Culinary

Black Forest ham originated from this region, and so, by name and reputation at least, did the Black Forest Cake. It also is known as the "Black Forest Cherry Cake" and is made with chocolate cake, cream, sour cherries and Kirsch. The Black Forest variety of *Flammkuchen* is a Badisch specialty made with ham, cheese and cream. *Pfannkuchen*, a crêpe or crêpe-like (*Eierkuchen* or *Palatschinken*) pastry, is also common.

Gallery

The Feldberg

Black Forest

Titisee, popular year-round

The Black Forest is known for its native clockmakers

Mummelsee

Lake Constance bordering Austria and Switzerland

Black Forest Train near Karlsruhe

Hohenzollern Castle; backdrop: Black Forest

See also

- Hercynian Forest
- Deutsches Uhrenmuseum

References

- Bremke, N. (1999). *Schwarzwald quer*. Karlsruhe: Braun. ISBN 3-7650-8228-7
- Lamparski, F. (1985). Der Einfluß der Regenwurmart Lumbricus badensis auf Waldböden im Südschwarzwald. *Schriftenreihe des Institut für Bodenkunde und Waldernährungslehre der Albert-Ludwigs-Universität Freiburg i. Br., 15.* ISSN 0344-2691. English summary [4]
- German Wikipedia "Pfannkuchen" disambiguation

- Barnes, K. J. (2007). *A Rough Passage: Memories of an Empire*

External links

- Tourist Info [5]

pnb:کالا جنگل

Cologne Cathedral

Cologne Cathedral*	
UNESCO World Heritage Site	

State Party	Germany
Type	Cultural
Criteria	i, ii, iv
Reference	292 [1]
Region**	Europe
Inscription history	
Inscription	1996 (20th Session)
Endangered	2004-2006

* Name as inscribed on World Heritage List. [2]
** Region as classified by UNESCO. [3]

Cologne Cathedral	
Cologne Cathedral was the world's tallest building from 1880 to 1884.[1]	
Record height	
Preceded by	Rouen Cathedral
Surpassed by	Ulm Minster
General information	
Status	Complete
Constructed	1248-1880
Height	
Antenna or spire	157.4 m (516 ft)
Fully habitable, self-supported, from main entrance to highest structural or architectural top; see the list of tallest buildings in the world for other listings.	

Cologne Cathedral (German: *Kölner Dom*, officially *Hohe Domkirche St. Peter und Maria*) is a Roman Catholic church in Cologne, Germany. It is the seat of the Archbishop of Cologne (currently Cardinal Joachim Meisner), and is under the administration of the archdiocese of Cologne. It is renowned as a monument of Christianity, of German Catholicism in particular, of Gothic architecture and of the continuing faith and perseverance of the people of the city in which it stands. It is dedicated to Saint Peter and the Blessed Virgin Mary. The cathedral is a World Heritage Site, one of the best-known architectural monuments in Germany, and Cologne's most famous landmark, described by UNESCO as an "exceptional work of human creative genius". It is visited by 30 thousand people every day.

Construction of Cologne Cathedral began in 1248 and took, with interruptions, until 1880 to complete. It is 144.5 metres long, 86.5 m wide and its towers are approximately 157 m tall. The cathedral is one of the world's largest churches and the largest Gothic church in Northern Europe. For four years, 1880-84, it was the tallest structure in the world, until the completion of the Washington Monument. It has the second-tallest church spires, only surpassed by the single spire of Ulm Minster, completed 10 years later in 1890. Because of its enormous twin spires, it also presents the largest façade of any church in the world. The choir of the cathedral, measured between the piers, also holds the distinction of having the largest height to width ratio of any Medieval church, 3.6:1, exceeding even Beauvais Cathedral which has a slightly higher vault.

Cologne's medieval builders had planned a grand structure to house the reliquary of the Three Kings and fit its role as a place of worship of the Holy Roman Emperor. Despite having been left incomplete during the medieval period, Cologne Cathedral eventually became unified as "a masterpiece of exceptional intrinsic value" and "a powerful testimony to the strength and persistence of Christian belief in medieval and modern Europe".

History

The Altarpiece of the Three Kings by Stephan Lochner.

Ancient site

When the present Cologne Cathedral was commenced in 1248, the site had been occupied by several previous structures, the earliest of which may have been a grain store, perhaps succeeded by a Roman temple built by Mercurius Augustus. From the 4th century the site was occupied by Christian buildings including a square edifice known as the "oldest cathedral" and commissioned by Maternus, the first Christian bishop of Cologne. A free-standing baptistery from the 6th century was located at the east end of the Cathedral. The baptistery was demolished to build the old cathedral in the 9th century. Now only the ruins of the baptistery and the octagonal baptismal font remain. The second church, the so-called "Old Cathedral", was completed in 818. This burned down on April 30, 1248.

Medieval beginning

In 1164, the Archbishop of Cologne, Rainald of Dassel had acquired relics of the Three Kings which had been taken from Milan, Italy by the Holy Roman Emperor, Frederick Barbarossa. The relics had great religious significance and could be counted upon to draw pilgrims from all over Christendom. It was important to church officials that they be properly housed. The loss of the old five-aisled cathedral prompted a building program in the new style of Gothic architecture based in particular on the French Cathedral of Amiens.

The foundation stone was laid on August 15, 1248, by Archbishop Konrad von Hochstaden. The eastern arm was completed under the direction of Master Gerhard, was consecrated in 1322 and sealed off by a temporary wall so it could be in use as the work proceeded. Eighty four misericords in the choir date from this building phase. In the mid 14th century work on the west front commenced under Master Michael. This work halted in 1473 leaving the south tower complete up to the belfry level and crowned with a huge crane which was destined to remain in place, and the landmark of Cologne for 400 years.

Some work proceeded intermittently on the structure of the nave between the west front and the eastern arm but during the 16th century, this ceased.

19th century completion

With the 19th century romantic enthusiasm for the Middle Ages and spurred on by the lucky discovery of the original plan for the façade, it was decided, with the commitment of the Protestant Prussian Court, to complete the cathedral. It was achieved by civic effort, the *Central-Dombauverein*, founded in 1842, raised two-thirds of the enormous costs (over US$ 1 billion in today's money), while the Prussian state supplied the remaining third. The state saw this as a way to improve its relations with the large number of Catholic subjects it had gained in 1815.

Work resumed in 1842 to the original design of the surviving medieval plans and drawings, but utilising more modern construction techniques including iron roof girders. The nave was completed and the towers were added. The bells were installed in the 1870s.

The completion of Germany's largest cathedral was celebrated as a national event in 1880, 632 years after construction had begun. The celebration was attended by Emperor Wilhelm I.

World War II and post-war history

The cathedral suffered seventy hits by aerial bombs during World War II. It did not collapse, but stood tall in an otherwise flattened city. The great twin spires are said to have been used as an easily recognizable navigational landmark by Allied aircraft raiding deeper into Germany in the later years of the war, which may be a reason that the cathedral was not destroyed. It has been claimed that in June 1945 American troops used the cathedral as a rifle range.

The repairs to the building were completed in 1956. In the northwest tower's base, an emergency repair carried out in 1944 with bad-quality brick taken from a nearby war ruin (see German Wikipedia "Kölner Domplombe") remained visible until 2005 as a reminder of the War, but then it was decided to reconstruct this section according to the original appearance. The brick-filling can be seen in the image on the left.

US soldier and destroyed Panther tank, 4 April 1945.

Some repair and maintenance work is constantly being carried out in some section of the building, which is almost never completely free of scaffolding, since wind, rain, and pollution slowly eat away at the stones. The *Dombauhütte*, which was established to build the cathedral and repair the cathedral, is said to employ the best stonemasons of the Rhineland. There is a common joke in Cologne that the leader of the *Dombauhütte*, the *Dombaumeister* (master builder of the cathedral), has to be Catholic and free from giddiness. The current Dombaumeisterin is Barbara Schock-Werner. Half of the costs of repair and maintenance are still borne by the Dombauverein.

On August 25, 2007, the cathedral received a new stained glass in the south transept window. With 113 square metres of glass, the window was created by the German artist Gerhard Richter. It is composed of 11,500 identically sized pieces of coloured glass resembling pixels, randomly arranged by computer, which create a colorful "carpet". Since the loss of the original window in World War II, the space had been temporarily filled with plain glass. The archbishop of the cathedral, Joachim Cardinal Meisner, who had preferred a figurative depiction of 20th-century Catholic martyrs for the window, did not attend the unveiling.

World Heritage Site

In 1996, the cathedral was added to the UNESCO World Heritage List of culturally important sites. In 2004 it was placed on the "World Heritage in Danger" list due to plans to construct a high-rise building nearby which would have visually impacted the site, as the only Western site in danger. The cathedral was removed from the List of In Danger Sites in 2006, following the authorities' decision to limit the heights of buildings constructed near and around the cathedral.

As a World Heritage Site, and with its convenient position on tourist routes, Cologne Cathedral is a major tourist attraction, the visitors including many who travel there as a Christian pilgrimage.

Visitors can climb 509 steps of the spiral staircase to a viewing platform about 98 metres above the ground.

On May 12, 2001, the American rock band R.E.M. performed a free concert in Roncalliplatz, the square to the south side of Cologne Cathedral. The concert was organised to promote the eradication of violence in schools, and was in part broadcast live on MTV Europe.

On August 18, 2005, Pope Benedict XVI visited the cathedral during his apostolic visit to Germany, as part of World Youth Day 2005 festivities. An estimated one million pilgrims visited the cathedral during this time. Also as part of the events of World Youth Day, Cologne Cathedral hosted a televised gala performance of Beethoven's Missa Solemnis, performed by the Royal Philharmonic Orchestra and the London Philharmonic Choir conducted by Sir Gilbert Levine.

Cologne Cathedral seen at night from the other side of the Rhine at Deutz.

Architecture

The design of Cologne Cathedral was based quite closely on that of Amiens Cathedral in terms of ground plan, style and the width to height proportion of the central nave. The plan is in the shape of a Latin Cross, as is usual with Gothic cathedrals. It has two aisles on either side, which help to support one of the very highest Gothic vaults in the world, being nearly as tall as that of the ill-fated Beauvais Cathedral, much of which collapsed. Externally the outward thrust of the vault is taken up by flying buttresses in the French manner. The eastern end has a single ambulatory, the second aisle resolving into a *chevet* of seven radiating chapels.

The nave looking east

Internally, the medieval choir is more varied and less mechanical in its details than the 19th century building. It presents a French style arrangement of very tall arcade, a delicate narrow triforium gallery lit by windows and with detailed tracery merging with that of the windows above. The clerestory windows are tall and retain some old figurative glass in the lower sections. The whole is united by the tall shafts which sweep unbroken from the floor to their capitals at the spring of the vault. The vault is of plain quadripartite arrangement.

The choir retains a great many of its original fittings, including the carved stalls, which is made the more surprising by the fact that French Revolutionary troops had desecrated the building. A large stone statue of St Christopher looks down towards the place where the earlier entrance to the cathedral was, before its completion in the late 19th century.

The nave is enhanced by a good many 19th century stained glass windows including a set of five on the south side called the "Bayernfenster" which were a gift from Ludwig I of Bavaria, a set highly representative of the painterly German style of that date.

Externally, particularly from a distance, the building is dominated by its huge spires which are entirely Germanic in character, being openwork like those of Ulm, Vienna and Regensburg Cathedrals.

Treasures

One of the Treasures of the cathedral is the High Altar which was installed in 1322. It is constructed of black marble, with a solid slab 15 feet long forming the top. The front and sides are overlaid with white marble niches into which are set figures, with the Coronation of the Virgin at the centre.

The Shrine of the Three Kings.

The most celebrated work of art in the cathedral is the *Shrine of the Three Kings*, a large gilded sarcophagus dating from the 13th century, and the largest reliquary in the Western world. It is traditionally believed to hold the remains of the Three Wise Men, whose bones and 2,000-year-old clothes were discovered at the opening of the shrine in 1864.

Near the sacristy is the *Gero-Kreuz*, a large crucifix carved in oak and with traces of paint and gilding. Believed to have been commissioned around 960 for Archbishop Gero, it is the oldest large crucifix north of the Alps and the earliest-known large free-standing Northern sculpture of the medieval period.

In the Sacrament Chapel is the *Mailänder Madonna* ("Milan Madonna"), dating from around 1290, a wooden sculpture depicting the Blessed Virgin Mary and the infant Jesus. The altar of the patron saints of Cologne with an altar piece by the International Gothic painter, Stephan Lochner is in the *Marienkapelle* ("St. Mary's Chapel"). Other works of art are to be found in the Cathedral Treasury.

The altar also houses the relics of Saint Irmgardis.

Jewish tablets

Embedded in the interior wall are a pair of tablets on which are carved the provisions worked out by Archbishop Englebert II (1262-67) under which Jews were permitted to reside in Cologne.

Bells

The cathedral has eleven church bells, four of which are medieval. The first was the 3.8-ton *Dreikönigenglocke* ("Bell of the Three Kings"), cast in 1418, installed in 1437, and recast in 1880. Two of the other bells, the *Pretiosa* (10.5 tons; at that time the largest bell in the Occident) and the *Speciosa* (5.6 tons) were installed in 1448 and remain in place today.

During the 19th century, as the building neared completion, there was a desire to extend the number of bells. This was facilitated by Kaiser Wilhelm I who gave French bronze cannon, captured in 1870-71, for this purpose. The 22 pieces of artillery were displayed outside the Cathedral on the 11th of May 1872. Andreas Hamm in Frankenthal used them to cast a bell of over 27,000 kilos on the 19th of August 1873. The tone was not harmonious and another attempt was made on the 13th of November 1873. The Central Cathedral Association, which had agreed to take over the costs, did not want this bell either. Another attempt took place on the 3rd of October 1874. The colossal bell was shipped to Cologne and on the 13th of May 1875, installed in the Cathedral. This *Kaiserglocke* was eventually dismantled in 1918 to support the German war effort.

The 24-ton *St. Petersglocke* ("Bell of St. Peter", "Dicke Pitter" in the Kölsch dialect), was cast in 1922 and is the largest free-swinging bell in the world. (See below: **Gallery**, Petersglocke)

Petersglocke, note person to right of bell clapper.

Bells of the ridge turret:

- Consecration Bell - 0.425 tons (*Wandlungsglocke*)
- Vespers Bell - 0.28 tons (*Mettglocke*)
- Angelus Bell - 0.763 tons (*Angelusglocke*)

Bells of the main bell cage in the south spire:

- Hail Bell - 0.83 tons (*Aveglocke*)
- Chapter Bell - 1.4 tons (*Kapitelsglocke*)
- St Joseph's Bell - 2.2 tons (*Josephglocke*)
- St Ursula's Bell - 2.55 tons (*Ursulaglocke*)
- Bell of the Three Kings - 3.8 tons (*Dreikönigenglocke*)
- Pretiosa - 10.5 tons
- Speciosa - 5.6 tons
- St Peter's Bell - 24 tons (*St. Petersglocke*)

Church music

Main article: Organs and organists of Cologne Cathedral

Cologne Cathedral has two pipe organs by Klais Orgelbau, the Transept Organ built in 1948 and the Nave Organ built in 1998. Cathedral organists have included Josef Zimmermann, Clemens Ganz (1985–2001) and Winfried Bönig (2001).

Dimensions

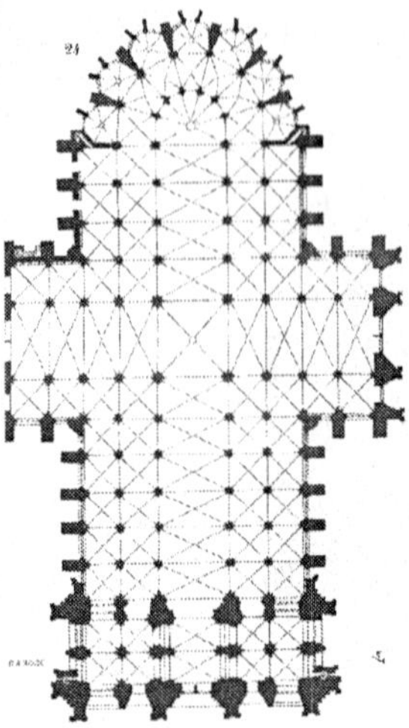

Groundplan.

Detail of a tower, from an albumen print taken ca. 1877-1880

External length	144.58 m
External width	86.25 m
Width of west façade	61.54 m
Width of transept façade	39.95 m
Width of nave (with aisles, interior)	45.19 m
Height of southern tower	157.31 m
Height of northern tower	157.38 m
Height of ridge turret	109.00 m
Height of transept façades	69.95 m
Height of roof ridge	61.10 m
Inner height of nave	43.35 m
Building area	7,914 m²
Window surface area	10,000 m²
Roof surface area	12,000 m²
Gross volume without buttresses	407,000 m³

Gallery

The exterior of one of the Cathedral's spires

Inside a spire showing the openwork construction.

Statue of the Blessed Virgin Mary on the central jamb of the door.

The main entrance shows the brittle repetitive nature of the 19th century decoration.

The earlier carving around this entrance is lively.

Inside the 19th century roofspace steel girders rise above the stone vaulting.

Interior of the Medieval east end, showing the extreme height.

The *Crucifix of Bishop Gero*, a famous 10th century sculpture, with a modern surround.

This "swallows' nest" organ was built into the gallery in 1998, to celebrate the cathedral's 700 years.

Detail of a window showing the patrons of the Cathedral, St. Peter and the Virgin Mary.

A lightshow in the Cathedral.

Cologne Cathedral floodlit.

See also

- Cathedral architecture of Western Europe
- Gero Crucifix
- Gothic architecture
- Gothic revival
- List of buildings
- List of highest church naves
- Middle Ages in history

Sources

- Wim Swaan, *The Gothic Cathedral*, Omega Books (1969), ISBN 090785348X
- Banister Fletcher, *A History of Architecture on the Comparative Method.*
- Howard Hubbard, *Masterpieces of Western Sculpture*, Thames and Hudson, ISBN 0500232784
- Wolff, Arnold, *Cologne Cathedral. Its History - Its Works of Arts*, Verlag (editor) Kölner Dom, Cologne: 2nd edition 2003, ISBN 9783774303423

External links

- Cologne Cathedral Official website [4] (English) (German)
- Cologne Cathedral and Pictures by GermanPlaces.com [5]
- unesco World Heritage Sites, Cologne Cathedral [6]
- unesco, Cologne Cathedral [7] (German)
- Web cam showing Cologne Cathedral [8] (German)
- Cologne Cathedral [9] at *Structurae*
- A photo essay on the Cologne Cathedral [10]

Geographical coordinates: 50°56′29″N 6°57′29″E

Bavarian State Archaeological Collection

The **Bavarian State Archaeological Collection** (Archäologische Staatssammlung) in Munich is one of the most important archaeological collections and cultural history museums in Germany.

The museum's foundation in 1885 was initiated by the anthropologist Johannes Ranke, a nephew of Leopold von Ranke.[*citation needed*] The museum houses the Bavarian state collection of Prehistory, represented by mostly local exhibits of the Paleolithic, the Neolithic, the Bronze Age, the Urnfield culture, the Hallstatt culture, the era of the Celts, the Roman Empire, the Migration Period and the Early Middle Ages. The collection has been structured in a chronological exhibition which is continued by the collection of the Bavarian National Museum. Since 1976, the Bavarian State Archaeological Collection is situated in an adjoining modern building.

The Bavarian State Archaeological Collection keeps several local branches in Bavaria such as the Celtic-Roman Museum Manching.

External links

- Museum website [1] (English)

Geographical coordinates: 48°08′38″N 11°35′28″E

Overview of Stuttgart

Stuttgart

Stuttgart

Stuttgart Schlossplatz (Castle square)

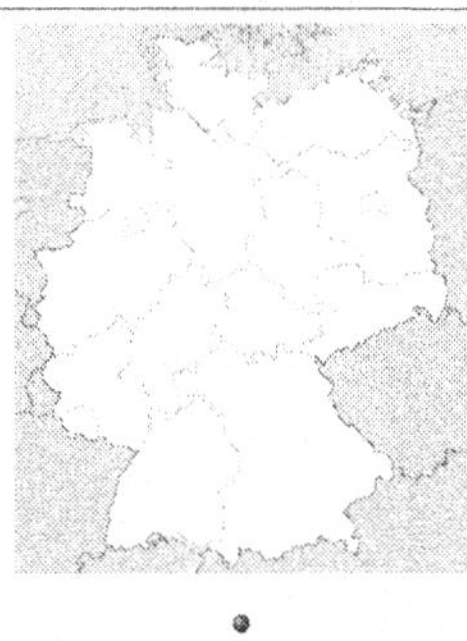

Stuttgart

Coordinates	48°46′43″N 9°10′46″E
Administration	
Country	Germany
State	Baden-Württemberg
Admin. region	Stuttgart

District	Urban district
City subdivisions	23 districts
Lord Mayor	Wolfgang Schuster (CDU)
Basic statistics	
Area	207.36 km^2 (80.06 sq mi)
Elevation	245 m (804 ft)
Population	600038 *(1 December 2008)*
- Density	2894 /km^2 (7495 /sq mi)
Founded	10th century
Other information	
Time zone	CET/CEST (UTC+1/+2)
Licence plate	S
Postal codes	70173–70619
Area code	0711
Website	stuttgart.de [1]

Stuttgart (German pronunciation: [ˈʃtʊtɡaɐ̯t]) is the capital of the state of Baden-Württemberg in southern Germany. The sixth-largest city in Germany, Stuttgart has a population of 600,038 (December 2008) while the metropolitan area has a population of 5.3 million (2008).

The city lies at the centre of a heavily populated area, circled by a ring of smaller towns. This area called Stuttgart Region has a population of 2.7 million making 'greater Stuttgart' the third biggest urban area in Germany after the Ruhr Area and Berlin. With over 5 million inhabitants, the larger Stuttgart Metropolitan Region is the fourth-biggest in Germany after the Rhine-Ruhr area, Berlin/Brandenburg and Frankfurt/Rhine-Main.

Stuttgart is spread across a variety of hills (some of them vineyards), valleys and parks - unusual for a German city and often a source of surprise to visitors who primarily associate the city with its industrial reputation as the 'cradle of the automobile'.

Stuttgart has the status of Stadtkreis, a type of self-administrating urban county. It is also the seat of the state legislature, the regional parliament, local council and the Protestant State Church in Württemberg as well as one of the two co-seats of the bishop of the Roman Catholic diocese of Rottenburg-Stuttgart.

The city of Stuttgart ranked 30 globally in Mercer's 2010 liveability rankings, and 7th in Germany behind top-ranked cities such as Frankfurt, Düsseldorf and Munich. For economic and social innovation the city was ranked 11 globally, 2nd in Germany after Hamburg and 7th in Europe in 2009 out of 256 cities.

The city's tourism slogan is "Stuttgart is more". Under current plans to improve transport links to the international infrastructure (as part of the Stuttgart 21 project), in March 2008 the city unveiled a new logo and slogan, describing itself as "*Das neue Herz Europas*" ("The new heart of Europe"). For business it describes itself as "*Standort Zukunft*", "Where business meets the future"). In 2007 the *Bürgermeister* marketed Stuttgart to foreign investors as "The creative power of Germany". In July 2010, Stuttgart unveiled a new city logo, designed to entice more business people to stay in the city and enjoy breaks in the area.

Stuttgart is nicknamed the *Schwabenmetropole* (Swabian metropolis), a reference to the Swabian dialect spoken by the locals. In that dialect, the city's name is pronounced *Schturget* or *Schtuagerd.*

Name and coat of arms

Stuttgart's coat of arms shows a black horse on its hind legs on a yellow background. It was first used in its current format in 1938; prior to this various designs and colours had been used, often with two horses. The canting seal pictured here reflects the origin of the name 'Stuttgart'. The name in Old High German was 'stuotgarten', with 'stuot' meaning mare, later cognate with the Old English term 'stod' (Modern English: 'stud', relating to the breeding of horses). The Old High German term 'garten' referred to the compound on the site of the original settlement. The logo of the Porsche automobile company features a modified version of Stuttgart's coat of arms at its centre.

Geography

Stuttgart lies about an hour from the Black Forest and a similar distance from the Swabian Jura. The city centre lies in a lush valley, nestling between vineyards and thick woodland close to, but not on the River Neckar. Thus, the city is often described as lying *"zwischen Wald und Reben"*, between forest and vines. In the hot summer months local residents refer to this area as the *Stuttgarter Kessel*, or Stuttgart cauldron, for its hot and humid climate which is frequently warmer than the surrounding countryside of Württemberg.

Stuttgart covers an area of 207 km^2 (80 sq mi). The elevation ranges from 207 m (679 ft) above sea level by the Neckar river to 549 m (1801 ft) on Bernhartshöhe hill. As a result there are more than 400 flights of stairs around the city (called "Stäffele" in local dialect), equivalent to approximately 20 km (12 mi) of steps. Many originate from the time when vineyards lined the entire valley. Even today there are vineyards less than 500 m (1640 ft) from the Main Station.

Panorama of Stuttgart looking South East. From the Neckar valley on the left the city rises to the city centre, backdropped by high woods to the south (television tower). Stuttgart South and Stuttgart West are to the right.

Stuttgart at night, looking north west

City districts

The city of Stuttgart is subdivided into a total of 23 city districts, 5 inner districts and 18 outer districts.

The inner districts are: Central Stuttgart (German: Stuttgart-Mitte), Stuttgart North (Stuttgart-Nord), Stuttgart East (Stuttgart-Ost), Stuttgart South (Stuttgart-Süd), and Stuttgart West (Stuttgart-West).

The outer districts are:

- Bad Cannstatt: home to Europe's second largest mineral spas, (second only to the ones in Buda, Hungary), the Cannstatter Wasen (site of the Stuttgart Spring Festival and the Cannstatter Volksfest (the world's second largest beer festival, every September/October)), Wilhelma zoo and botanical garden , the Schleyer-Halle, the Porsche Arena, the Mercedes-Benz Museum, the VfB Stuttgart Bundesliga football team and their home ground, the Mercedes-Benz Arena, and adjacent to it the Robert Schlienz Stadium. The greenhouse of Gottlieb Daimler, where he developed his cars, motorcycles and motorboats can also be found in Cannstatt, as well as the oldest remaining residential building in Stuttgart, the *Klösterle* ("little monastery", a Beguin residence erected in 1463). The largest city district of Stuttgart, Cannstatt was suggested as the future capital of Württemberg by Gottfried Leibniz in 1696.[*citation needed*] Cannstatt is also famous for the Pleistocene mammals preserved in the local travertine deposited by the mineral springs, some of which are on exhibit at the State Museum of Natural History Stuttgart. The leading German chocolate brand Ritter Sport was first produced in Cannstatt. In 1930 the company was relocated to Waldenbuch.
- Degerloch: the world's first television tower, Stuttgarter Kickers football team and their home ground, the Waldaustadion (where reserve team VfB II currently play as the Cannstatt Robert Schlienz Stadium is not approved for third division matches).
- Möhringen: musical theatres, U.S. Army's Kelley Barracks, seat of the United States Africa Command.
- Plieningen: campus of University of Hohenheim, Schloß Hohenheim (castle).

- Stammheim: location of high-security Stammheim Prison and court (see Red Army Faction terrorists).
- Untertürkheim: Daimler AG headquarters and original Mercedes-Benz plant, the Württemberg mountain, eponymous to the historic territory of Württemberg, site of the Württemberg Mausoleum.
- Vaihingen: not to be confused with nearby Vaihingen (Enz), home to one of two University of Stuttgart campuses and Patch Barracks, the headquarters of U.S. armed forces in Europe (USEUCOM).
- Zuffenhausen [2]: Porsche headquarters and museum. Kennel name adopted by UK Dobermann enthusiasts
- Feuerbach: home of the original Bosch plant and Behr.
- as well as Birkach, Botnang, Hedelfingen, Mühlhausen, Münster, Obertürkheim, Sillenbuch, Wangen, and Weilimdorf.

Stuttgart agglomeration and metropolitan region

Stuttgart's agglomeration (the political entity 'Stuttgart Region') consists of the nearby towns of Ludwigsburg with its enormous baroque palace, Böblingen, the old Free Imperial City of Esslingen, Waiblingen, Göppingen and their respective homonymous rural districts (*Landkreise*, the exception being the Waiblingen district, called Rems-Murr-Kreis).

The Stuttgart Metropolitan Region is a wider regional concept, that, in addition to the districts of the *Stuttgart Region*, encompasses most of North, Central, and East Württemberg, consisting of the cities of Heilbronn/Schwäbisch Hall, Reutlingen/Tübingen as well as Aalen/Schwäbisch Gmünd and their respective districts and regions, i.e. Heilbronn-Franken, Neckar-Alb and Ostwürttemberg.

Climate

Stuttgart experiences an oceanic climate (Köppen climate classification *Cfb*). In the summer months, the nearby Black Forest and Swabian Alb hills act as a shield from severe weather but the city can also be subject to thunderstorms in the summer months and periods of snow lasting several days in the winter. The centre of the city, referred to by locals as the "Kessel" (cauldron) experiences more severe heat in the summer and less snow in the winter than the suburbs. Lying as it does at the centre of the European continent, the temperature range between day and night or summer and winter can be extreme. On average Stuttgart enjoys 1693 hours of sunshine per year.

Winters last from December to March. The coldest month is January with an average temperature of 0 °C (32 °F). Snow cover tends to last no longer than a few days although it has been known to last several weeks at a time as recently as 2010. The summers are warm with an average temperature of 20 °C (68 °F) in the hottest months of July and August. The summers last from May until September.

Climate data for Stuttgart													
Month	**Jan**	**Feb**	**Mar**	**Apr**	**May**	**Jun**	**Jul**	**Aug**	**Sep**	**Oct**	**Nov**	**Dec**	**Year**
Average high °C (°F)	3 (37)	4 (40)	9 (49)	12 (54)	17 (63)	20.5 (69)	24 (75)	23 (73)	19 (66)	14 (57)	8 (46)	4 (40)	13 (56)
Average low °C (°F)	-3 (27)	-3 (27)	0.5 (33)	3 (37)	7 (45)	10.5 (51)	13 (56)	12 (54)	8 (49)	5 (41)	0.5 (33)	-2 (29)	4 (40)
Precipitation cm (inches)	4.8 (1.9)	4.6 (1.8)	4.3 (1.7)	6.1 (2.4)	8.6 (3.4)	8.6 (3.4)	7.4 (2.9)	8.6 (3.4)	5.8 (2.3)	4.6 (1.8)	4.6 (1.8)	5.1 (2.0)	73.4 (28.9)
Source: Weatherbase													

History

Pre 19th century

The first known settlement of Stuttgart was around the end of the 1st century AD with the establishment of a Roman fort in the modern district of Cannstatt on the banks of the river Neckar. Early in the 3rd century the Romans were pushed by the Alamanni back past the Rhine and the Danube. Although nothing is known about Cannstatt during the period of Barbarian Invasion it is believed that the area remained inhabited as it is mentioned in Abbey of St. Gall archives dating back to 700 AD.

Stuttgart itself was probably founded around 950 AD shortly before the Battle of Lechfeld by Duke Liudolf of Swabia, one of the sons of Holy Roman Emperor Otto I the Great. The town was used for breeding cavalry horses in fertile meadows at the very centre of today's city, although recent archaeological excavations indicate that this area was already home to Merovingian farmers.

The 'Old Castle' which dates back to 950

A gift registry from Hirsau Abbey dated around 1160 mentioned 'Hugo de Stuokarten', confirmation of the existence of the Stuttgart of today.

Between this time and the 14th century, the settlement was owned by the Margraves of Baden and the Württemberg towns of Backnang and Besigheim.

The 'New Castle' on Schlossplatz which was built between 1746 and 1807

Around 1300, Stuttgart became the residence of the Counts of Württemberg, who expanded the growing settlement into the capital of their territory (*Territorialstaat*). Stuttgart was elevated to the status of city in 1321 when it became the official royal residence. The territory around Stuttgart was known as the County of Württemberg before the counts were elevated to dukes by the Holy Roman Emperor in 1495, when Stuttgart became the Duchy capital and Ducal residence.

The name Württemberg originates from a steep hill in Stuttgart, formerly known as *Wirtemberg*.

In the 18th century, Stuttgart temporarily surrendered its residence status after Eberhard Ludwig founded Ludwigsburg to the north of the city. In 1775, Karl Eugen requested a return to Stuttgart, ordering the construction of the New Castle.

19th and 20th century

In 1803, Stuttgart was proclaimed capital of Württemberg *Kurfürstentum* (ruled by a Prince-elector) until Napoleon Bonaparte's breakup of the Holy Roman Empire in 1805 when Stuttgart became capital of the Kingdom of Württemberg. The royal residence was expanded under Frederick I of Württemberg although many of Stuttgart's most important buildings, including the Wilhelm Palace, Katharina Hospital, the State Gallery, the Villa Berg and the Königsbau were built under the reign of King Wilhelm I.

Stuttgart's development as a city was impeded in the 19th century by its location. It was not until the opening of the Main Station in 1846 that the city underwent an economic revival. The population at the time was around 50,000.

During the revolution of 1848/1849, a democratic pan-German national parliament (Frankfurt Parliament) was formed in Frankfurt to overcome the division of Germany. After long discussions, the parliament decided to offer the title of the German emperor to King Frederick William IV of Prussia. As the democratic movement became weaker, the German princes regained control of their independent states. Finally, the Prussian king declined the revolutionaries' offer. The members of parliament were driven out of Frankfurt and the most radical members (who wanted to establish a republic) fled to Stuttgart. A short while later, this rump parliament was dissolved by the Württemberg military.

By 1871 Stuttgart boasted 91,000 inhabitants, and by the time Gottlieb Daimler invented the automobile in a small workshop in Cannstatt, the population had risen rapidly to 176,000.

In 1871, as an autonomous kingdom, Württemberg joined the German Empire created by Otto von Bismarck, Prime Minister of Prussia, during the unification of Germany.

At the end of the First World War the Württemberg monarchy broke down: William II of Württemberg refused the crown - but also refused to abdicate - under pressure from revolutionaries who stormed the Wilhelm Palace. The Free State of Württemberg was established, as a part of the Weimar Republic. Stuttgart was proclaimed the capital.

In 1920 Stuttgart became the seat of the German National Government (after the administration fled from Berlin, see Kapp Putsch).

Under the Nazi regime, Stuttgart began deportation of its Jewish inhabitants in 1939. Around sixty percent of the German Jewish population had fled by the time restrictions on their movement were imposed on 1 October 1941, at which point Jews living in Württemberg were forced to live in 'Jewish apartments' before being 'concentrated' on the former Trade Fair grounds in Killesberg. On 1 December 1941 the first deportation trains were organised to Riga. Only 180 Jews from Württemberg held in concentration camps survived.

During the period of Nazi rule, Stuttgart held the "honorary title" *Stadt der Auslandsdeutschen* (City of the Germans living outside of the Reich).

During World War II, the centre of Stuttgart was nearly completely destroyed in Allied air raids. Some of the most severe bombing took place in 1944 at the hands of Anglo-American bombers. The heaviest raid took place on 12 September 1944 when the Royal Air Force bombed the old town of Stuttgart dropping over 184,000 bombs including 75 blockbusters. More than 1000 people perished in the resulting firestorm. In total Stuttgart was subjected to 53 bombing raids, resulting in the destruction of 68% of all buildings and the death of 4477 people.

Stuttgart *Rathaus* (city hall) in 1907. All but the rear of the building was destroyed by allied bombing in the Second World War.

In 1945 the Allied Forces took control of Germany, spearheaded by the French army which occupied Stuttgart until the city fell into the American military occupation zone. An early concept of the Marshall Plan aimed at supporting reconstruction and economic/political recovery across Europe was presented during a speech given by US Secretary of State James F. Byrnes at the Stuttgart Opera House. His speech led directly to the unification of the British and American occupation zones, resulting in the 'bi-zone' (later the 'tri-zone' including the French). When the Federal Republic of Germany was founded on 23 May 1949, Stuttgart, like Frankfurt, was a serious contender to become the federal capital, but finally Bonn succeeded.

Parts of the former German States of Baden and Württemberg were merged in 1952 leading to the founding of the new state of Baden-Württemberg, now Germany's third largest state.

Recent

During the Cold War, Stuttgart became home to the joint command centre of all United States military forces in Europe, Africa and the Atlantic (US European Command, EUCOM). EUCOM is still headquartered there today. U.S. Army bases in and around Stuttgart include or included the following: Patch Barracks (HQ EUCOM), Robinson Barracks, Panzer Kaserne, Kelley Barracks (HQ AFRICOM)

In the late 1970s, the district of Stammheim was centre stage of one of the most controversial periods of German post-war history during the trial of Red Army Faction members at Stammheim high-security court. After the trial, Ulrike Meinhof, Andreas Baader, Gudrun Ensslin and Jan-Carl Raspe committed suicide in Stammheim. Several attempts were made to free the terrorists by force or blackmail during the 'German Autumn' of 1977, culminating in the abduction and murder of the German industrialist and President of the German Employers' Association Hanns Martin Schleyer as well as the hijacking of Lufthansa flight LH181.

First Stuttgart coat of arms in 1286

In 1978 Stuttgart's suburban railway came into operation.

Landmarks, sights and culture

The inner city

At the centre of Stuttgart lies its main square, Schlossplatz. As well as being the largest square in Stuttgart, it stands at the crossover point between the city's shopping area, *Schlossgarten* park which runs down to the river Neckar, Stuttgart's two central castles and major museums and residential areas to the south west. Königstraße, Stuttgart's most important shopping street which runs along the northwestern edge of Schlossplatz, claims to be the longest pedestrianised street in Germany.

The *Stiftskirche*, seen from the west (Stiftstraße)

Although the city centre was heavily damaged during World War II, many historic buildings have been reconstructed and the city boasts some fine pieces of modern post-war architecture. Buildings and squares of note in the inner city include:

Schillerplatz square

The *Alte Kanzlei* on Schillerplatz square

- The *Stiftskirche* (the Collegiate Church), dates back to the 12th century, but was changed to the Late Gothic style in the 15th century and is a Protestant church since 1534. Exterior: Romanesque/Gothic; interior: Romanesque/Gothic/Modern. Reconstructed with simplified interior after WWII.
- *Altes Schloss* (the Old Castle), mostly dating from the late 15th century, some parts date back to 1320. Renaissance style; reconstructed
- *Alte Kanzlei* (the Old Chancellery) on Schillerplatz square which backs onto the 1598 Mercury Pillar
- *Neues Schloss* (the New Castle), completed in 1807. Baroque/Classicism); reconstructed with modern interior, currently houses government offices. The cellars with a collection of stone fragments from the Roman times are open to visitors
- *Wilhelmpalais* (the King Wilhelm Palais), 1840
- *Königsbau* (the King's Building), 1850. Classicism; reconstructed
- The *Großes Haus* of Stuttgart National Theatre, 1909–1912
- *Markthalle* Market Hall, 1910. (Art Nouveau)
- The *Hauptbahnhof* (Main Railway Station) was designed in 1920; its stark, functional lines are typical of the artistic trend 'Neue Sachlichkeit' (New Objectivity)
- The *Württembergische Landesbibliothek* state library, rebuilt in 1970.
- *Friedrichsbau Varieté* (Friedrich Building), rebuilt in 1994 on the site of the former art nouveau building

Architecture in other districts

A number of significant castles stand in Stuttgart's suburbs and beyond as reminders of the city's royal past. These include:

- Castle Solitude, 1700–1800. Baroque/Rococo)
- Ludwigsburg Palace, 1704–1758. Baroque, with its enormous baroque garden.
- Castle Hohenheim, 1771–1793

The *Haus der Wirtschaft* (House of Commerce)

Other landmarks in and around Stuttgart include (*see also museums below*):

- Castle Rosenstein (1822–1830). Classical
- Württemberg Mausoleum (1824) which holds the remains of Catherine Pavlovna of Russia and King William I of Württemberg
- *Wilhelma* Zoo and Botanical Gardens (1853)
- Weissenhof Estate (1927), (International Style)
- The TV Tower (1950), the world's first concrete TV tower
- Stuttgart Airport Terminal Building, 2000. In neighbouring Leinfelden-Echterdingen

Parks, lakes, cemeteries and other places of interest

At the centre of Stuttgart lies a series of gardens which are popular with families and cyclists. Because of its shape on a map, the locals refer to it as the *Green U*. The Green U starts with the old Schlossgarten, castle gardens first mentioned in records in 1350. The modern park stretches down to the river Neckar and is divided into the upper garden (bordering the Old Castle, the Main Station, the State Theater and the State Parliament building), and the middle and lower gardens - a total of 61 hectares. The park also houses Stuttgart planetarium.

At the far end of Schlossgarten lies the second *Green U* park, the larger Rosensteinpark which borders Stuttgart's Wilhelma zoo and botanical gardens. Planted by King William I of Württemberg, it contains many old trees and open areas and counts as the largest English-style garden in southern Germany. In the grounds of the park stands the former Rosenstein castle, now the Rosenstein museum.

Beyond bridges over an adjacent main road lies the final *Green U* park, Killesbergpark or 'Höhenpark' which is a former quarry that was converted for the Third Reich garden show of 1939 (and was used as a collection point for Jews awaiting transportation to concentration camps). The park has been used to stage many gardening shows since the 1950s, including the Bundesgartenschau and 1993 International Gardening Show, and runs miniatures trains all around the park in the summer months for children and adults. The viewing tower (Killesbergturm) offers unique views across to the north east of Stuttgart.

On the northern edge of the Rosensteinpark is the famous 'Wilhelma', Germany's only combined zoological and botanical garden. The whole compound, with its ornate pavilions, greenhouses, walls and gardens was built around 1850 as a summer palace in moorish style for King Wilhelm I of Württemberg. It currently houses around 8000 animals and some 5000 plant species and contains the biggest magnolia grove in Europe.

Other parks in Stuttgart include the historic Botanischer Garten der Universität Hohenheim and Landesarboretum Baden-Württemberg at Castle Hohenheim (which date back to 1776 and are still used to catalogue and research plant species), Uhlandshöhe hill (between the city centre, Bad Cannstatt and Frauenkopf, and home to Stuttgart observatory), the Weißenburgpark (a five hectare park in the Bopser area of Stuttgart South which dates back to 1834 and is now home to a 'tea house' and the 'marble room' and offers a relaxing view across the city centre), the Birkenkopf (at 511 metres (1677 ft) the highest point in central Stuttgart, where many ruins were laid to commemorate the Second World War), the Eichenhain park in Sillenbuch (declared a nature reserve in 1958 and home to 200 oak trees, many 300–400 years old).

There are a number of natural and artificial lakes and ponds in Stuttgart. The largest is the Max-Eyth-See which was created in 1935 by reclaiming a former quarry and is now an official nature reserve. It is surrounded by an expansive open area overlooked by vineyards on the banks of the river Neckar near Mühlhausen.

There are expansive areas of woodland to the west and south west of Stuttgart which are popular with walkers, families, cyclists and ramblers. The most frequented lakes form a 3 km (1.9 mi) trio made up of the Bärensee, Neuer See and Pfaffensee. The lakes are also used for local water supplies.

In the Feuersee area in the west of Stuttgart lies one of two 'Feuersee's (literally fire lakes), striking for its views of the church across the lake, surrounded by nearby houses and offices. The other Feuersee can be found in Vaihingen.

Feuersee, in the area of the same name in Stuttgart West.

Cemeteries in Stuttgart include:

- The Hoppenlaufriedhof in Central Stuttgart, the oldest remaining cemetery which dates back to 1626, an infirmary graveyard last used in 1951
- The Waldfriedhof, the 1913 forest cemetery that is connected to Südheimer Platz by funicular railway

- The Pragfriedhof, with its Art Nouveau crematorium. Established in 1873 it was extended to include Jewish graves in 1874 and also now houses the Russian Orthodox Church of Alexander Nevsky
- The Uff-Kirchhof cemetery in Bad Cannstatt which stands at the crossroads of two ancient Roman roads and Cannstatter Hauptfriedhof, the largest graveyard in Stuttgart which has been used as a Muslim burial ground since 1985.

The city boasts the largest mineral water deposits in Europe after Budapest, with over 250 springs within the urban area.

Culture and events

Stuttgart is known for its rich cultural heritage, in particular its State Theatre (*Staatstheater*) and State Gallery (*Staatsgalerie*). The *Staatstheater* is home to the State opera and three smaller theatres and it regularly stages opera, ballet and theatre productions as well as concerts. The Staatstheater was named Germany/Austria/Switzerland 'Theatre of the year' in 2006; the Stuttgart Opera has won the 'Opera of the year' award six times. Stuttgart Ballet is connected to names like John Cranko and Marcia Haydée.

The State Opera House

The city also offers two broadway-style musical theatres, the Apollo and the Palladium Theater (each approx. 1800 seats). Ludwigsburg Palace in the nearby town of Ludwigsburg is also used throughout the year as a venue for concerts and cultural events.

The Schleyerhalle sports arena is regularly used to stage rock and pop concerts with major international stars on European tour.

Stuttgart's Swabian cuisine, beer and wine have been produced in the area since the 17th century and are now famous throughout Germany and beyond. For example, Gaisburger Marsch is a stew that was invented in Stuttgart's Gaisburg area of Stuttgart South.

In October 2009 the Stuttgart Ministry of Agriculture announced that the European Union was to officially recognise the pasta dish Maultaschen as a "regional speciality", thus marking its significance to the cultural heritage of Baden-Württemberg.

The Cannstatter Volksfest in the district of 'Bad Cannstatt'

In 1993 Stuttgart hosted the International Garden Show in the suburb of Killesberg. In 2006 it was also one of the host cities of the Football World Cup. In 2007, Stuttgart hosted the 2007 World Artistic Gymnastics Championships. In 2008 it was host to the World Individual Debating and Public Speaking Championships.

Regular events that take place in Stuttgart:

- The world-famous annual 'Volksfest', originally a traditional agricultural fair which now also hosts beer tents and a French village and is second in size only to the Oktoberfest in Munich. Unlike Munich, however, there is also a Spring festival on the same grounds in April of each year.
- With more than 3.6 million visitors in 2007 and more than 200 stands, Stuttgart's Christmas Market is the largest and one of the oldest and most beautiful traditional Christmas markets in Europe. It is especially renowned for its abundant decorations and takes place in the four weeks leading up to Christmas.
- The Fish Market (*Hamburger Fischmarkt*, late July) with fresh fish, other food and beer from Hamburg.
- The Summer Festival (*Stuttgart Sommerfest*, usually in early August) with shows, music, children's entertainment and local cuisine in Schlossplatz, Stuttgart and adjacent parks
- The Lantern Festival (*Lichterfest*, early July) in Killesberg park with its famous firework display and fairground attractions
- The Wine Village (*Weindorf*, late August/early September) - vintages are sold at this event held at Schlossplatz and Upper Palace Garden

Museums

Stuttgart is home to five of the eleven state museums in Baden-Württemberg. The foremost of these is the old State Gallery (opened in 1843, extended in 1984) which holds art dating from the 14th to 19th century including works by Rubens, Rembrandt, Monet, Renoir, Cézanne and Beuys. Next door to the Old State Gallery is the New State Gallery (1980) with its controversial modern architecture. Among others, this gallery houses works from Max Beckmann, Dalí, Matisse, Miró, Picasso, Klee, Chagall and Kandinsky.

Entrance to the Old State Gallery

The Old Castle is also home to the State Museum of Württemberg which was founded in 1862 by William I of Württemberg. The museum traces the rich history of Württemberg with many artefacts from the its dukes, counts and kings, as well as earlier remants dating back to the stone age. On the Karlsplatz side of the Old Castle is a museum dedicated to the memory of Claus Schenk Graf von Stauffenberg, former resident of Stuttgart who attempted to assassinate Adolf Hitler on 20 July 1944.

Other leading museums in Stuttgart include:

- The History Museum (*Haus der Geschichte*, 1987), examining local history, finds, the conflict between modern society and its cultural history
- State Museum of Natural History Stuttgart (SMNS) in Park Rosenstein housed in Castle Rosenstein (with an emphasis on biology and natural history) and Löwentor Museum (paleontology and geology, home of the Steinheim Skull and many unique fossils from the triassic , jurassic and tertiary periods
- The Mercedes-Benz Museum (1923, moved in 2006), now the most visited museum in Stuttgart (440,000 visits per year. The museum traces the 120 year history of the automobile from the legendary silver arrow to the Mercedes-Benz brand of today
- Stuttgart Art Museum (*Kunstmuseum Stuttgart*, 2005), the number two museum in Stuttgart in terms of visitors with a strong leaning towards modern art (the foremost exhibition of Otto Dix works. The museum stands on the corner of Schlossplatz, Stuttgart in a huge glass cube, in strong contrast to the surrounding traditional architecture.
- The Porsche Museum (1976, reopened in 2008 on new premises).
- Hegel House (*Hegelhaus*), birthplace of the philosopher Georg Wilhelm Friedrich Hegel which documents his life works
- The Linden Museum, established in 1911, a leading international ethnological museum
- Stuttgart Tram Museum in Zuffenhausen, a display of historical vehicles dating back to 1868
- Theodor Heuss House (*Theodor-Heuss-Haus*, 2002) in Killesbergpark, a tribute to the life and times of the former German president

- The North Station Memorial (*Gedenkstätte am Nordbahnhof Stuttgart*) in memory of the 2000 or so Jewish holocaust victims deported by the Nazis from the now disused North Station

Churches

Stuttgart is the seat of a Protestant bishop (Protestant State Church in Württemberg) and one of the two co-seats of the bishop of the Roman Catholic diocese of Rottenburg-Stuttgart. The Stuttgart-based Pentecostal *Biblische Glaubens-Gemeinde* is the largest place of worship (megachurch) in Germany.

The Protestant Stiftskirche (originally built in 1170) pictured around 1900. In the foreground: the memorial on *Schillerplatz* square.

Demographics

The population of Stuttgart declined steadily between 1960 (637,539) and 2000 (586,978). Then low levels of unemployment and attractive secondary education opportunities led to renewed population growth, fuelled especially by young adults from the former East Germany. For the first time in decades, in 2006 there were also more births in the city than deaths. In April 2008 there were 590,720 inhabitants in the city.

In 2000, 22.8% of the population did not hold German citizenship, in 2006 this had reduced to 21.7%. The largest groups of foreign nationals were Turks (22,025), Greeks (14,341), Italians (13,978), Croats (12,985), Serbs (11,547) followed by immigrants from Bosnia-Herzegovina, Slovenia, Portugal, Poland, Austria and France. 39% of foreign nationals come from the European Union.

Religion

The religious landscape in Stuttgart changed in 1534 as a direct result of the Reformation. Since this time Baden-Württemberg has been predominantly Protestant. However since 1975 the number of Protestants in Stuttgart has dropped from around 300,000 to 200,000. In 2000, 33.7% of inhabitants were Protestant and 27.4% were Roman Catholic. 39% of the population fall into 'other' categories: Muslims, Jews and those who either follow no religion or follow a religion not accounted for in official statistics.

Unemployment

Stuttgart Town Hall (Rathaus)

Unemployment in the Stuttgart Region is low compared to other metropolitan areas in Germany. In November 2008, before the annual winter rise, unemployment in the Stuttgart Region stood at 3.8%, 0.1% lower than the rate for Baden-Württemberg, in February 2009 it was 4.7%. Unemployment in the actual city of Stuttgart during the same periods stood at 5.2% and 6.0% (Nov 08 and Feb 09 respectively). By comparison: unemployment for the whole of Germany stood at 7.1% (Nov 08) and 8.5% (Feb 09).

Crime rates

Stuttgart ranks as one of the safest cities in Germany. In 2003, 8535 crimes were committed in Stuttgart for every 100,000 inhabitants (versus the average for all German cities of 12,751). Figures for 2006 indicate that Stuttgart ranked second behind Munich. 60% of Stuttgart crimes were solved in 2003, ranking second behind Nuremberg.

Politics

Stuttgart's current Bürgermeister (mayor) is Wolfgang Schuster of the conservative CDU party (Christian Democratic Union of Germany).

City government past and present

When Stuttgart was run as a county (or within the Duchy of Württemberg), it was governed by a type of protectorate called a Vogt appointed by the Duke. After 1811 this role was fulfilled by a City Director or 'Stadtdirektor'. After 1819 the community elected its own community mayor or 'Schultheiß'. Since 1930 the title of Oberbürgermeister (the nearest equivalent of which would be an executive form of Lord Mayor in English) has applied to Stuttgart and all other Württemberg towns of more than 20,000 inhabitants.

At the end of the Second World War, French administrators appointed the independent politician Arnulf Klett as Burgomaster, a role he fulfilled without interruption until his death in 1974. Since this time Stuttgart has been governed by the CDU. The previous mayor was Manfred Rommel (son of perhaps the most famous German field marshal of World War II, Erwin Rommel).

As the capital of Baden-Württemberg, Stuttgart is an important political centre in Germany and the seat of the State Parliament, or Landtag as well as all Baden-Württemberg state departments.

In June 2009, for the first time the Greens gained the most seats in a German city with more than 500,000 inhabitants, effectively changing the balance of power in the city council. For the first time since 1972 the CDU no longer held the most seats, toppling its absolute majority shared with the Independent Party and the FDP. According to the German newspaper Die Welt, the main reason for the Greens' victory was disgruntlement with the controversial Stuttgart 21 rail project.

Recent election results

Party Year	Regional 1999	European 1999	State 2001	National German parliament 2002	Regional 2004	European 2004	City Council 2009 (seats)	National German parliament 2005	European 2009
CDU	42.5 %	42.9 %	37.1 %	35.1 %	35.6 %	37.4 %	24.2 % (15)	32.7 %	29,1%
SPD	24.5 %	27.6 %	36.3 %	35.7 %	24.4 %	21.2 %	17.0 % (10)	32.0 %	18,0%
FDP	5.5 %	6.2 %	9.2 %	8.5 %	5.3 %	7.7 %	10.9 % (7)	12.8 %	14,5%
Green Party	14.1 %	14.3 %	11.5 %	16.2 %	17.2 %	22.1 %	25.3 % (16)	15.0 %	25,0%
Independent	5.6 %	-	-	-	8.5 %	-	10.3 % (6)	-	1,2%
Republicans	3.6 %	3.6 %	4.7 %	1.0 %	4.0 %	3.3 %	2.5 % (1)	0.8 %	2,0%
PDS	-	-	-	1.4 %	1.7 %	1.9 %	4.5 % (2)	4.4 %	4,5%
SÖS	-	-	-	-	-	-	4.6 % (3)	-	-
Others	1.5 %	5.4 %	1.2%	2.1 %	3.4 %	6.5 %	0.7 % (0)	2.3 %	6,7 %
Election turnout	59.1 %	46.6 %	65.5 %	81.0 %	54.0 %	51.9 %	48.7 %	79.1 %	52,3%

Source =Stuttgart election results

Economy

The Stuttgart area is known for its high-tech industry. Some of its most prominent companies include Daimler AG, Porsche, Bosch, Celesio, Hewlett-Packard and IBM -- all of whom have their world or European headquarters here.

Stuttgart is home to Germany's ninth biggest exhibition centre, Stuttgart Trade Fair which lies on the city outskirts next to Stuttgart Airport. Hundreds of SMEs are still based in Stuttgart (often termed *Mittelstand*), many still in family ownership with strong ties to the automotive, electronics, engineering and high-tech industry.

Stuttgart has the highest general standard of prosperity of any city in Germany. Contact Air, a regional airline and Lufthansa subsidiary, is headquartered in Stuttgart.

Its nominal GDP per capita is €57,100 and GDP purchasing power parity (PPP) per capita is €55,400. Total GDP of Stuttgart is €33.9 billion, of which service sector contributes around 65.3%, industry 34.5%, and agriculture 0.2%. [*citation needed*]

The cradle of the automobile

The motorbike and four-wheel automobile were invented in Stuttgart (by Gottlieb Daimler and Karl Benz and subsequently industrialised in 1887 by Gottlieb Daimler and Wilhelm Maybach at the Daimler Motoren Gesellschaft). As a result it is considered by many to be the starting point of the worldwide automotive industry and is sometimes referred to as "The cradle of the automobile". Mercedes-Benz, Porsche and Maybach are all produced in Stuttgart and nearby towns. The very first prototypes of the VW Beetle were manufactured in Stuttgart based on a design by Ferdinand Porsche. Also automotive parts giants Bosch and Mahle are based in the city. A number of auto-enthusiast magazines are published in Stuttgart.

Science and R&D

The region currently has Germany's highest density of scientific, academic and research organisations. No other region in Germany registers so many patents and designs as Stuttgart. Almost 45% of Baden-Württemberg scientists involved in R&D are based directly in the Swabian capital. More than 11% of all German R&D costs are invested in the Stuttgart Region (approximately 4.3 billion euros per year). In addition to several universities and colleges (e.g. University of Stuttgart, University of Hohenheim, Stuttgart Institute of Management and Technology and several Stuttgart Universities of Applied Sciences), the area is home to six Fraunhofer institutes, four institutes of collaborative industrial research at local universities, two Max-Planck institutes and a major establishment of the German Aerospace Centre (DLR).

The 'Königsbau' on Schlossplatz, former home to the Stuttgart Stock Exchange

Financial services

The Stuttgart Stock Exchange is the second largest in Germany (after Frankfurt). Many leading companies in the financial services sector are headquartered in Stuttgart with around 100 credit institutes in total (e.g. LBBW Bank, Wüstenrot & Württembergische, Allianz Life Assurance).

A history of wine and beer

Vineyards on the Neckar river in the Mühlhausen area of Stuttgart

Wine-growing in the area dates back to 1108 when, according to State archives, Blaubeuren Abbey was given vineyards in Stuttgart as a gift from 'Monk Ulrich'. In the 17th century the city was the third largest German wine-growing community in the Holy Roman Empire. Wine remained Stuttgart's leading source of income well into the 19th century.

Stuttgart is still one of Germany's largest wine-growing cities with more than 400 hectares of vine area, thanks in main to its location at the centre of Germany's fourth largest wine region, the Württemberg wine growing area which covers 11522 hectares (28470 acres) and is one of only 13 official areas captured under German Wine law. The continuing importance of wine to the local economy is marked every year at the annual wine festival ('Weindorf').

Stuttgart also has several famous breweries such as Stuttgarter Hofbräu, Dinkelacker, and Schwaben Bräu.

Education and research

Stuttgart and its region have been home to some significant figures of German thought and literature, the most important ones being Georg Wilhelm Friedrich Hegel, Friedrich Schiller and Friedrich Hölderlin.

The new building of the State University of Music and Performing Arts, designed by James Stirling

The city, in its engineering tradition as the cradle of the automobile, has also always been a fruitful place of research and innovation. Stuttgart has Germany's second-highest number of institutions (six) of applied research of the Fraunhofer Society (after Dresden).

The city is not considered a traditional university city, but nevertheless has a variety of institutions of higher education. The most significant of them are:

- the University of Stuttgart, it is the fourth biggest university in Baden-Württemberg after Heidelberg, Tübingen and Freiburg. Founded in 1829, it was a *Technische Hochschule* ("Technical University") until 1967, when it was renamed to "university". Its campus for social sciences and architecture is located in the city centre, near the main train station, while the natural science campus is in the southwestern city district of Vaihingen. Historically, its been especially renowned for its faculty of architecture (*Stuttgarter Schule*). Today, its main focus is on engineering and other technical subjects.
- the University of Hohenheim, founded in 1818 as an academy for agricultural science and forestry. While these subjects are still taught there today, its other focus today is on business administration. It is located in Hohenheim quarter of the southern city district of Plieningen.
- the State University of Music and Performing Arts Stuttgart, founded in 1857, located in the city centre, next to the Neue Staatsgalerie.
- the State Academy of Visual Arts Stuttgart, one of the biggest art colleges in Germany, founded in 1761, located in the Killesberg quarter of the northern city district Stuttgart-Nord.
- the College of Media, founded in 2001, a merger of the former *College of Printing and Publishing* and the *College of Librarianship*, located in Vaihingen.
- the University of Applied Science Stuttgart, founded in 1832 as a college for craftsmanship, university of applied science since 1971, located in the city centre, near the University of Stuttgart's city-centre campus.
- the University of Cooperative Education Baden-Württemberg, founded in 1974, with a focus on practical experience, subjects are business, technology and social work.

Media and publishing

One of the headquarters of the public Südwestrundfunk (SWR; *Southwest Broadcasting*) channels (several radio and one TV channel; regional focus on the southwestern German States of Baden-Württemberg and Rhineland-Palatinate) is located in Stuttgart (the other ones being Baden-Baden and Mainz). It also has a *Landesmedienzentrum*, a State media centre.

Furthermore, the city is a significant centre of publishing and specialist printing, with renowned houses such as Georg von Holtzbrinck Publishing Group, Klett Verlag (schoolbooks), Kohlhammer Verlag, Metzler Verlag and Motor Presse having their head offices there. The Reclam Verlag is located in nearby Ditzingen.

The newspapers Stuttgarter Zeitung (StZ; regional, with significant supra-regional, national and international sections) and Stuttgarter Nachrichten (StN; regional) are published here as well as a number of smaller, local papers such as *Cannstatter Zeitung*.

Transport

Following the suit of other German cities such as Berlin, Cologne and Hanover, on 1 March 2008 a Low Emission Zone (LEZ) came into effect in Stuttgart with the aim of improving air quality. This affects all vehicles entering the Stuttgart 'Environmental zone' (*Umweltzone*), including vehicles from abroad.

Local transport

The Stadtbahn underground

Stuttgart has a light rail system known as the Stuttgart Stadtbahn. In the city centre and densely built-up areas, the Stadtbahn runs underground. Stations are signposted with a 'U' symbol, which stands for *Unabhängig* (independent). Until 2007, Stuttgart also operated regular trams. Stuttgart also has a large bus network. Stadtbahn lines and buses are operated by the Stuttgarter Straßenbahnen AG (SSB).

The outlying suburbs of Stuttgart and nearby towns are served by a suburban railway system called the Stuttgart S-Bahn, using tracks supplied by the national Deutsche Bahn AG (DBAG).

The *Zahnradbahn* in 1917

A peculiarity of Stuttgart is the *Zahnradbahn*, a rack railway that is powered by electricity and operates between Marienplatz in the southern inner-city district of the city and the district of Degerloch. It is the only urban rack railway in Germany. Stuttgart also has a *Standseilbahn*, a funicular railway that operates in the Heslach area and the forest cemetery (Waldfriedhof). In Killesberg Park, on a prominent hill overlooking the city, there is the miniature railway run by diesel (and on weekends with steam).

Rail links

Stuttgart is a hub in the InterCityExpress and InterCity networks of Deutsche Bahn AG (DBAG), with through services to most other major German cities. It also operates international services to Strasbourg, Vienna, Zürich and Paris (four times a day, journey time 3 hours 40 minutes).

Stuttgart Hauptbahnhof (main train station)

Long distance trains stop at Stuttgart Hauptbahnhof, the city's main line terminus which is also used by regional DBAG RegionalExpress and RegionalBahn for services to stations in the Stuttgart metropolitan area. The local rail networks (see above) operate underneath the terminus.

Stuttgart also has its own rail freight centre with marshalling yards and a container terminal in the Obertürkheim area of Hedelfingen.

Rail: The *Stuttgart 21* project

After years of political debate and controversy, plans were approved in October 2007 to convert the existing above-ground main train station to an underground through station. The *Stuttgart 21 project* will include the rebuilding of surface and underground lines connecting the station in Stuttgart's enclosed central valley with existing railway and underground lines. Building work started in 2010 and should be completed in 2020.

Air transport

Stuttgart Airport

Stuttgart is served by Stuttgart Airport (German: *Flughafen Stuttgart*, airport code *STR*), an international airport approximately 13 km (8 mi) south of the city centre on land belonging mainly to neighbouring towns. It takes 30 minutes to reach the airport from the city centre using S-Bahn lines S2 or S3. Stuttgart airport is Germany's only city airport with one runway. Despite protests and local initiatives, surveys are currently underway to assess the impact of a second runway.

The A8 motorway running under the car park next to Stuttgart Airport and Stuttgart Trade Fair

Road transport

Stuttgart is served by Autobahn A8, that runs east-west from Karlsruhe to Munich, and Autobahn A81 that runs north-south from Würzburg to Singen. The Autobahn A831 is a short spur entering the southern side of Stuttgart.

Besides these Autobahns, Stuttgart is served by a large number of expressways, many of which are built to Autobahn standards, and were once intended to carry an A-number. Important expressways like B10, B14, B27 and B29 connect Stuttgart with its suburbs. Due to the hilly surroundings, there are many road tunnels in and around Stuttgart. There are also a number of road tunnels under intersections in the center of Stuttgart.

Waterways

Stuttgart has an inland port in Hedelfingen on the River Neckar.

Sport

Football

As in the rest of Germany, football is the most popular sport in Stuttgart which is home to 'The Reds' and 'The Blues'. 'The Reds', VfB Stuttgart, are the most famous and popular local club. An established team in the German Bundesliga, VfB was founded in 1893 and has won five German titles since 1950, most recently in 1992 and 2007. VfB is based at the Mercedes-Benz Arena in Bad Cannstatt.

VfB Stuttgart's home ground, the Mercedes-Benz Arena in Bad Cannstatt. In the background: the Stuttgart Spring Festival

'The Blues', Stuttgarter Kickers, are the second most important football team. They currently play in the Regionalliga Süd (fourth division) at the smaller Gazi Stadium close to the TV tower in Degerloch.

Other lower-division football teams are *Sportfreunde Stuttgart* - most famous for taking part in the Sir Thomas Lipton Trophy in 1908, considered the first *World Cup* - and FV Zuffenhausen.

Other sports

Stuttgart is home to VfL Pfullingen/Stuttgart, a local handball team that played in the national league from 2001 to 2006 in the Schleyerhalle. Its three-times German champion women's volleyball team, CJD Feuerbach, has now stopped playing for financial reasons but there is now Stuttgart Volleyball Club with a women's team in the 2nd southern league.

Stuttgart's ice hockey team, Stuttgarter EC plays at the Waldau ice rink in Degerloch. The strongest local water polo team is SV Cannstatt which won the German championship in 2006.

Stuttgart has two American Football teams, the Stuttgart Nighthawks American football team which plays in the Western Europe Pro League and Stuttgart Scorpions which plays in Stuttgarter Kickers' Gazi Stadium.

TC Weissenhof is a Stuttgart-based women's tennis team that has won the German championship four times. Another women's team is TEC Waldau Stuttgart (German champions in 2006).

HTC Stuttgarter Kickers is one of the most successful field hockey clubs in Germany, having won the German championship in 2005 and a European title in 2006.

Sporting events

Stuttgart has a reputation for staging major events, including the FIFA World Cup 1974, the UEFA Euro 1988, and the World Championships in Athletics 1993. It was also one of the twelve host cities of the FIFA World Cup 2006. Six matches, three of them second round matches, including the 3rd and 4th place playoff, were played at the Gottlieb Daimler Stadium (today Mercedes-Benz Arena). Stuttgart was also 2007 'European Capital of Sports', hosting events such as the UCI World Cycling Championships Road Race and the IAAF World Athletics Final.

Other famous sports venues are the Weissenhof tennis courts, where the annual Mercedes Cup tennis tournament is played, the Porsche Arena (hosting tennis, basketball and handball) and the Schleyerhalle (boxing, equestrianism/show jumping, gymnastics, track cycling etc.).

International relations

See also: List of twin towns and sister cities in Germany

Stuttgart is twinned with the following cities:

- St Helens in England, UK *(since 1948)*
- Cardiff in Wales, UK *(since 1955)*
- St. Louis in Missouri, USA *(since 1960)*
- Strasbourg in France *(since 1962)*
- Mumbai *(formerly known as Bombay)* in India *(since 1968)*
- Menzel Bourguiba in Tunisia *(since 1971)*
- Cairo in Egypt *(since 1979)*
- Łódź in Poland *(since 1988)*
- Brno in Czech Republic *(since 1989)*
- Samara in Russia *(since 1992)*

Stuttgart also has *'special friendships'* with the following cities:

- Ōgaki in Gifu Prefecture, Japan *(since 1988)*
- Shavei Zion in Israel
- Nanjing in People's Republic of China
- The city district of *Bad Cannstatt*, which has the second largest mineral water sources in Europe, has a partnership with Újbuda, the 11th district of Budapest, Hungary, which has the largest mineral water sources in Europe.

Notable residents

Notable people born in Stuttgart or residents who influenced the history of the city:

- Rosalie Abella - Justice, Supreme Court of Canada
- Günther Behnisch - architect
- Robert Bosch - inventor (founded the Robert Bosch GmbH)
- Fred Breinersdorfer - writer and film producer
- Wilhelm Camerer - pediatrician
- Gottlieb Daimler - inventor of the motorbike and automobile, founded what would become Mercedes-Benz
- Roland Emmerich - film producer, director and writer
- Gerhard Ertl - Nobel Prize laureate in chemistry 2007
- Sascha Gerstner - Guitarist of German power metal band Helloween
- Bernd Glemser - international concert pianist [citation needed]
- Georg Wilhelm Friedrich Hegel - philosopher
- Theodor Heuss - First German Post-War President
- Jürgen Klinsmann - football player, former coach of the German football squad
- Klaus von Klitzing - German physicist (1985 Nobel Prize in Physics)
- Helmut Lachenmann - composer [citation needed]
- Mark Landler - *The New York Times* European economic correspondent
- Maximilian Herre - Influential musician and part founder of the Kolchose
- Hermann Lang - Grand Prix race car driver
- Fritz Leonhardt - structural engineer
- Jerri Manthey - Survivor contestant, actress
- Wilhelm Maybach - inventor together with Gottlieb Daimler
- Frei Otto - architect (designer of the roof on the Olympic stadium in Munich)
- Ferdinand Porsche - creator of the VW Beetle, founder of the Porsche car company
- Manfred Rommel - Mayor of Stuttgart 1974–1996, son of Erwin Rommel
- Friedrich von Schiller - famous German poet
- Peter Schilling - popular musician and *Neue Deutsche Welle* artist
- Claus Schenk Graf von Stauffenberg - member of the German Resistance who tried to kill Hitler
- Friedrich Wilhelm Seiffer - neurologist
- Bernard Tomic - Tennis child prodigy
- Carmen Vincelj - Professional dancer and nine times Latin dance World Championship winner
- Dorothea Wendling - soprano for whom the role of Ilia was created by Mozart in his *Idomeneo*
- Richard von Weizsäcker - former German President, Mayor of Berlin

Gallery

Stuttgart from Weinsteige Road

Castle Solitude

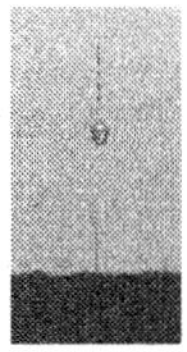

The 1956 Radio masts and towersTV Tower

New Castle (Stuttgart)Neues Schloss at night

The Hegel Museum, birthplace of Georg Wilhelm Friedrich HegelHegel

References

Bibliography

- [3], Mercer Quality of Living 2008 Press Release - Full City Rankings.
- McLachlan, Gordon (2004). *The Rough Guide to Germany*. Rough Guides. ISBN 9781843532934.
- Peters, Kurt; Andrea Schulte-Peevers, Sarah Johnstone, Etain O'Carroll, Jeanne Oliver, Tom Parkinson, Nicola Williams (2004). *Germany*. Lonely Planet. ISBN 9781740594714.

External links

- Stuttgart travel guide from Wikitravel
- Official homepage of Stuttgart [1]
- Official Stuttgart Tourist Board [4]
- Stuttgart International Airport [5]
- Stuttgart Public Transportation System [6]

frr:Stuttgart pnb:□راگ□□س

Things to See in and Around the City

State Museum of Natural History Stuttgart

The **State Museum of Natural History Stuttgart** (German: Staatliches Museum für Naturkunde Stuttgart, short: SMNS) is one of the two state of Baden-Württemberg's natural history museums. Together with the State Museum of Natural History Karlsruhe (Staatliches Museum für Naturkunde Karlsruhe) it is one of the most important repositories for state-owned natural history collections.

Exhibitions are shown in two buildings, both situated in the Rosenstein park in Stuttgart: the Löwentor Museum (German: Museum am Löwentor) houses the paleontology and geology exhibitions, while the Museum Rosenstein in Rosenstein Palace focuses on biology and natural history. Every year, the SMNS is visited by about 110,000 people.

History

Prior to World War II, the natural history collection of Baden-Württemberg was located at the Neckarstraße in downtown Stuttgart. A part of the exhibits were destroyed during the war, when the original building was destroyed by fire after Allied bombing. Luckily, most of the exhibits were sourced out and survived the war. Some specimens were also recovered form the rubble of the destroyed old museum building, including a spectacular plesiosaur today mounted in 3D in the Löwentor Museum exhibition.

The biological specimens of the State's collection are displayed at the castle Rosenstein since 1954. For the paleontological collection, the construction of a new exhibition building began in 1981 and was finished in 1985.

The principal exhibition area of Löwentor Museum consists of a single room, made up of three floors and over 3500 square meters (37'600 square feet) of exhibition area. The room has a height of up to 11 meters.

Permanent exhibition

The Museum am Löwentor exhibition focueses mainly on fossils from its home state of Baden-Württemberg in southwestern Germany, and other localities in Germany. The state is rich in fossils, including several famous classical localities. Especially well exposed are terrestrial and marine Triassic, marine Jurassic and terrestrial Cenozoic sediments. Therefore, the museum exhibits the early prosauropod dinosaur *Plateosaurus* and other terrestrial animals from the Lower and Upper Triassic

(Buntsandstein and Keuper, respectively), a wide range of marine fossils, mainly invertebrates, from the Muschelkalk, and a plethora of ichtyosaurs, pliosaurs and plesiosaurs, as well as sharks from the Posidonia Shale and other Lower Jurassic formations. Furthermore, exquisite Jurassic ammonites and other invertebrates are shown in large numbers. The Cenozoic is represented by invertebrates and mainly vertebrates from various German localities, including a pleistocene elephant and a copy of a mammuth mummy. Also on exhibit is the skull of the prehistoric man of Steinheim (*Homo steinheimensis*). The museum also houses a spectacular collection of plant and animal fossils in amber.

Geographical coordinates: 48°48′19″N 9°11′25″E

External links

Official website [1] (German)

References

Part of this article was translated from the German Wikipedia article (June 20, 2009), version [2].

Württemberg Mausoleum

The **Württemberg Mausoleum** is a memorial in the Rotenberg part of Untertürkheim in Stuttgart, Germany. The mausoleum stands on the peak of Württemberg Hill at the westernmost end of Schurwald woods overlooking the Neckar river. The memorial was built for Catherine Pavlovna of Russia (1788–1819), the second wife of William I of Württemberg (1781–1864). The remains of William I and his daughter Maria Friederike Charlotte of Württemberg (1816–1887) are also housed in the mausoleum.

The Württemberg Mausoleum

History

The mausoleum was built after the death of Queen Catherine between 1820 and 1824 based on a design drafted by Giovanni Salucci. The location on the former site of Fort Wirtemberg was chosen as the home of the House of Württemberg.

Between 1825 and 1899 the mausoleum was used as a Russian Orthodox Church place of worship. The memorial is still used to this day for a Russian Orthodox service every Pentecost.

The mausoleum at night

Architecture

The mausoleum is inspired by the Villa Capra "La Rotonda" build by Andrea Palladio. The building stands by itself in the middle of the vineyards along the river Neckar making it visible from afar.

The former fort of Württemberg on which the Mausoleum stands today

External references

- Official website [1]
- Information and images on www.historisches-wuerttemberg.de (German) [2]

Geographical coordinates: 48°46′55″N 9°16′07″E

Kunstmuseum Stuttgart

The **Kunstmuseum Stuttgart** is a recently opened (March 2005) art museum in Stuttgart, Germany.

The cubic museum building with 5000 m² of display space was designed by Berlin architects Hascher and Jehle. During the day it looks like a glass cube, and at nights the interior lighted limestone walls become visible.

The museum's collection comes from the previous "Galerie der Stadt Stuttgart". The city's collection goes back to a gift from the Marchese Silvio della Valle di Casanova in 1924. It contains one of the most important collections of the work of Otto Dix and also works from Willi Baumeister, Adolf Hölzel, Dieter Roth, and others.

External links

- http://www.kunstmuseum-stuttgart.de/- Museum site
- http://www.hascher-jehle.de/kunstmuseum-stuttgart/index.htm - Architects' site with construction photos

Geographical coordinates: 48°46′42″N 9°10′40″E

Porsche Museum, Stuttgart

The **Porsche Museum** is an automotive museum in the Zuffenhausen district of Stuttgart, Germany on the site of carmaker Porsche.

The new museum

The new Porsche museum stands on a conspicuous junction just outside Porsche Headquarters in Zuffenhausen. The display area covers 5600 square meters featuring around 80 exhibits, many rare cars and a variety of historical models.

The museum was designed by the architects Delugan Meissl. The exhibition spaces were designed by HG Merz who was also involved in the building of the award winning Mercedes-Benz Museum.

Construction

New Porsche-Museum under construction, September 2007

The original Porsche museum opened in 1976 in a side-road near the Porsche factory. It was a relatively small *works museum* with little parking space and it was only big enough to hold around 20 exhibits (in rotation).

Porsche built the museum as a kind of "rolling museum" with rotating exhibits from a stock of 300 restored cars, many in pristine condition and still in full driving order. Originally there was discussion that the new museum would be built alongside a new Mercedes-Benz museum on former trade fair grounds in the Killesberg area of Stuttgart. After the new Mercedes-Benz Museum opened in the east of Stuttgart in 2006, Porsche went ahead with plans to upgrade and extend its museum in the northern district of Zuffenhausen next to the company headquarters. Originally costs were set at 60 million euros but days before the official opening ceremony on 29 January 2009, it was confirmed that the actual costs hit 100 million euros.

The new museum, still under construction in November 2008

Work on the concept for the new Porsche Museum began in 2003. A storyboard comprising relevant topics, exhibits and their presentation was drawn up and a permanent exhibition was designed.

The result is an exhibition that focuses firmly on the vehicles showcased. All ancillary architectural, media and typographic elements are designed to be unobtrusive and complement the cars.

Main Portal from Porsche-Platz

The museum, which is as flexible as it is exclusive, functions as a home base for the vehicles.

References

- Official Porsche company information on the new museum [1]

Selected exhibits

Four wheel drive Porsche 360 *Cisitalia* (1947)

Porsche 356 Nr. 1 Roadster (1948)

Porsche 917 Short coupé (1970)

The 1100 hp Porsche 917/30 Spider (1973)

McLaren TAG Porsche F1 (1985)

Porsche 911 GT1 '98, with Le Mans starting number 25 (1998)

External links

- Website Porsche Museum [2]
- Porsche Automuseum Gmünd
- Porsche Museum on Design Build Network [3]

Geographical coordinates: 48°50′07″N 9°09′06″E

Landesmuseum Württemberg

The **Landesmuseum Württemberg** (Württemberg State Museum) is the main historical museum of the Württemberg part of the German state of Baden-Württemberg. It emerged from the 16th century "Kunstkammer" (art chamber) of the dukes, later kings, of Württemberg who resided in Stuttgart. As a museum it was founded in 1869 by King William I.

Old Castle in Stuttgart, museum main building

The museum's main location is the Old Castle in Stuttgart. The nearby granary and the cellar of the New Castle also contain parts of the collections as well as Waldenbuch Castle outside of Stuttgart. The collections are grouped into three divisions:

- archeology: paleolithic, neolithic, bronze age, iron age, antiquity, Romans in Württemberg, early middle ages, antique glass, and the Roman lapidarium (located in the New Castle)
- history of art and cultural history: modern era glass, Württemberg crown jewels, medieval art, art chamber of the Württemberg rulers, modern glass painting, musical instruments (located in the granary), clocks and scientific instruments
- folklore (located at the Museum of Popular Culture in Waldenbuch Castle): labor, belief and piety, graphic design, clothing, merchandise, culture of living.

Apart from these collections the museum regularly features special exhibitions.

The museum presents a whole range of archeological treasures and a notable collection of medieval art. It also includes the inventories of the former army and manufacturing museums. Some of the most valuable possessions of the museum were already acquired by the dukes for their art chamber: two of only four preserved aztec feather shields from before 1521 and the oldest preserved card game, about 1430, richly decorated and expensive already at the time of production. Exhibits of local origin include a celestial globe of 1493 by Johannes Stöffler, a 11-digit mechanical calculator of 1774 by Philipp Matthäus Hahn, first to build functional calculators to Gottfried Leibniz' design for all four arithmetic operations, and, less unique, but probably the museum's most symbolic exhibit: the royal Württemberg crown of 1797.

The museum today has a further seven branches throughout Württemberg referring to special topics:

- Schlossmuseum Aulendorf (Aulendorf Castle museum): old toys and art of the classicism period
- Schloss Urach (Urach Castle): sleighs of state, 25 specimens, world's biggest collection of this kind
- Museum für Kutschen, Chaisen, Karren (museum for carriages, chaises, carts), Hellenstein Castle, Heidenheim
- Deutsches Spielkartenmuseum (German Playing Card Museum), Leinfelden-Echterdingen: 15000 card decks and 500000 cards from seven centuries, biggest public collection of playing cards in Europe
- Fashion museum, Ludwigsburg Palace
- Ceramics museum, Ludwigsburg Palace
- Dominican museum, Rottweil: archeological collection on arae flaviae (Rottweil), oldest town (AD 73)in Baden-Württemberg; medieval religious art collection; contemporary art collection of the Rottweil area

Several other former branches now belong to the separate Baden-Württemberg State Archeological Museum (Archäologisches Landesmuseum Baden-Württemberg), which has been founded in 1990 due to the ever increasing findings of archeological heritage in the state.

Selected exhibits of Landesmuseum Württemberg

neolithic wooden bucket, c. 3700 BC

glass window from Alpirsbach monastery, Strassburg, c. 1160–1170

Jesus on donkey carving used for donkey walks, late 14th century

Maria Cleophae and Alphaeus by Tilman Riemenschneider, c. 1505–1510

Württemberg Crown, 1797 with later modifications

External links

- Official web site [1]
- Playing Card Museum [2] (German)

Geographical coordinates: 48°46′37″N 9°10′44″E

Mercedes-Benz Museum

The **Mercedes-Benz Museum** is an automotive museum housed in Stuttgart, Germany. Stuttgart is home to the Mercedes-Benz brand and the international headquarters of Daimler AG. The current building, which stands directly outside the main gate of the Daimler factory in Stuttgart-Untertürkheim, was designed by UN Studio. It is based on a unique cloverleaf concept using three overlapping circles with the center removed to form a triangular atrium. The building was completed and opened in 2006. Previously, the museum was housed in a dedicated building within the factory complex and visitors had in recent decades been transported from the main gate by a secured shuttle.

The building's height and "double helix" interior were designed to maximise space, providing 16,500 square metres of exhibition space on a footprint of just 4,800 square metres. The museum contains more than 160 vehicles, some dating back to the very earliest days of the motor engine.

The museum provides visitors with free audio tours in a variety of languages. In 2007 the museum was visited by 860,000 people.

Mercedes-Benz Welt, with the museum (left) and sales center (right)

See also

- Mercedes-Benz World at Brooklands, UK

Further reading

- *Buy Me a Mercedes-Benz: The Book of the Museum.* ACTAR. ISBN 978-84-96540-37-8.

External links

- Official Site [1]
- PERI GmbH - Unrivalled formwork technology [2]
- Technical profile of the building of the museum in *Specifier Magazine* [3]

Geographical coordinates: 48°47′15″N 9°14′00″E

Linden Museum

Linden Museum *(Linden-Museum Stuttgart)*	
Established	May 28, 1911
Location	Stuttgart, Germany
Collection size	Ethnological
Website	www.lindenmuseum.de [1]

The Linden Museum (German: *Linden-Museum Stuttgart. Staatliches Museum für Völkerkunde*) is an ethnological museum located in Stuttgart, Germany. It is one of the principal ethnological museums in the world.

The museum traces its origins to the collection of objects amassed by the Verein für Handelsgeographie (Association for Trade Geography) in the 19th century. The namesake of the museum is Karl Graf von Linden (1838-1910) who, as president of the Stuttgart Verein für Handelsgeographie, took an interest in assembling and organizing the collection, and invited explorers of the caliber of Sven Hedin and Roald Amundsen to Stuttgart.

In 1911, the collection was established as a private museum and its current building was constructed. After suffering extensive damage during World War II, the building was restored in the 1950s and the municipality became its custodian. Since 1973, the museum has been jointly administrated by the city of Stuttgart and the state of Baden-Württemberg.

Staatsgalerie Stuttgart

The **Staatsgalerie Stuttgart** (*State Gallery*) is an art gallery and art museum in Stuttgart, Germany, opened in 1843. In 1984 the opening of the Neue Staatsgalerie (*New State Gallery*) designed by James Stirling transformed the once provincial gallery into one of Europe's leading museums.

Alte Staatsgalerie

Originally, the classicist building of the *Alte Staatsgallerie* was also the home of the royal art school. Built in 1843, it was extended by two further wings during 1881-1887. After being totally destroyed in World War II, it was rebuilt from 1946 and reopened in 1948.

Alte Staatsgalerie

It houses the following collections:

- Old German paintings 1300-1550
- Italian paintings 1300-1800
- Dutch paintings 1500-1700
- German paintings of the baroque period
- Art from 1800-1900 (romanticism, impressionism)

Notable works

- Max Beckmann's *Journey on the Fish*
- Salvador Dalí's *The Raised Instant* (1938)
- George Grosz's *The Funeral* (1918)
- Franz Marc's *The Small Yellow Horses* (1912)
- Henri Matisse's *With the Toilet (La Hair-style)* (1907)
- Joan Miró's *The Bird with the Calm View, the Wings in Flames* (1952)
- Piet Mondrian's *Composition in White, Red and Blue* (1936)
- Pablo Picasso's *Tumblers (Mother and Son)* (1905), *Laufende Frauen am Strand* (1922), *The Breakfast in the Free One* (1961)
- Works by: Paul Klee, Marc Chagall, Wassily Kandinsky

Neue Staatsgalerie

Main article: Neue Staatsgalerie

Neue Staatsgalerie

The *Neue Staatsgalerie*, a controversial{Sudjic, D. (1986). Norman Foster, Richard Rogers,James Stirling: New Directions in British Architecture . London: Thames and Hudson. p. 10{Citation needed|date=September 2009}} architectural design by James Stirling, opened on March 9, 1984 on a site right next to the old building. It houses a collection of 20th-century modern art — from Pablo Picasso to Oskar Schlemmer, Joan Miró and Joseph Beuys.

External links

- Official Website [1]

Geographical coordinates: 48°46′49″N 9°11′13″E

Neue Staatsgalerie

Façade

The **Neue Staatsgalerie** in Stuttgart, Germany was designed by the British firm James Stirling, Michael Wilford and Associates, although largely accredited solely to partner James Stirling. It was constructed in the 1970s and opened to the public in 1984.

History

Entrance

The gallery occupies a site next to the Staatsgalerie Stuttgart. A car park is located below the building.

Style

The building incorporates warm, natural elements of travertine and sandstone to contrast the industrial pieces of green steel framing system and the bright pink and blue steel handrails. The building's most prominent feature is a central circular atrium. This outdoor, enclosed space houses the sculpture garden. It is circumvented by a public footpath that leads pedestrians through the lot, turning the architecture into an "architectural landscape." This feature allows the public to reach the higher elevation behind the museum from the lower front of the building's main face. Throughout the building Stirling alludes to other architectural works.[*citation needed*]

Neue Staatsgalerie

Influence

It is believed by some that this building, being a much acclaimed example of British architecture, was one of the principal reasons Stirling received the Pritzker Prize in 1981.

External links

- http://www.staatsgalerie.de/(Official Site, German)
- http://www.greatbuildings.com/buildings/Neue_Staatsgalerie.html
- http://www.greatbuildings.com/models/Neue_Staatsgalerie_mod.html

Geographical coordinates: 48°46′49″N 9°11′13″E

Stiftskirche (Stuttgart)

The **Stiftskirche Stuttgart** (*Collegiate Church*) is an inner-city church in Stuttgart, the capital of Baden-Württemberg, Germany. It is the main church of the Evangelical-Lutheran Church in Württemberg (*Evangelische Landeskirche in Württemberg*) as well as the parish church of the evangelical (Lutheran) inner-city church district of Stuttgart.

History and structure

Structures of a small Romanesque church from the 10th and 11th centuries could recently be traced as having been exactly in today's church outline.

In 1240, a stately three-naved church with two towers is built in the Romanic style, apparently by the Counts of Württemberg who from around that time are residing in the nearby Old Castle. From the end of the 13th century a double tomb is preserved in today's South tower chapel. It contains the remains of Ulrich I, Count of Württemberg and his second wife, Countess of Württemberg, Agnes von Schlesien-Liegnitz (both died in 1265).

View on the Stiftskirche from the west

With Stuttgart the new residence of the rulers of Württemberg, a new Gothic chancel was built from 1321 to 1347. To it was added a Late Gothic nave in the second half of the 15th century by Ulrich V.

In 1500, a coloured, later (from the 19th century) golden pulpit was added.

With the adoption of the Lutheran Protestant Reformation in Württemberg in 1534, all pictures and altars are removed from the naves, pewage and a gallery is added. The tombstones are moved to the interior of the church.

The Lutheran reformer Johannes Brenz (died 1570), the main Protestant Reformer of Württemberg, was buried under the chancel.

From 1574, small statues of all the Counts of Württemberg (i.e. since Ulrich I) are added at the North wall of the chancel.

In 1608, a new grave crypt or burial vault is added. All of the Württemberg rulers until 1677 are buried there. Catherine Pavlovna of Russia, Queen of Württemberg from 1816 until 1819, was buried here from 1819 to 1824, before her remains were brought to a mausoleum on the Württemberg mountain.

In 1826, the roof of the chancel was renovated, as was most of the interior of the church in the 1840s.

Towards the end of the Second World War, the church was heavily destroyed by the bombing raids on Stuttgart in 1944.

In the 1950s, the church was restored, however, not in all historical detail.

The latest major renovation took place from 1999 to 2003.

Evangelical-Lutheran Church in Württemberg

The **Evangelical-Lutheran Church in Württemberg** (Evangelische Landeskirche in Württemberg; analoguous translation in English: *Evangelical State Church in Württemberg*) is a Protestant church in the German former state of Württemberg, now the part of the state Baden-Württemberg. The seat of the church is in Stuttgart.

It is a full member of the Evangelical Church in Germany (EKD), and is a Lutheran Church. The presiding bishop (Landesbischof) of the church is Frank Otfried July (2005). There are four regional bishops (Regionalbischöfe).

The Evangelical Lutheran Church of Württemberg is one of 22 Lutheran, united and reformed churches of the EKD. The church has 2,286,893 members (31. Dezember 2007) in about 1,400 parishes. It's the most important Protestant denomination in Eastern Baden-Württemberg.

The Evangelical Lutheran Church of Württemberg is a member church of the Community of Protestant Churches in Europe. It is neither a member of the United Evangelical Lutheran Church of Germany, nor a member of the Lutheran World Federation, but has a guest status in both. The Church runs a minister training house at Tübingen called Tübinger Stift.

The most prominent churches of the Evangelical Lutheran Church of Württemberg are the Stiftskirche in Stuttgart, the Minster in Ulm, the Kilians church in Heilbronn, the St. Mary's Church, Reutlingen, the city church St. Dionysius in Esslingen as well as the church St. Michael in Schwäbisch Hall.

The ordination of women like in all other EKD churches has been allowed.

History

In 1534 Ulrich, Duke of Württemberg enforced in his Duchy of Württemberg the Protestant Reformation. The Duke, later on the respective King of Württemberg was therefore head of the state church as so called summus episcopus, meaning the respective ruler united secular and religious power in his person. The former Catholic bishops lost all privileges. Johannes Brenz was deployed as reformer of the state in terms of Martin Luther. He is entombed in the Stuttgart Stiftskirche.

The Evangelical State Church in Württemberg was therefore from the beginning on a Lutheran church, however the form of church service is bound to reformed tradition, meaning that it is rather plain. The otherwise in Lutheran parishes form of the Lutheran mass is hardly ever practiced. Up to 1806 the Duchy of Württemberg was a purely evangelical territory. Only when Württemberg became kingdom and due to Napoleon larger Catholic territories (Upper Swabia) were added, the uniform religious structure ended. Since the late 19th century also in former Catholic territories of (southern) Württemberg evangelical parishes were founded.

After the end of World War I King William II of Württemberg was forced to resign. The church therefore formally had no ruler anymore. But the church was prepared for this vacuum, since his issue was disqualified for royal succession due to inadequate marriage. Therefore since the 1890s the head of a Catholic ducal branch line of the royal house was enacted as successor, whom the Lutheran state church would not accept as summus episcopus. Therefore leading clergymen took over the church. After the exiled King William II had died (October 1921) the Evangelical State Church in Württemberg gave itself a new constitution in 1923/24 and put in a church president as the lead of the church, who in 1933 received the title *Landesbischof.*

From 1945 on the Hohenzollern provincial Protestant deanery (Kirchenkreis) of the Evangelical Church of the old-Prussian Union adopted the provisional supervision by the Evangelical State Church in Württemberg. On April 1, 1950 the deanery joined that church body and thus terminated its subordination to the supervision by the prior old-Prussian Ecclesiastical Province of the Rhineland.

From 20 July - 27 July 2010 the Evangelical State Church in Württemberg will host of the 11th General Assembly of the Lutheran World Federation in Stuttgart, Germany.

Leading persons and bishops in history

- 1924–1929: Johannes von Merz, church president
- 1929–1948: Theophil Wurm, bishop (until 1933 church president)
- 1948–1962: Dr. Martin Haug, bishop
- 1962–1969: Dr. Erich Eichele, bishop
- 1969–1979: Helmut Claß, bishop
- 1979–1988: Hans von Keler, bishop
- 1988–1994: Theo Sorg, bishop
- 1994–2001: Eberhardt Renz, bishop
- 2001–2005: Gerhard Maier, bishop
- 2005 – today: Frank Otfried July, bishop

Synod

The election of the synod is for six years.

External links

- Official web site (German) [1]
- International Information (English) [2]
- Association for Württemberg Church History (German) [3]
- Evangelic Community Paper of Württemberg (German) [4]
- Evangelical Church in Germany [5]

Blaubeuren Abbey

Blaubeuren Abbey (*Kloster Blaubeuren* in German) was a house of the Benedictine Order located in Blaubeuren, Baden-Württemberg, Germany.

History: Catholic

The monastery was founded in 1085 by the Counts of Rück and Tübingen, against the background of the Investiture Controversy and the Hirsau Reforms. The first abbot, Adzelinus, and monks were from Hirsau Abbey.

Abbot Fabri was closely involved with the foundation of the University of Tübingen in 1477. In 1493 the high altar was created. The choir stalls by Jörg Syrlin the younger are of a similar date.

The Reformation saw the end of the Roman Catholic monastery, from which the monks were expelled in 1535, returning for a short time between 1549 and 1562.

Reredos of the high altar (central detail), by Michael Erfurt

History: Protestant

In 1563 the first Protestant abbot was appointed, and in 1565 a choir school was opened in the premises.

During the Thirty Years' War the monks returned again in 1630 and yet again in 1648, but were expelled; the choir school closed in 1630 and reopened in 1650. It was finally shut down in 1807.

A few years later in 1817 Blaubeuren became a Protestant seminary with an attached boarding school, which has remained to the present, except for a closure during World War II.

The school now operates in co-operation with the similar establishment at Maulbronn Abbey: see Evangelical Seminaries of Maulbronn and Blaubeuren.

External links

- (German) Website of Blaubeuren Protestant Seminary [1]

Geographical coordinates: 48°24′55″N 9°47′4″E

Wilhelm Palais

The **Wilhelmspalais** is a Palais located on the Charlottenplatz in Stuttgart-Mitte. It was the living quarters of the last Württemberg King Wilhelm II. Nowadays, the central library of the Stadtbücherei Stuttgart is situated in this building.

Hohenheim

Stuttgart-Hohenheim (also known simply as *Hohenheim*) is a quarter of Plieningen, one of the 18 outer districts of Stuttgart, the state capital of Baden-Württemberg, Germany. Hohenheim is famous for Hohenheim Palace built in 1782 by Duke Karl Eugen of Württemberg, today the site of Stuttgart's oldest university, the University of Hohenheim.

After the duke had acquired the former manor of the *Hohenheim* noble family - with Philipp von Hohenheim called Paracelsus as its most notable member - in 1768, he gave it to his mistress Franziska Leutrum von Ertingen, including the title of a *Reichsgräfin von Hohenheim*. From 1772 Karl Eugen had the manor house rebuilt as a water castle surrounded by an extended English garden featuring several midget replicas of historic buildings, an arboretum and numerous exotic plants. The construction of the present-day palace started in 1782 but discontinued with the duke's death in 1793.

In 1818 King William I of Württemberg established an agricultural school at Hohenheim, the predecessor of the nowadays university. Today the gardens comprise the Landesarboretum Baden-Württemberg and the Botanischer Garten der Universität Hohenheim.

External links

- Hohenheim Palace [1]

This article incorporates text from a publication now in the public domain: Chisholm, Hugh, ed (1911). *Encyclopædia Britannica* (Eleventh ed.). Cambridge University Press.

Old Castle (Stuttgart)

The **Old Castle** (German: *Altes Schloss*) is located in the centre of Stuttgart, the capital of the German State of Baden-Württemberg. It dates back to the 10th century.

Old Castle in Stuttgart

The first castle dated back to around 950 when Stuttgart was a settlement for breeding horses. In the 14th century it became the residence of the sovereign Counts of Württemberg. In the 16th century dukes Christopher and Ludwig ordered it to be converted into a Renaissance castle. Moats around the castle were removed in the 18th century.

In 1931 the castle was severely damaged by a fire and before it could be reconstructed it was damaged by bombing in the Second World War. The castle was finally renovated in 1969.

Today the Old Castle is home to the Württemberg State Museum.

King Charles I of Württemberg and his wife Olga are buried beneath the castle church. The inner courtyard houses a monument to Eberhard I. The Old Castle stands adjacent to its replacement, the New Castle, which was built in the late 18th century.

On the Karlsplatz side of the Old Castle is a museum dedicated to the memory of Claus Schenk Graf von Stauffenberg a former resident of Stuttgart who attempted to assassinate Adolf Hitler on 20 July 1944.

See also

- Duchy of Württemberg
- Kingdom of Württemberg

Gallery

Inner courtyard

Castle chapel

Monument of count Eberhard I

The south west corner

External links

- http://www.landesmuseum-stuttgart.de
- Altes Schloss Stadt-Panorama [1] - Interactive 360° Panorama of the Old Castle

Geographical coordinates: 48°46′38″N 9°10′45″E

New Castle (Stuttgart)

The **New Castle** (German: "das Neue Schloss") is a building which stands on the south edge of Schlossplatz, the central square in Stuttgart, Germany. The castle is built in late Baroque style.

From 1746 to 1797 and from 1805 to 1807, it served as a residence of the kings of Württemberg. The castle, which is more of a palace, stands adjacent to the Old Castle.

The castle was almost completely destroyed by Allied bombing during the Second World War and was reconstructed between 1958 and 1964. During this time most of the inside of the castle was also restored and the building was used by the Baden-Württemberg State Parliament. Today it is used by the State Ministries of Finance and Education. Public tours of the building are only permitted by special arrangement.

Schlossplatz stands next to two other popular squares in Stuttgart: Karlspatz to the south and Schillerplatz to the south west.

See also

- List of Baroque residences

Gallery

New Castle at Night

The New Castle viewed from the New Gallery

Fountains in front of the New Castle at night

Geographical coordinates: 48°46′41″N 9°10′55″E

Castle Solitude

<table>
<tr><th colspan="2">Schloss Solitude</th></tr>
<tr><td colspan="2">
Castle Solitude</td></tr>
<tr><td>Town</td><td>Stuttgart</td></tr>
<tr><td>Country</td><td>Germany</td></tr>
</table>

Castle Solitude in Stuttgart, Germany (German: *Schloss Solitude*), was built as a hunting lodge between 1764 and 1769 under Duke Karl Eugen of Württemberg. It is not a true castle, but rather a rococo palace. Since 1956 the area is part of the urban district of Stuttgart-West. The castle is located on a high plain between the towns of Leonberg, Gerlingen and Stuttgart city. The castle offers views to the north over Weilimdorf, Korntal and Ludwigsburg.

History

Schloss Solitude was originally designed to act as a *refugium*, a place of quiet, reflection and solitude (thus the name). Construction of the castle was plagued by political and financial difficulties. Karl Eugen had taken Württemberg into the Seven Years' War on the losing side against Prussia. The building exceeded the budget allocated by the duchy of Württemberg. Further, political wrangling between the duke and influential Stuttgart land barons led to the duke moving temporarily from Stuttgart to Ludwigsburg. In the long run, the castle was prohibitively expensive to keep just as a temporary residence. In 1770 it housed a high school founded by Duke Eugen. In 1775, the Karlsschule academy moved to Castle Solitude. It served as an academy of arts, a military academy, and later a general university for children of the elite. Eventually, maintenance costs led to its closure as a school after the Duke's death late in the 18th century. Between 1972 and 1983, the Federal Republic of Germany restored the castle.

Current use

Since 1990, the annexed buildings (*Officen*-building and *Kavaliers*-building) have housed the 'Castle Solitude' academy. The *Kavaliers* building incorporates living quarters for students.

Architecture

Castle Solitude was designed by a working group at the ducal court under the guidance of Philippe de La Guêpière with active input from Duke Karl Eugen and master craftsmen. Its exterior is typical Rococo. On the inside, however, the style is characteristic of classicism: instead of the irregular lively forms typical of Rococo, the proportions of the rooms and wall are typically classical in design.

Solitude avenue

The northern main gate of the castle marks the beginning of *Solitudeallee*, a partially tree-lined straight avenue leads directly to Ludwigsburg over 13 km. Duke Karl-Eugen commissioned the building of the avenue from 1764 to 1768 as a connecting route to the residence palace in Ludwigsburg. The avenue, which is still largely intact today, leads via Stuttgart-Weilimdorf past Stuttgart-Zuffenhausen and Stuttgart-Stammheim. Only in Weilimdorf, where it intersects the main street, and in Ludwigsburg, where it is interrupted by the railway, are there minor irregularities. According to a plaque inside the castle, the avenue served as the baseline for the Württemberg land survey of 1820 and measures exactly 40,118.718 Paris feet or 13,032.14 meters.

Race track

After 1903 Castle Solitude was the finishing point of hill races. In later years, the grounds of the castle served as a hostel for drivers. From 1935 to 1965, the 11.3 kilometers Solituderennen course south of the castle was used for World Championship motorcycle Grand Prix racing. From 1961 to 1965, a series of non-championship Formula 1 races were also held on the same weekends, welcoming drivers such as John Surtees, Jim Clark, Dan Gurney and Jack Brabham. In their heyday, the Solitude races attracted crowds of 288,000 spectators, but they were abandoned in 1966.

In 2003, a *revival* competition was staged in and around the castle with former competitors and ex-world champions such as Giacomo Agostini. A rally to commemorate the 50th anniversary of races was held in 2004.

Suburb

The area of Castle Solitude first belonged to Weilimdorf. After the middle of the 19th century it belonged to Gerlingen until the 31st of March 1942, at which point it was assigned to the suburb of Botnang before being integrated into the district of Stuttgart-West in 1956.

See also

- List of Baroque residences

External links

- Memorial site of the Solitude races [1] (German)

Geographical coordinates: 48°47′13″N 9°05′03″E

Rosenstein Castle

Castle Rosenstein in the Bad Cannstatt district of Stuttgart, Germany was built between 1822 and 1830 by the court builder Giovanni Salucci (1769–1845) in the classical style for King Wilhelm I.

The palace stands in Park Rosenstein on a height overlooking the Neckar river valley. Formerly called the Kahlenstein (literally 'bald rock', because it was bare of trees), the hill was renamed Rosenstein ('rose rock'), and a rose garden was planted to the south-east of the palace.

Today, Schloss Rosenstein houses that part of State Museum of Natural History Stuttgart (SMNS) dealing with extant lifeforms.

Geographical coordinates: 48°48′04″N 9°12′22″E

Hegel House

The **Hegel House** (German: *Hegelhaus*) is a museum in Stuttgart, Germany, located in the house where the philosopher Georg Wilhelm Friedrich Hegel was born.

Born in 1770, Hegel lived in Stuttgart for the first 18 years of his life; he died in Berlin in 1831. The Hegel House is on Eberhardstraße, and dates from the 16th century.

The ground floor contains an exhibition about Stuttgart during Hegel's lifetime. Another exhibition is devoted to Hegel's life story, and includes his famous beret and his *Stammbuch* (an early form of friendship book). A third room contains a text collage of key quotations from Hegel, and various editions of his works in different languages.

External links

- http://www.stuttgart.de/hegelhaus Hegel House entry on the city of Stuttgart's home page. (German)

  This article incorporates information from this version [1] *of the equivalent article on the German Wikipedia.*

Schillerplatz (Stuttgart)

Schillerplatz is a square in the old city centre of Stuttgart, Germany named in honour of the German poet, philosopher, historian, and dramatist Friedrich Schiller. Schillerplatz stands to the south west of Stuttgart's main square, Schlossplatz.

Schillerplatz showing the Fruchtkasten building on the left and Prinzenbau on the right. In the centre: the Schiller memorial

Buildings around Schillerplatz

Starting in the south west corner, Schillerplatz is surrounded by the *Stiftskirche* (the Collegiate Church), the *Fruchtkasten* building, the *Prinzenbau* (which now houses the Baden-Württemberg Ministry of Justice, the *Alte Kanzlei* (Old Chancellery) and *Altes Schloss* (the Old Castle).

A street market takes place twice a week on Schillerplatz. The square is also used for major events taking place on *Marktplatz* (Stuttgart's Market Square) such as the annual Christmas Market. Hidden underneath Schillerplatz's cobblestones is an underground car park.

The late Gothic *Fruchtkasten* building in the corner of Schillerplatz is now used by the State Museum of Württemberg to house a collection of musical instruments.

The Schiller memorial

The Schiller memorial

At the centre of the cobblestone square is a memorial to Friedrich Schiller which was erected in 1839 by the Danish sculptor Bertel Thorvaldsen. Thorvaldsen's statue was the first memorial to Schiller to be erected in Germany.

History

Alte Kanzlei (The Old Chancellery)

The first known brick building in Stuttgart - the *Stuthaus* or mare house - stood next to the adjacent Stiftskirche (collegiate church). It is therefore supposed that the square was originally used as a horse breeding area around 1000 years ago (in keeping with Stuttgart's history). After the 12th century the square was probably covered in simple houses before other stone houses such as the *Fruchtkasten* were built. In the mid-14th century the *Dürnitzbau* wing of the Old Castle (next to

Schillerplatz) was erected. The Old Chancellery was built in 1542 shortly before completion of the *Arkadenflügel* wing of the Old Castle. The area between the Old Castle and the Chancellery became a moat.

In 1594 Duke Friedrich I asked his master builder Heinrich Schickhardt to turn today's Schillerplatz into a Renaissance square. Residents' houses were bought and demolished. The new square was laid with cobblestones and called 'Castle and Chancellery Square'. The dimensions of the square have not changed since.

The Collegiate Church from Schillerplatz

In 1607 work began on the *Gesandtenhaus* (a type of ambassador's house) which is now known as the *Prinzenbau* and was finally completed in 1677. In 1711 the Prinzenbau was extended behind the Old Chancellery with an arch in the northernmost corner of Schillerplatz. On the opposite, southern side of the square between the Old Castle and Stiftskirche the first Stuttgart Café opened in 1712. It was replaced in 1798 by the *König von England* inn (King of England Inn). This was shortly after the moat surrounding the Old Castle had finally been filled in leaving the square the way it stands today.

The square was officially renamed Schillerplatz in 1934 in memory of one of Baden-Württemberg's most famous writers and intellectuals.

During the Second World War of the buildings around Schillerplatz were burnt down but all were reconstructed after the war with the exception of the *King of England Inn.*

The underground car park was built in 1972-3.

External references

- Harald Schukraft: *Stuttgarter Straßen-Geschichte(n).* German. Silberburg Publishing, ISBN 3-925344-05-5

The Old Castle

Schillerplatz around 1900

Schillerplatz in 1839

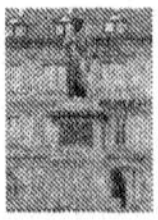

The Schiller memorial

Geographical coordinates: 48°46′37.76″N 9°10′42.48″E

Schlossplatz, Stuttgart

Schlossplatz is the largest square in the centre of the city of Stuttgart and home to the New Castle which was built between 1746 and 1807.

Schlossplatz looking towards the New Castle

Schlossplatz stands next to two other popular squares in Stuttgart: Karlspatz to the south and Schillerplatz to the south west.

The entire square was last fully renovated in 1977 to mark the staging of the Bundesgartenschau (State Garden Show) in Stuttgart. The lawns and flowerbeds were renewed in 2006 following the staging of the 2006 World Cup Finals.

Public transport

- Schlossplatz lies almost directly on the B27 road.

- Bus routes 42 and 44, all 17 night buses, the U5, U6, U7 and U15 lines of the Stuttgart underground stop directly on Schlossplatz.

The new art gallery

Events

Every year Schlossplatz is home to major outdoor events such as open air concerts, children's fairs and parts of the Christmas market including an outdoor ice rink. During the 2006 World Cup Finals the square regularly held more than 40,000 spectators who watched live matches on 3 huge screens.

Schlossplatz featured the United Buddy Bears exhibition in summer 2008 - an array of 144 two metre-high sculptures, each designed by a different artist, touring the world as a symbol of cultural understanding, tolerance and mutual trust.

Other images

The centre of arts

The Alte Kanzlei (Old chancellery), viewed from neighbouring Schillerplatz

The Mercury Pillar, completed in 1598

New Castle (Stuttgart)Neues Schloss at night

References

- Schlossplatz panorama [1] – Interactive 360° Panorama

Geographical coordinates: 48°46′42.78″N 9°10′47.68″E

Staatstheater Stuttgart

The *Großes Haus* of Stuttgart National Theatre

The ***Staatstheater Stuttgart*** **(Stuttgart National Theatre)** is an opera house in Stuttgart, Germany. It is also known locally as the *Grosses Haus*, having been the larger of two theatres of the former *Königliche Hoftheater*.

Designed by the noted Munich architect, Max Littmann, who won a competition to create new royal theatres, it was constructed between 1909 and 1912 as the *Königliche Hoftheater*, a royal theatre of the Kingdom of Württemberg with a *Grosses Haus* and a *Kleines Haus*.

In 1919 the theatres were renamed the *Landestheater*, and later, the *Staatstheater*. The *Small House* was destroyed by bombing during the Second World War and, today, the site is occupied by a new *Kleines Haus* ,which opened in 1962.

The *Grosses Haus* is the only major German opera house to survive the bombing of the Second World War. Between 1982 and 1984, extensive renovations restored it to its original condition and it now seats 1,399.

The theatre is presently the home of the Staatsoper Stuttgart.

See also

- Staatsoper Stuttgart
- List of opera houses

External links

- (German) Staatsoper Stuttgart website [1]

Geographical coordinates: 48°46′48.61″N 9°11′05.89″E

Stuttgart Ballet

The Stuttgart National Theatre, home to the Stuttgart Ballet

Stuttgart Ballet was the first major German ballet company. It rose to fame in the 1960s under Artistic Director John Cranko. The company, which is renowned for presentations of full-length narrative ballets including *Romeo and Juliet*, *Eugene Onegin*, *The Taming of the Shrew*, Neumeier's *Die Kameliendame* and *Streetcar Named Desire*, continues to be defined critically as one of the world's best ballet theatres for its combination of classical, story and new modern ballets.

Stuttgart Ballet has a tradition of producing new and exciting dance while giving young choreographers and dancers opportunity to express themselves and flourish[citation needed]. Famous dancers who have emerged from the ranks of the company to become some of the world's most well-known choreographers include John Neumeier, William Forsythe, Uwe Scholz, John Alleyne, Jiri Kylian and Renato Zanella.

The modern Stuttgart Ballet evolved from the royal ballet that resided at the court of the Duke of Württemberg as early as 1609. Previous directors include Glen Tetley and Marcia Haydee. Reid Anderson has been the artistic director since 1996. Stuttgart Ballet is known for its enthusiastic and knowledgeable audiences and performs in the Stuttgart Opera House and (slightly smaller) playhouse. The company is recognised all over the world and is regularly invited to perform on the most distinguished stages, giving approximately twenty shows a season across a variety of countries.

Current Artists

As of April 2010:

Principal dancers

- Alicia Amatriain
- Bridget Breiner
- Maria Eichwald
- Sue Jin Kang
- Elizabeth Mason
- Anna Osadcenko
- Katja Wünsche
- Filip Barankiewicz
- Douglas Lee
- Evan McKie
- Marijn Rademaker
- Jason Reilly
- Friedemann Vogel
- Alexander Zaitsev

Soloists

- Oihane Herrero
- Laura O'Malley
- Myriam Simon
- Nikolay Godunov
- Alexander Jones
- William Moore
- Damiano Pettenella

Demi soloists

- Magdalena Dziegielewska
- Hyo-Jung Kang
- Katarzyna Kozielska
- Alessandra Tognoloni
- Linda Waasdorp
- Angelina Zuccarini
- Laurent Guilbaud
- Roland Havlica
- Dimitri Magitov
- Arman Zazyan

Corps de ballet

- Maria Alati
- Francesca Berruto
- Anais Bueno Garces
- Rachele Buriassi
- Christina Burnell
- Jelena Buschuyeva
- Annabel Fawcett
- Nathalie Guth
- Catherine Hamer
- Miriam Kacerova
- Daniela Lanzetti
- Daisy Long
- Julie Marquet
- Elizabeth Wisenberg
- Renee Wright
- Bilyana Yancheva
- Özkan Ayik
- Attila Bako
- Daniel Camargo
- Matthew Crockard-Villa
- Tomas Danhel
- Lee Fennell
- Sébastien Galtier
- David Moore
- Roman Novitzky
- Ludovico Pace
- Brent Parolin
- Mikhail Soloviev
- Petros Terteryan
- Demis Volpi
- Yaosheng Weng

Apprentices

- Elisa Badenes
- Mariya Batman
- Valeria Busdraghi
- Heather MacIsaac
- Ami Morita
- Lea Zoe Weidner
- Lionel de Bayser
- Doruk Demirdirek

External links

- Official website of the Stuttgart Ballet [1] Accessed Feb. 26, 2010

Birkenkopf

The Birkenkopf	
The Birkenkopf	
Elevation	511 m (1677 ft)
Location	
Location	Stuttgart, Baden-Württemberg, Deutschland
Coordinates	48°45′55″N 9°7′54″E
Geology	
Type	Schuttberg

This article incorporates information from the equivalent article on the German Wikipedia.

The memorial plaque fixed to one of the rubble pieces

The **Birkenkopf** is a hill of height 511m within Stuttgart. It is the highest point of the inner regions of Stuttgart and is almost 300m higher than the river Neckar on which Stuttgart lies. The hill lies in the Stuttgart-West city region. It is in part a Schuttberg, an artificial hill built from the ruins and rubble from World War II.

Between 1953 and 1957, 15 million cubic metres of rubble from 53 bombing missions during World War II were built on top of the hill, which resulted in an increase in height of around 40 metres. At the summit there are many recognisable facades from the ruined buildings. The locals colloquially call the Birkenkopf "Monte Scherbelino", which roughly translates as "Mount Shards" but in childlike language. One of the pieces of rubble has a plaque attached to it, which says: *Dieser Berg nach dem Zweiten Weltkrieg aufgetürmt aus den Trümmern der Stadt steht den Opfern zum Gedächtnis den Lebenden zur Mahnung*. This translates roughly as: *This mountain was built after the Second World War from the rubble of the town to stand as a memorial of the dead and a warning to the living*.

From the summit the whole city centre can be seen, and on a clear day the view extends to the Swabian Alb, to the Black Forest, and the lowlands of Württemberg. On the summit there is a steel cross, which in 2003 replaced the original 1953 wooden cross. In the summer, early morning services are sometimes held here.

External links

- Stuttgarter Zeitung: Der Birkenkopf [1] (in German)
- 360° Panorama of the Birkenkopf [2] (in German)

Stuttgart Observatory

Sternwarte Stuttgart (Observatory Stuttgart)

Sternwarte Stuttgart (**Stuttgart Observatory**) is an astronomical observatory owned and operated by the association Schwäbische Sternwarte e.V.. It is located on the Uhlandshöhe in Stuttgart, Germany. Public tours have been held since 1920 and the observatory claims to be one of the oldest in Germany.

External links

- Stuttgart Observatory [1]

Geographical coordinates: 48°52′30″N 9°35′48″E

Observation Tower Burgholzhof

The **Observation Tower Burgholzhof** in Burgholzhof, since 1998 a separate community within Bad Cannstatt in Stuttgart, Baden-Württemberg, Germany, is an 1891 brick observation tower constructed by the Cannstatt municipal architect Friedrich Keppler on behalf of the *Verschönerungsverein Cannstatt e. V.* ("Society for the Beautification of Cannstatt"), in the style of a Roman tower, at an elevation of 359 meters above sea level, at 9°11'41 east and 48°49'08" north. It was formally opened on 19 September 1891 in the presence of the then Crown-Prince Wilhelm of Württemberg. It has extensive views over East Stuttgart, Bad Cannstatt and along the Neckar valley as far as Esslingen am Neckar.

During World War II the tower was used by anti-aircraft spotter personnel keeping a look-out for Allied bomber attacks.

Burgholzhof observation tower was restored in 1987/88, on the initiative of the local amenity group *Pro Bad Cannstatt*, and since then has again been accessible during the summer.

Nearby, to the north of the tower, is a point-to-point radio tower used for military purposes, at 48°49'11 north.

The tower, in an anthropomorphic form known as "Burgi", is the mascot of the new community of Burgholzhof.

Geographical coordinates: 48°49′08″N 9°11′41″E

Sources and external links

- Stuttgart Burgholzhof website [1] (German)
- Photos [2]

Tagblatt-Turm

The **Tagblatt-Turm** (English translation: **Tagblatt-Tower**) was one of the earliest German high-rises. This landmark is located in Stuttgart, Baden-Württemberg; its address is Eberhardstraße 61.

2006 Tagblatt-Tower

The Tagblatt-Turm was designed by architect Ernst Otto Oßwald. It was constructed between 1924 and 1928 and made from crushed stone and cement. With a height of 61 m, the 16-floor tower was the tallest building in the city after the old 1905 city hall, and the highest office building in Germany. Its modern design caused controversy during construction, however, the building has since been recognized as a cultural and architectural landmark. The earliest high-rise office building erected from cement and steel was the Zeiss Building in Jena, built by the Dywidag company of Nuremberg in 1912 to house Zeiss' corporate headquarters.

From 1928 to 1943, the tower was the seat of the editorship and publishing house of the *Stuttgarter Neues Tagblatt*, a local newspaper; the building derives its name from this original tenant. After World War II until 1978, the tower served as the headquarters for the two newspapers *Stuttgarter Zeitung* and the *Stuttgarter Nachrichten*. In 2004, after extensive renovations, the tower was converted into a cultural center with several theatres under the name *Kultur unterm Turm*.

References

- **Wörner, Martin**: *Stuttgart - Ein Architekturführer*. 2nd edition, 1997. Dietrich Reimer Verlag. Berlin (Germany). ISBN 3-496-01157-2 (in German)

External links

- Tagblatt Tower [1] at *Structurae*

Geographical coordinates: 48°46′22″N 9°10′34″E

Fernsehturm Stuttgart

The **Fernsehturm Stuttgart** (TV Tower Stuttgart) is the world's first TV tower built from concrete (and prototype for many towers of that kind all over the world).

It is located on the so-called "Hoher Bopser" hill in the southern Stuttgart district of Degerloch. After a construction period of 20 months it was placed in service February 5, 1956, by Süddeutscher Rundfunk (today: Südwestrundfunk – SWR). The tower broadcasts several public FM radio stations and transmitted the ARD TV network's analogue service until 2006. The digital television services have moved to nearby Fernmeldeturm Stuttgart, which also broadcasts private FM radio stations in the area. Although controversial at first, it quickly became a well known landmark of Stuttgart and tourist attraction. From the two observation decks there is a view of Stuttgart, from the forests and vineyards in and around Stuttgart to the Swabian Jura and the Black Forest. On clear days the Swiss Alps are visible.

- Engineer: Professor Dr. Ing. Fritz Leonhardt
- Altitude: Foot of tower 483 m (1585 ft) above sea level
- Overall height to the antenna point: 216.8 m (711 ft)
- Height of upper observation deck: 153.5 m (504 ft)
- Height of lower observation deck: 150 m (490 ft)
- Diameter of foundation: 27 m (89 ft)
- Total weight of tower: approximately 3000 tons
- Weight of foundation: approximately 1500 tons
- Speed of elevators: 4 m per second
- Panorama Café on a platform of the tower basket
- Maximum diameter of tower basket: 15 m (49 ft)

The tower can be reached by the Stuttgart public transport system (see Stuttgart external links) and is open for visitors from 9:00 until 23:00.

History

- 10 January 1954: Start of construction
- 5 February 1956: Inauguration
- October 1965 until December 1965: Extension of antenna, hence today the tower is 216.8 meters tall.

Air traffic warning lights

The tower carries beside the conventional red air traffic warning lights three rotating Xenon-lamps similar to those used on lighthouses just above the observation deck.

Other Transmission Towers in Stuttgart (not accessible to public)

- Fernmeldeturm Frauenkopf (height: 192.4 m)
- Vodafone-Funkturm Stuttgart-Vaihingen (height: 98.6 m)
- Funkturm Stuttgart (height: 93 m)
- Directional Radio Tower Stuttgart-Möhringen (height: 93 m)

Similar towers

- Rheinturm in Düsseldorf
- Sentech Tower in Johannesburg
- Donauturm in Vienna
- CN Tower in Toronto
- Oriental Pearl Tower in Shanghai
- Macau Tower in Macau
- Sky Tower in Auckland City

Literature

- Fernsehturm Stuttgart. Fernsehturm-Betriebs-GmbH, Stuttgart 1991
- Walther Drechsel: Turmbauwerke. Wiesbaden, Berlin, 1967
- Jörg Schlaich, Matthias Schüller: Ingenieurbauführer Baden-Württemberg. Bauwerk Verlag, Berlin 1999; pp. 486-488.

External links

- TV tower Stuttgart [1]
- Stuttgart Television Tower [2] at *Structurae*
- Satellite Image [3]

Geographical coordinates: 48°45′24″N 9°11′29″E

Cannstatter Wasen

The **Cannstatter Wasen** is a 35 hectare festival area on the banks of the Neckar river in the part of Stuttgart known as Bad Cannstatt.

The Cannstatter Wasen form part of the Neckar Park Fairground.

Each year the Wasen hosts the Cannstatter Volksfest and the Stuttgart Spring Festival, along with other events such as concerts and circuses.

See also

- Beer festival

Cannstatter Volksfest

The **Cannstatter Volksfest** is an annual three-week festival in Stuttgart, Germany. It is sometimes also referred to by foreign visitors as the Stuttgart Beer Festival although it is actually more of an autumnal fair. Locals to Stuttgart variously refer to the festival as the **Cannstatter Wasen** or just **Wasen**.

The Volksfest takes place from the end of September to the beginning of October on an area called the Cannstatter Wasen. The extensive Wasen area is located in the Stuttgart city district of Bad Cannstatt, near the river Neckar. A smaller variant of the Stuttgart Festival - the Stuttgart Spring Festival is also held each year on the Wasen.

Background

Although the Volkfest is not strictly speaking a beer festival, it is considered by many to be the second largest beer festival in the world after the Munich Oktoberfest. According to estimates about 4.2 million people visited the festival in 2006. The Volksfest begins one week later than the Oktoberfest.

Cannstatter Volksfest 2004

History

Cannstatter Volksfest – Wasen From an agricultural event to a famous festival

Colorful flashing lights, the squealing and rattling of unknown machines, the smell of burned almonds, "Göckele" (roasted chicken) and stockfish affects all your senses. Above the noise you can hear the bandmaster shouting out typical slogans like "die Krüge hoch". No doubt, it's "Volksfest" time in Bad Cannstatt. Annually around four million festival people gather at the biggest carnival festival in the world since 1818.

In 1815 a gigantic eruption of the Vulcano Tambora in Indonesia led to a climatic catastrophe even in Europe. The incredible explosion hurled around 100 cubic km of rocks, ashes and dust up to 70 km high and darkened the sky. The blast equalled to 170.000 Hiroshima bombs. The shockwave could be felt 1.500 km away. 10.000 people died due to the eruption. Another 100.000 died because of the aftermath. The dust particles were distributed by the jet stream around the world and caused crop failure and famine in Europe.

The winter of 1815/16 in Wurttemberg was the coldest since weather records were kept. Snow until May, no summer, alternating rain, whipping hail and thunderstorms continued into the growth season. This made bringing in a harvest in those years not possible. Throughout Germany, people were starving. The little existing flour was stretched with sawdust and the planted potatoes were dug up again. The need of the people was indescribable.

When the young King Wilhelm I. became mayor of Wurttemberg in 1816, the crisis of the people couldn't be any worse. His brother in law, Czar Nikolaus of Russia, helped him to relive the biggest misery with deliveries of grain.

Then, in 1817, when the first harvest wagon was brought in, King Wilhelm and his Russian wife Katharina had the glorious idea to sponsor a harvest festival. This should take place annually on the King's birthday on September, 28th in the area of the Cannstatter Wasen.

The first festival in 1818 lasted one day and had more than 30,000 visitors. At the time the village of Canstatt had a population of 3000. The Royal Couple donated cash prizes and honorary awards for outstanding agricultural accomplishment. The festival was designed to encourage the farmers.

At the same time the popular monarch couple established an agricultural school in castle Hohenheim. This set the foundation for today's agricultural university. Due to this and other outstanding efforts the young monarch was titled "King of the farmers" and "Farmer amongst kings". In the German Agricultural Museum many of the developments, e.g. the double bladed plow, can still be seen.

From agricultural festival to people festival

The most important activities of the festival had been the award for breeding performance and the display of agricultural efficiency of the Wurttemberg farmers. The first food shops and carnies showed up with the first festival. The vendors attracted the people with sauerkraut, sausage and a lot of sweet fancy foods. A market completed the culinary choices. The carnies presented the strongest men, the fattest women and a lot of other curiosities. Through the years the festival grew larger and larger and transformed from the "Agricultural festival of Kannstadt" to the "Cannstatter Volksfest".

During the 19th century the first festival lasted one day, by 1920 it was extended to five days and since 1972 the Volksfest has been celebrated for 16 days.

In the beginning, there had only been a few Volksfest-carnies and beer counters. They were moved to the edge of the festival in favour of the royal lounge and the tribune for the dignitaries. In 1860 the layout of the festival was three main streets and numerous side streets to handle the yearly increasing crowd. Today with around 350 companies, the Cannstatter Volksfest is the biggest carnival-festival worldwide. 4 to 5 million visitors are attracted to it.

King Wilhelm assigned his royal builder Nikolaus Thouret to create an emblem next to the royal lounge in the middle of the festival areal. He created the fruit pillar as a symbol for thanksgiving which is still the emblem of the Volksfest. Placed on top of the 23 m high pillar sits a bowl with fruits. Only the highest mobile Ferris wheels of the world is towering above it.

Today, the parade on the first festival Sunday is one of the most popular events of the Canstatter Volksfest. Nearly one hundred historical groups of town militia, Shepard-dancing-groups, festival wagons representing different crafts, groups dressed in traditional clothing and groups of musicians, create this colorful "Lindworm". There are still groups in traditional clothes and professional period groups, which have taken part in the festival since 1841.

Based on the German article: "Fruchtsäule, Festzelt, Ferkel" by Wulf Wagner Translated by Lewia Flournoy, Katja Freiler, Dirk Krause and Boris Michalski

Attractions

The festival offers a variety of attractions ranging from booths to roller coasters, carousels, roundabouts and fairground rides. One of the largest attractions at the Cannstatter Volksfest is the world's largest mobile Ferris wheel which measures 60 meters in diameter.

Fruit column

The fruit column in 2005 with two beer tents behind

Symbolic of the Cannstatter Wasen is its "fruit column", a wooden pillar decorated with fruit, 26 metres high and weighing 3.5 tons. After World War I, with the beginning of the Weimar Republic, the fruit column was removed from the Cannstatter Wasen as it was considered a relic of the monarchy. Since 1935, the 100th anniversary, it has been back in its traditional place. Until recently the fruit column, the design of which has changed over the years, was dismantled after each Volksfest. Every few years it is redesigned. Since 1995 it has been left in place throughout the year and is thus also on display at the Stuttgart spring festival. In recent years only the tip has been dismantled leaving the lower portion in place housing information stands and the Cannstatter "city can".

Fairground rides

Typical rides include

- 60 meter Ferris wheel (biggest mobile Ferris wheel in the world)
- 47 metre Ferris wheel
- Alpina roller coaster
- Free fall "Powertower", height 66 meters
- Imperator (weight: 350t)
- Wild water coaster
- "Wild mouse"
- Airwulf carousel
- Transformer carousel
- Turboforce carousel
- "Black Hole" indoor roller coaster
- Boosters revolution

as well as 73 stands ranging from shooting galleries to raffles, some 95 food stands and a chandler's market with 60 market stalls and a boxing show.

Beer tents

Today, there are seven large beer tents on the Cannstatter Wasen for people to celebrate in. They either have their own name or carry the name of the brewery supplying the beer:

- Schwaben Bräu tent of Alexander Laub, remodeled in 2006 and now offering room for about 5200 people
- Stuttgarter Hofbräu tent of Hans-Peter Grandl, room for 5000
- Dinkelacker tent of Dieter and Werner Klauss seating 4500 visitors
- Fürstenberg tent

  From 2000 to 2004, Walter Weitmann organized a tent with about 5000 seats for the Fürstenberg Brewery, which courted the other breweries' resentment by both its size and the origin (Fürstenberg is from Baden). In 2005, a smaller tent (room for 2800) run by Peter Brandl replaced Weitmann's.

- *Festzelt Göckelesmaier* established in 1938 as *Maiers Karle*, renamed because of the fried chicken (Swabian: *Göckele*) served there; seats 2500, also serves *Stuttgarter Hofbräu* beer
- *Festzelt Wasenwirt*: room for 2200, *Stuttgarter Hofbräu*
- *Arcadia Erlebniszelt* established in 2005; 1800 seats, an artificial waterfall and *Dinkelacker* brew

Since 1982 the tents of Laub, Grandl and Klauss have been located by the fruit column. Each tent takes it in turn to host the opening ceremony. The price for a *Maß* is usually the same in all tents.

French Village and Alpine Village

For years the French village was an integral part of the Cannstatter Volksfest. By 2004, there were 33 food stands offering French meals and beverages along with traditional French music. The village was relaunched as an Alpine village in October 2008.

Parade

Traditionally a parade also takes place at the Wasen, usually on the first Sunday. In 1954 a record number of spectators attended the parade along the route from Stuttgart's central square to the Wasen site: 300,000.

Fireworks

German Reunification is marked every year on the 3rd of October by a firework display.

Agriculture exhibition

Every three years an agricultural exhibition (*Landwirtschaftliches Hauptfest*) is included in the main celebration. This was the original Cannstatter Wasen Volksfest. Unlike the Volksfest, there is an entrance fee to visit the exhibition. The last exhibition of this kind was in 2006.

Dates

The festival is opened by a ceremony in which the incumbent Lord Mayor of Stuttgart tries to tap the first barrel of beer with as few hits as possible. This takes place on a Friday in late September, so that the duration of the festival is actually 17 days.

- 2009: 25 September – 11 October
- 2010: 24 September – 10 October

Opening hours

The food stands, fixed tents and carousels are open between Sunday and Friday from 11am to 11pm. On Saturdays and before Bank Holidays the Volksfest is open until 11.30pm although music is stopped at 11pm.

Trivia

In Philadelphia (Pennsylvania) a Cannstatter Volkfest is celebrated each year on Labor Day, including German beer and food ([1]).

See also

- Beer festival

Fruit Column

The **fruit column (Fruchtsäule)** is a 26 metre high wood column heavy decorated with fruits in Stuttgart, Germany.

Fruit Column at Cannstatter Volksfest

It weighs 3.5 tons and is the landmark of the Cannstatter Wasen in Stuttgart although it is nowadays towered above by numerous roundabouts. Already at the first people celebration in 1818 there was a fruit column as landmark, which had been sketched and built by the master of building of yards of Wuerttemberg at that time, Nikolaus Thouret.

After the First World War, with which beginning of the first German republic became, the fruit column was banned as "monarchistic" leftover from the Cannstatter Wasen. Since 1935, it stands for the 100th anniversary again on its traditional place. The fruit column, whose design was changed in the course of the years, was dismantled until recently annually after conclusion of the people celebration. Every few years a new fruit column with other Design was established again and again. Starting in 1995 it was experimentally let long all-season stand by way of trial and was thus also on Stuttgart spring celebrations to be seen for the first time. Since a few years only the column is dismantled and the underbody, in which some statuses of information are and which carries the Cannstatter city can during the spring celebration, left untouched.

External links

- http://skyscraperpage.com/diagrams/?b41549

The fruit column from above

See also

List of towers

Stuttgart Spring Festival

Stuttgart Spring Festival (in german called **Stuttgarter Frühlingsfest** or sometimes vernacular **Cannstatter Wasen** or just **Wasen**) is an annual fair that takes place in the German city of Stuttgart between the middle of April and the beginning of May. The festival takes place on the *Cannstatter Wasen*, traditional fairgrounds in Stuttgart's Bad Cannstatt district. It is slightly smaller than the festival in the autumn (and therefore occasionally also called the "small Wasen"). Like the autumn fair, the Frühlingsfest offers a variety of fairground attractions. The tallest attraction is the 47 meter Ferris wheel and the fair almost invariably features a major roller coaster.

Ferris wheel and Fruit Column

The Frühlingsfest starts on a Saturday with the traditional opening of a beer barrel by the Stuttgart mayor.

The Fruit Column, a tall wooden structure decorated with fruits, was introduced to the Stuttgarter Frühlingsfest in 1995. Originally it was only present at the autumn Volksfest but in 1995 it was left to stand on the festival site all year round. However, in recent years, this practice was changed and once again the column began to be dismantled in the autumn of each year, leaving just the base. This carries a large can during the Stuttgarter Frühlingsfest.

The fruit column and beer tents in 2005

Periods of operation

- The festival opens Monday - Friday at noon, Saturday, Sunday and holidays at 11 am.
- Closing time is 11 pm on Sunday - Thursday and midnight on Friday, Saturday and before holidays.
- Musical performances end in the main tents half an hour before closing.

See also

- Beer festival
- The autumn fair in Stuttgart (Cannstatter Wasen)

External links

- Stuttgarter Fruehlingsfest Official Website [1]

Stuttgart Trade Fair

Type	German limited (GmbH)
Industry	Trade fairs and exhibitions
Founded	1940
Headquarters	Stuttgart, Germany
Key people	Ulrich Kromer von Baerle
Products	Trade exhibitions
Revenue	€ 61 million (2006)
Employees	237 (2006)
Website	www.messe-stuttgart.de [1]

Messe Stuttgart is an exhibition centre and trade fair next to Stuttgart Airport, 7 miles south of Stuttgart, Germany. It is the ninth biggest trade fair in Germany.

The new exhibition grounds, which were completed in 2007, are right next to the A8 autobahn (motorway). The centre can be accessed via the local suburban railway network. Buses also travel to the trade fair from nearby Esslingen, Göppingen, Reutlingen and Tübingen. As part of the Stuttgart 21 Project, there are plans to link the trade fair and airport to the intercity train route between Stuttgart and Wendlingen–Ulm by 2019.

Exhibition halls

Stuttgart exhibition centre encompasses seven standard halls measuring 10,500m² and a high hall with a net display area of 26,800m² which is also designed to cater for sports events and concerts. The exhibition centre also includes a communication and events centre, the *Internationale Congresscenter* or ICS, which includes a congress hall (4900m²), a congress room (2600m²) and conferencing facilities encompassing 25 meeting rooms.

Car park

One of the most striking features of Stuttgart Messe is its huge car park which spans the A8 Autobahn. The car park has space for 4200 vehicles on five stories. Display rights for the 4 ton logo on both sides of the car park bridge were sold to Robert Bosch GmbH which paid around 20 million euros for exclusive advertising space. The logo is the second largest illuminated sign in the world and the biggest logo in the world after the unlit Hollywood Sign.

Brief history

Before completion of the new site next to Stuttgart Airport, Stuttgart Messe was based for more than 50 years in the Killesberg suburb of Stuttgart. As nearby housing estates encroached on trade fair parking and roads, the old fair was closed down to make way for social housing for old aged pensioners and apartments.

Criticism

Immediately after opening, Stuttgart Messe was plagued by a number of unexpected teething problems, ranging from faulty barcode readers at the entrances to poor signage.

Construction of the new site, which was originally approved in 1993, was subject to frequent delay. First of all, local farmers refused to sell their land after successful lobbying by nearby residents. After compulsory repossession of land was approved by the Baden-Württemberg State Government, demonstrations came to a peak resulting in a string of court cases between landowners and the company commissioned to build the new trade fair. Eventually agreement was reached between the local government and landowners, amid cries from local residents that the farmers had "sold out" to the politicians and had only gone along with lobbyists in the first place to maximise returns on the sale of land.

External references

- Messe Stuttgart official website [1]
- Messe Stuttgart plans (German) [2]

Geographical coordinates: 48°41′37″N 9°11′13″E

Christmas Market, Stuttgart

Stuttgart Christmas Market, known in German as the *Stuttgarter Weihnachtsmarkt* is a Christmas market that takes place every year during Advent in the German city of Stuttgart.

History

The *Stuttgarter Weihnachtsmarkt* was first mentioned in city records in 1692 when it was described as a 'traditional Stuttgart event'. The modern Christmas Market encompasses around 200 stands and is visited by around 3.6 million people every year, making it one of the largest of its kind in Germany. In terms of area, Stuttgart Christmas Market is claimed by organisers to be the largest in Europe.

Location

A traditional stand selling teddy bears

The market stretches from the west and northern edge of Stuttgart's central square (*Schlossplatz*, where there is a children's 'fairytale land' alongside a miniature railway and ice rink) to the old squares and alleyways of Stuttgart, including *Schillerplatz*, *Karlsplatz* (featuring a Finnish Christmas Market and a Christmas collectors' fair) and *Marktplatz*.

The Christmas market opens every year on the last Thursday in November in the Renaissance inner quadrangle of Stuttgart Old Castle. It is open Monday to Saturday from 10am to 9pm and on Sundays from 11am to 9pm. The market finishes on Christmas Eve.

External links

- Listing of Christmas Markets in Germany [1] Official Website of the German National Tourist Board

Schocken Department Store, Stuttgart

The **Schocken Department Store** (**Kaufhaus Schocken**, later Merkur Department Store) was a department store in the south German town of Stuttgart.

It was built by the Schocken department store chain owned by Salman Schocken. The architect was Erich Mendelsohn, who also built the *Kaufhaus Schocken* in Nuremberg (1925/26) and Chemnitz). The Stuttgart store was the most significant of the latter's projects in the sphere of retail store construction. The inspiration for the design came to Mendelsohn while he was attending a concert of music by Bach.

The building was a department store with a modern style in an urban context. It was constructed of brick and concrete. The shopping area within the building had mainly wooden furnishings and, in the absence of air conditioning, had a large number of windows. Again owing to the absence of air conditioning, the food hall was situated in the basement. The name of the store was displayed in lettering some 7.5 in height and illuminated after dark. The booklet which he designed for the opening features Mendelsohn's coloured sketch. He also created a logo and branding style based on the lettering on the façade of the store.

The department store, together with the Tagblatt-Turm of Ernst-Otto Oßwald across the way, constituted an impressive ensemble of modern architecture, and was damaged only slightly in World War II. In 1960, the local authority demolished the store, despite international protest. In its place today stands Egon Eiermann's unremarkable department store building (Galeria Kaufhof, previously Horten).The building was re-leased in 1960.

See also

- Schocken Department Stores

Attractions

Killesbergpark

The **Killesbergpark** (Höhenpark Killesberg) is an urban public park of half a square kilometre (123 acres) in Stuttgart, Germany. It is just north of the state capital, and borders the city's fairgrounds. The park dates back to the horticultural show of 1939. Before the show, a large area of the park had been a quarry. It was transformed into a park with exhibition sites for the show, and has remained, hosting horticultural events on a regular basis, including the Bundesgartenschau and the IGA.

Killesbergpark and Killesberg tower

Every July the park hosts the popular Lichterfest Stuttgart. Thousands of lanterns are placed around the park, decorating the park for a variety of family activities throughout. After dark, there is a fireworks show accompanied by music. Visitors often bring blankets to sit on for the show.

Killesberg railway

Since its opening, the park has been home to the 381-millimetre (15-inch) narrow-gauge Killesberg railway. In the summer months, visitors can see two diesel and two steam locomotives, which have been fixtures in the park since 1950. The horticultural show of 1939 saw the opening of the railway, when two borrowed steam engines from Leipzig traversed a short stretch of track. During World War II, the steam engines were returned to Leipzig for use there. New locomotives were purchased, and today there are two diesel and two steam engines in use.

Killesberg tower

Completed in 2000 the Killesberg tower is an observation tower, 40m high overlooking the park. It is cable-stayed tower construction designed by Jörg Schlaich, using cable-stayed bridge technology.

Other features

From the 1950s until the 1980s there was a chair lift for visitors to enjoy views of the fairgrounds and parklands.

The twenty-metre high Bismarck tower stands one kilometre south-west of the exhibition halls. It was built on the Gaehkopf, the highest point in northern Stuttgart, giving good views of Stuttgart itself and in all directions. It was one of many towers built to commemorate Otto von Bismarck. The building of over 410 Bismarck towers worldwide was planned, and 238 were actually built. The building of the tower was begun in 1902 by the students of the technical university in Stuttgart. The Stuttgart Bismarck tower was opened on 16 July 1904. In 2004, for its 100th anniversary, it was comprehensively renovated.

Surroundings

- Near the Bismarck tower is the Theodor Heuss house, the house of the first German Federal President, which has been converted into a museum.
- An open-air swimming pool borders the fairground buildings to the north.
- To the southwest lies the Weissenhof Settlement of 1927, a protected monument, exhibiting "the dwelling" as initiated by the German work federation.

External links

- Stuttgart.de [1]
- Die Parkeisenbahn von 1939 [2]
- Killesberg Tower [3]
- Aussichtsturm Killesberg: Technische Daten [4]
- Lichterfest-Stuttgart [5]

Geographical coordinates: 48°48′26″N 9°10′19″E

Schönbuch

Map of the Schönbuch

Birkensee, a bog in the Schönbuch

The **Schönbuch** is an almost completely wooded area south west of Stuttgart and part of the Southern German Escarpment Landscape (German: "südwestdeutsches Schichtstufenland"). In 1972 the centre zone of the Schönbuch became the first natural park in Baden-Württemberg. Today the 156 km² large reserve is referred to as Schönbuch whereas the original, more comprehensive area is usually called Schönbuch-Region.

The natural park Schönbuch is an important recreational area of the Stuttgart region, also because it is intersected by relatively few roads only.

Transport

The commuter train called the Schönbuchbahn runs though the Schönbuch connecting Dettenhausen to Böblingen where it connects with the S-Bahn system.

Location

The Schönbuch is located in central Baden-Württemberg – approximately 25 km south of the city center of Stuttgart, about 15 km south west of Stuttgart Airport. It is also close to Reutlingen (south east), the university city of Tübingen (south), Herrenberg (southwest) and Böblingen (northwest).

Geographical coordinates: 48°35′N 9°03′E

Landesarboretum Baden-Württemberg

The **Landesarboretum Baden-Württemberg** (16.5 hectares) is a historic arboretum now maintained by the University of Hohenheim. It is located next to the Botanischer Garten der Universität Hohenheim, the university's botanical garden, on Garbenstrasse in the Hohenheim district of Stuttgart, Baden-Württemberg, Germany.

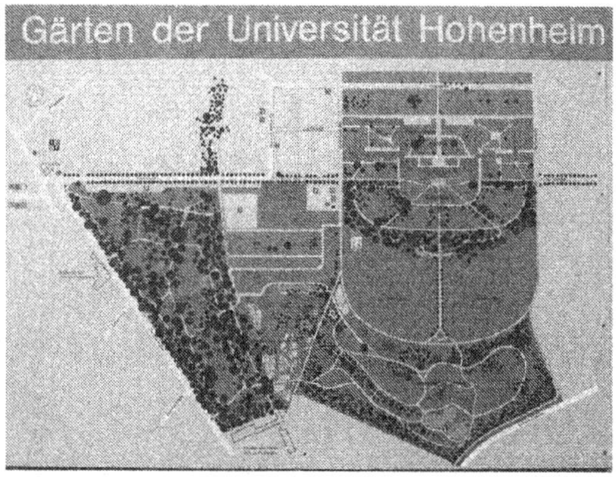

University of Hohenheim gardens, with the *Exotischer Garten* at left. The newer *Hohenheimer Landschaftsgarten* is not shown.

The arboretum was begun as a landscape garden in the years 1776-1793 by Karl Eugen, Duke of Württemberg, on a site southwest of Schloss Hohenheim. It contained two major collections - a botanical garden of plants from the Württemberg region, and an arboretum of North American trees (the *Exotischer Garten*) - which by 1783 contained a total of 120 species. After the Duke's death in 1793, the garden was opened to the public, and during the nineteenth and early twentieth centuries was used for cultivation of seedlings for the Duke's gardens, study of exotic trees for local forestry, and student botanical studies.

The garden suffered substantial losses in 1930-31, after which its nursery was demolished and the garden returned to approximately its original state. In 1953 the former Exotischer Garten became the Landesarboretum Baden-Württemberg. Its collections were substantially enhanced beginning in 1996 when an adjacent 7.4 hectares were devoted to a new *Hohenheimer Landschaftsgarten* (Hohenheimer Landscape Garden), with first trees were planted in 1997 and an additional 200 plants added in 1998. Plantings have continued since.

Today's arboretum comprises two linked sections, the old Exotischer Garten and the newer Hohenheimer Landschaftsgarten. Together they contain about 2450 taxa of deciduous and coniferous woody plants, representing 270 species from over 90 plant families. Particularly noteworthy are historic specimens dating to the arboretum's creation, including tulip trees planted in 1779, oaks (1790), and yellow buckeye (1799).

See also

- Botanischer Garten der Universität Hohenheim
- List of botanical gardens in Germany

External links

- Landesarboretum Baden-Württemberg [1]
- Arboretum plant list [2]
- Arboretum map [3]
- Hohenheimer Landschaftsgarten map [4]
- Hermann von Helmholtz-Zentrum entry [5]

Geographical coordinates: 48°42′30″N 9°12′31″E

Botanischer Garten der Universität Hohenheim

The **Botanischer Garten der Universität Hohenheim** (10 hectares) is a botanical garden maintained by the University of Hohenheim. It is located next to the historic Landesarboretum Baden-Württemberg on Garbenstrasse in the Hohenheim district of Stuttgart, Baden-Württemberg, Germany, and is sometimes called the *Neuer Botanischer Garten* to distinguish it from the arboretum.

University of Hohenheim gardens, with the *Botanischer Garten der Universität Hohenheim* at bottom. The newer *Hohenheimer Landschaftsgarten* is not shown.

The garden was established in 1974 and focuses on vegetation in south-west Germany since the last Ice Age. It contains about 7,000 plant taxa in various groupings, including a systematic garden of about 5,000 taxa (2 hectares), a medicinal plant garden, and tropical and subtropical greenhouses containing about 1,200 taxa, including about 250 Begoniaceae species. Other collections include *Gymnocalycium* (65 species),

Peperomia (41 species), *Viscum* (40 species), and *Maranthes* (14 species), as well as collections of useful plants and North American trees and shrubs.

See also

- Landesarboretum Baden-Württemberg
- List of botanical gardens in Germany

External links

- Botanischer Garten der Universität Hohenheim [1]
- Neuer Botanischer Garten der Universität Hohenheim [2]
- Garden map (overall context) [3]
- Garden map (*Neuer Botanischer Garten* proper) [4]
- BGCI entry [5]
- Hermann von Helmholtz-Zentrum entry [6]
- Stuttgart-Tourist description [7]
- Stuttgart description [8]

Geographical coordinates: 48°42′30″N 9°12′53″E

Wilhelma

This article is about the zoo. For the templer settlement, see Wilhelma, Palestine

Wilhelma, built as a royal palace, is now a zoo in the northern suburbs of Stuttgart, Baden-Württemberg, Germany. It is Europe's only large combined zoological and botanical garden and is home to over 8,000 animals from over 1,000 different species and exotic plants from over 5,000 species.

The zoo is famous for keeping all four kinds of great apes, all in families with offspring, as well as for its aquarium featuring animals and plants from all over the world. The botanical gardens are renowned for containing Europe's biggest magnolia grove. It was also the home of the polar bear Wilbär.

The Wilhelma was originally a royal palace, in Moorish Revival style, and echoes such buildings as the Alhambra Palace. After the Second World War, it was gradually converted to its present day use. Besides animals and plants, the Wilhelma is therefore also worth visiting for its architecture, which is intact from the mid-19th century.

As is common in many German zoos, barriers between spectators and animals are minimal.

A particularly unusual feature is the "hatchery" were chicks can be watched hatching and mother birds feed their chicks at very close quarters.

The upper section of the zoo includes an impressive stand of sequoia trees.

The zoo immediately adjoins a public park to its west, laid out in the 'English landscape style' of rolling grass and informal groups of trees. In landscape terms this perfectly complements the landscape of the zoo.

Transport

The zoo sits next to a main arterial route from the city centre and is easily accessed by car. The road can be very busy on holidays and weekends.

A tram line (U12) connects the zoo to the city centre.

Breeding of invasive plant

The aquarium staff was responsible for altering the genes of *Caulerpa taxifolia*, such that it became a highly invasive plant known as "Killer Algae" which "has had severe negative consequences for biodiversity".

Insectarium

There is an extensive insectarium on the grounds. There are many types of insects grown and kept live for the public to see, including african colored scarab beetles, among many others. There are butterflies, spiders, millipedes, and several beetle species that are continually cultivated and kept living, by breeding generation after generation of the individual species of choice.

See also

- List of botanical gardens in Germany

External links

- Official website [1]
- Stuttgart Zoo [2] at (in English)

Geographical coordinates: 48°48′19″N 9°12′11″E

VfB Stuttgart

Full name	Verein für Bewegungsspiele Stuttgart 1893 e. V.
Nickname(s)	*Die Roten* *Die Schwaben*
Founded	9 September 1893
Ground	Mercedes-Benz Arena, Stuttgart (Capacity: 41,000)
President	Erwin Staudt
Director of sport	Fredi Bobic Jochen Schneider
Coach	Jens Keller
League	Bundesliga
2009–10	Bundesliga, 6th
Website	Club home page [1]

Home colours	**Away colours**	**Third colours**

Verein für Bewegungsspiele Stuttgart 1893 e. V., commonly known as **VfB Stuttgart**, is a German sports club based in Stuttgart, the capital of Baden-Württemberg. The club is best known for its football team, which has participated in all but two Bundesliga seasons. The team has won the national championship five times in total—most recently in the 2006–07 season—and the DFB-Pokal (German cup) three times.

The football team plays its home games at the Mercedes-Benz Arena, situated in the Cannstatter Wasen sports complex. It is famous for its talented reserve team, VfB Stuttgart II, which currently plays in the 3rd Liga, two divisions below the first team, in the highest division allowed for a reserve team.

VfB Stuttgart is a membership-based club and with 45.037 (as of: January 2009), *VfB* is the largest sports club in the state and the fifth largest in the country. In addition to the successes of the professional, amateur and youth football teams, athletes from the club's athletics department have won numerous titles and medals. The club also has departments for fistball, hockey, table-tennis and football referees. These five departments only compete at amateur level. The club also maintains a social department, the *VfB-Garde*.

History

Foundation to WWII

Verein für Bewegungsspiele Stuttgart was formed through the 2 April 1912 merger of predecessor sides Stuttgarter FV and Kronen-Club Cannstatt following a meeting in the Concordia hotel in Cannstatt. Each of these clubs was made up of school pupils with middle class roots who learned new sports such as rugby union and football from English pioneers.

FV Stuttgart

Stuttgarter Fußballverein was founded at the *Zum Becher* hotel in Cannstatt on 9 September 1893. *FV* were initially a rugby club, playing games at Stöckach-Eisbahn before moving to Cannstatter Wasen in 1894. The rugby club established a football section in 1908. The team drew players primarily from local schools, under the direction of teacher Carl Kaufmann, and quickly achieved its first success; in 1909 they were runners-up to *FSV 1897 Hannover* in the national rugby final, losing 6-3. Rugby was soon replaced by football within the club, as spectators found the game too complicated to follow.

In 1909 *FV* joined the Süddeutschen Fußballverband (*Southern Germany Football Association*), playing in the second tier *B-Klasse*. In their second season *FV* won a district final against future merger partner *Kronen-Klub Cannstatt* before being defeated by *FV Zuffenhausen* in the county championship that would have seen the side promoted. They eventually advanced to the senior Südkreis-Liga in 1912.

Kronen-Klub Cannstatt

Cannstatter Fußballklub was formed as a rugby club in 1890 and also quickly established a football team. This club was dissolved after just a few years of play and the former membership re-organized themselves as *FC Krone Cannstatt* in 1897 to compete as a football-only side. The new team joined the Süddeutschen Fußballverband (SFV) as a second division club and won promotion in 1904. *Cannstatt* possessed their own ground, which still exists today as the home of *TSV Münster*.

Following the 1912 merger of these two clubs, the combined side played at first in the *Kreisliga Württemberg* and then in the *Bezirksliga Württemberg-Baden*, earning a number of top three finishes and claiming a title there in 1927. The club also made several appearances in the final rounds of the SFV in the late 20s and early 30s.

1933–1945

In 1933 German football was re-organized under the Third Reich into sixteen top-flight divisions called Gauligen. *Stuttgart* played in the Gauliga Württemberg and enjoyed considerable success there, winning division titles in 1935, 1937, 1938, 1940, and 1943 before the Gauliga system collapsed part way through the 1944–45 season. The club had an intense rivalry with *Stuttgarter Kickers* throughout this period.

VfB's Gauliga titles earned the team entry to the national playoff rounds, with their best result coming in 1935 when they advanced to the final where they lost 4–6 to defending champions *Schalke 04*. After a third place result at the national level in 1937, *Stuttgart* was not able in subsequent appearances to advance out of the preliminary rounds.

1950s championships

After the war *VfB* continued to play first division football in the Oberliga Süd, capturing titles there in 1946, 1952, and 1954. The team also made regular appearances in the German championship rounds emerging as national champion in 1950 and 1952, and finishing as runner-up in 1953. In the 1950s, the club also twice won the German Cup (1954 and 1958). The team which won four titles in eight years was led by Robert Schlienz who had lost his left arm in a car crash. No player from Stuttgart had been selected for the team that won the 1954 FIFA World Cup though.

1963 Bundesliga

Due to international competition that led to disappointing results in the 1958 and 1962 World Cup, DFB introduced a single professional league in 1963. *Stuttgart*'s consistently good play throughout the 1950s earned them a place among the sixteen clubs that would make up the original Bundesliga. The club, as an amateur organisation and due to proverbial *Swabian austerity*, hesitated to spend money, and some players continued to work in an everyday job. Throughout the balance of the decade and into the mid-70s the club would generally earn mid-table results. One of the few stars of the time was Gilbert Gress from Strasbourg.

In 1972–1973 the team qualified for the UEFA Cup for the first time and advanced to the semi-finals of the 1974 tournament where they were eliminated by eventual winners *Feyenoord Rotterdam* (1–2, 2–2).

1975–2000 era of president MV

VfB Stuttgart was in crisis in the mid 1970s, having missed new trends like sponsorship. Attempts to catch up with new levels of professionalism by spending money failed. Towards the end of the 1974–75 season, with the team in imminent danger of being relegated to Second Bundesliga, local politician Gerhard Mayer-Vorfelder was elected as new president. Yet, a tie in the final game meant that VfB would be ranked 16th and lose its Bundesliga status. The first season in second league, considered the worst in its history, ended with VfB being ranked 11th, having even lost a home game against local rival SSV Reutlingen in front of only 1200 spectators.

With new coach Jürgen Sundermann and new talents like Karlheinz Förster and Hansi Müller, the team around Ottmar Hitzfeld scored *hundred goals* in 1976–77 and thus returned to top flight play after just two seasons.

The young team was popular for offensive and high-scoring play, but suffered from lack of experience. At the end of 1977–78, the VfB was ranked 4th, but the average attendance of over 53,000 set the league record until the 1990s. They made another UEFA Cup semi-final appearance in 1980 and delivered a number of top four finishes on their way to their first Bundesliga title – the club's third national title – in 1984, now under coach Helmut Benthaus.

In 1986, VfB lost the German Cup final 2–5 to Bayern Munich. In the 1989 UEFA Cup Final, with Jürgen Klinsmann in their ranks, they lost out to Napoli (1–2, 3–3) where Diego Maradona was playing at the time.

In 1991–92, the club clinched its fourth title, in one of the closest races in Bundesliga history, finishing ahead of Borussia Dortmund on goal difference. Internationally, they had been eliminated from UEFA Cup play that season (1991–92) after losing their second round match to Spanish side Osasuna (2–3). As national champions, the club qualified to play in the UEFA Champions League in 1992–93, but was eliminated in the first round by Leeds United after a tie-breaking third match in Barcelona which was required due to coach Christoph Daum having substituted a fourth non-German player in game two.

VfB did not qualify for any European competition again until 1997, by way of their third German Cup win, with coach Joachim Löw. They enjoyed a measure of success on their return, advancing to the 1998 European Cup Winners' Cup final in Stockholm, where they lost to Chelsea in what was the penultimate year of the competition. Only one player of the *magic triangle*, captain Krassimir Balakov, remained after Giovane Elber and Fredi Bobic left. Löw's contract was not renewed, he was replaced by Winfried Schäfer who in turn was sacked after one season.

However, *Stuttgart*'s performance fell off after this as the club earned just mid-table results over the next two seasons despite spending money on the transfer market and for veterans like Balakov.

2000–2007 The post-MV-era return to success

Due to high debts and the lack of results, Gerhard Mayer-Vorfelder finally resigned from VfB in 2000 to take over offices at German Football Association, UEFA and FIFA. New president Manfred Haas had to renegotiate expensive contracts with players that seldom appeared on the field anyway. As in 1976, when *MV* had taken over, the team had to be rebuilt by relying on talents from the youth teams. The *VfB* has Germany's most successful program in the de:Deutsche Jugendmeisterschaft (Fußball).

Coach Ralf Rangnick had started a restructuring of the team that won the UI Cup, but the resulting extra strain of the UEFA cup participation ended in barely escaping from relegation in 2001 by clinching 15th spot. Rangnick was replaced by Felix Magath.

With players like Andreas Hinkel, Kevin Kurányi, Timo Hildebrand or Alexander Hleb earning themselves the nickname *the young and wild*, the club soon re-bounded and finished as Bundesliga runners-up in the 2002–03 season.

Champions League 2003–04

Thus, VfB qualified for their second Champions League appearance and, beating Manchester United and Rangers once and Panathinaikos twice, they advanced out of group play to the first knock out round where they were eliminated by their old nemesis Chelsea (0–1 and 0–0) (see also UEFA Champions League 2003-04).

They continued to play as one of the top teams in the country, earning fourth and fifth place Bundesliga finishes, and again taking part in the UEFA Cup, but without great success. In addition, coach Magath and several players left for stronger clubs: Kevin Kurányi for Schalke 04, Philipp Lahm for Bayern Munich and Aliaksandr Hleb for Arsenal.

Halfway through the disappointing 2005–06 season, Giovanni Trapattoni was sacked and replaced by Armin Veh. The new coach was designated as a stop-gap due to having resigned from Hansa Rostock in 2003 to focus on his family and having no football job since 2004 except coaching his home team Augsburg for a season. Supported by new manager Horst Heldt, Veh could establish himself and his concept of focusing on promising inexpensive players rather than established stars. Team captain Zvonimir Soldo retired, and other veterans left the team that slipped to ninth place and did not qualify for European competition for the first time in four years.

Bundesliga champions 2006–07

Despite early-season losses and ensuing criticism in 2006–07, including a 3–0 loss at home to Nuremberg, Veh managed to turn the collection of new players like Mexicans Pável Pardo, and Ricardo Osorio, and Brazilian Antônio da Silva and fresh local talents, including Mario Gómez, Serdar Tasci and Sami Khedira, into a strong contender that led the league on 12 November 2006 for the first time in two years. Stuttgart established themselves among the top five and delivered a strong challenge for the Bundesliga title by winning their final eight games. In the penultimate week on 12 May 2007, Stuttgart beat VfL Bochum 3–2 away from home, took the Bundesliga lead from Schalke 04 and secured a spot in the 2007-08 UEFA Champions League. After trailing 0–1 in the final match of the season against Energie Cottbus, Stuttgart came back to win 2–1 and claim their first Bundesliga title in 15 years. The victory celebrations in Stuttgart (250,000 people) even topped those of Germany's third place win over Portugal in the 2006 World Cup.

In addition, VfB had their first ever chance to win the *double* as they also reached the final of the German Cup for the first time since their victory there ten years former. Their opponents in the cup final in Berlin were Nuremberg, a team that had beaten them twice by 3 goals in regular season, 3–0 and 4–1, but last had won the cup in 1962. With the game level at 1–1 in the first half, Stuttgart's scorer Cacau was sent off. Nuremberg gained a 2–1 lead early in the second half, but the ten men of VfB managed to fight back and equalize. In the second half of extra time, with both teams suffering from exhaustion and the humid conditions, Nuremberg scored the winning goal.

Champions League 2007–08

The 2007–08 UEFA Champions League draw on August 30, 2007 paired the German champions with Spanish giants Barcelona, French champions Lyon and Scottish Old Firm side Rangers. Like in the 2003–04 Champions League season, Stuttgart's 2007–08 European campaign started with a match at Glasgow's Ibrox Park against Rangers. It ended in a 2–1 defeat. The second match at home against Barcelona was lost, too, 0–2, as well as the 3rd match, against Lyon at home, with the visitors coming out 2–0 winners from 2nd half strikes. Five defeats and just one win (over Rangers) meant the early exit on the European stage. In the league they managed to become 6th after a poor start. New Germany star Mario Gómez scored 19 goals.

Subsequently, UEFA Cup qualification was ensured in the summer by succeeding in the UEFA Intertoto Cup 2008.

2008-09 season

The 2008-09 season, like the one before it, came off to a bad start. After matchday 14 in November, VfB was only 11th in the table. As a result, Armin Veh was sacked and replaced by Markus Babbel. After exiting the German FA Cup after a thrashing 1-5 defeat to FC Bayern Munich in January, things improved considerably and the team ended up third, with 2nd place just being missed after a loss to Bayern Munich on the last matchday. That meant the chance of making the Champions League again.

Internationally, VfB mastered the group stages of the UEFA Cup 2008-09, but lost to Cup defenders FC Zenit Saint Petersburg in the round of the last 32 in February.

2009-10 season: returning to the Champions League

VfB went into the season with Mario Gomez gone, but Pavel Pogrebnyak arriving from FC Zenit and Aliaksandr Hleb returning (on loan from FC Barcelona).

On the European level, VfB started the season with a huge success by qualifying for the group stage of the UEFA Champions League 2009-10. VfB entered that competition for the third time in six years (after 2003 and 2007) by defeating Romanian side FC Timisoara in the Champions League qualification "play-off round" on August 18 and 26, 2009. VfB were drawn into Group G against Spanish side Sevilla, Scottish champions Rangers, against whom they had also been drawn against in their previous two Champions League Group Stage appearances, and Romanian champions Unirea Urziceni. With two wins (one each against Rangers and Unirea), three draws (one each against all opponents) and a loss (to Sevilla) they managed 2nd spot in the group, thus qualifying for the round of the last 16, where they had to face title holders FC Barcelona in late winter. After a superb home game against *Barca* which *VfB*, however, did not manage to win (1-1), they were eliminated in a 4-0 rout at the Camp Nou.

In the 2009-10 German Cup, they didn't proceed further than the last 16 either, losing to second-tier side Greuther Fürth. That defeat came in the course of a disappointing first half of the 2009-10 Bundesliga season. As a consequence of slipping to 16th spot in December, young coach Markus Babbel was fired after matchday 15 and replaced by the more experienced Swiss Christian Gross. Under his tenure, *VfB* improved their situation domestically as well as internationally before the winter break. During that break, Thomas Hitzlsperger, Jan Simak and Ludovic Magnin left the club; Cristian Molinaro was loaned out from Juventus Turin. In the later half of the season, the team - as in 2008-09 - had a fantastic, almost unbroken, winning streak. As the best team of that second (return) round of the Bundesliga, the Swabians under Christian Gross climbed into the upper half of the table and, after a sensational rally, eventually managed to qualify for European football next season (i.e. the UEFA Europa League 2010-11).

Stadium

The home ground of *VfB Stuttgart* is the Mercedes-Benz Arena which was originally built in 1933. It lies close to the River Neckar on Bad Cannstatt's Mercedes-Straße near the new Mercedes-Benz Museum and Mercedes-Benz factory. After being renovated several times, the stadium can hold a maximum capacity of 55,896 spectators (50,000 for international matches). Unlike most other Bundesliga stadiums, the former *Neckarstadion* retains the traditional athletic track around the playing field despite intentions to convert it into a football-only stadium. As for the 1974 FIFA World Cup, *Gottlieb-Daimler-Stadion* was one of the venues for the 2006 FIFA World Cup, hosting five preliminary round matches, a First Knockout Round match (England vs. Ecuador) and the third place play-off (Germany vs. Portugal). Since the 2008–09 season, the stadium was named the Mercedes-Benz-Arena, starting with a pre-season friendly against Arsenal on July 30, 2008. The stadium is currently undergoing extensive restructuring and rebuilding as it is being converted into a pure football arena. As building work continues, the capacity is reduced to around 41,000, while the final capacity will reach 60,000 at the end of 2011 (projected).

Rivalries, friendships and cooperations

The longest rivalry of *VfB* is the city rivalry with Stuttgarter Kickers (*Die Roten/Reds* against *Die Blauen/Blues*). However, the respective first teams of the two clubs haven't played each other since *Kickers* were relegated to the 2. Bundesliga in 1992. Thus, this derby has increasingly been overtaken in importance by the *Baden-Württemberg-Derby* between VfB and Karlsruher SC, *KSC*, for short. In this derby, old Badenian-Württembergian animosities are played out. The rivalry with Bavarian side FC Bayern München (*Süd-/South Derby*) is mainly one-sided, as VfB fans are angry at Bayern for buying some of Stuttgart's best players and coaches in recent years, such as Giovane Elber, Felix Magath and Mario Gómez.

Regional friendships exist between VfB and the South Württemberg side SSV Reutlingen (*little brother* of VfB) as well as with North Württembergers SpVgg Ludwigsburg.

In 2005, a cooperation treaty between VfB and Swiss Super League side FC St. Gallen was signed, especially with regard to the youth sectors of both clubs.

Honours

National

- **German championship:**
  - **Winners (5):** 1950, 1952, 1984, 1992, 2007
  - Runners-up (4): 1935, 1953, 1979, 2003
- **German Cup:**
  - **Winners (3):** 1954, 1958, 1997
  - Runners-up (2): 1986, 2007
- **German Super Cup:**
  - **Winners (1):** 1992
- **German League Cup:**
  - Runners-up (3): 1997, 1998, 2005

Regional

- **Oberliga Süd I:**
    - **Winners (3):** 1945-46, 1951–52, 1953–54
    - Runners-up (3): 1949-50, 1952–53, 1955–56
- **2nd Bundesliga Süd II:**
    - **Winners (1):** 1977
- **Bezirksliga Württemberg-Baden:**
    - **Winners (2):** 1926-27, 1929–30
    - Runners-up (1): 1925-26
- **Gauliga Württemberg:**
    - **Winners (4):** 1934-35, 1936–37, 1937–38, 1942–43
    - Runners-up (4): 1938-39, 1939–40, 1940–41, 1941–42

International

- **UEFA Cup:**
    - Runners-up (1): 1988-89
- **UEFA Cup Winners' Cup:**
    - Runners-up (1): 1997–98
- **UEFA Intertoto Cup:**
    - **Winners (3):** 2000, 2002, 2008
- **Uhrencup:**
    - **Winners (1):** 2010

Youth

- **German Under 19 championship**
    - **Champions**: 1973, 1981, 1984, 1988, 1989, 1990, 1991, 2003, 2005
    - **Runners-up**: 1972, 1977, 1982, 1999, 2002
- **German Under 17 championship**
    - **Champions**: 1986, 1994, 1995, 1999, 2004, 2009
    - **Runners-up**: 1988, 1990, 1998, 2002, 2003
- **Under 19 Bundesliga South/Southwest**
    - **Champions**: 2005, 2008

Trivia

- The merger that created *VfB* was held in the Concordia hotel in Bad Cannstatt, a district of the city of Stuttgart.
- *VfB* are nicknamed "the Reds" for their team colours, featuring a red *chest ring* on white jerseys. Local rivals Stuttgarter Kickers, wearing blue and white, are "the Blues".

Club management

- Dieter Hundt, chairman, entrepreneur
- Erwin Staudt, CEO & president since 26 June 2003
- Fredi Bobic, director of sport since 27 July 2010
- Jochen Schneider, director of sport

Players

As of August 31, 2010. For recent transfers, see List of German football transfers summer 2010, and List of German football transfers winter 2009–10.

Current squad

Note: Flags indicate national team as has been defined under FIFA eligibility rules. Players may hold more than one non-FIFA nationality.

No.	Position	Player
1	GK	Sven Ulreich
2	DF	Philipp Degen *(on loan from Liverpool)*
3	DF	Cristian Molinaro
5	DF	Serdar Tasci
6	DF	Georg Niedermeier
7	FW	Martin Harnik
8	MF	Zdravko Kuzmanović
9	FW	Ciprian Marica
11	MF	Johan Audel
12	GK	Alexander Stolz
13	MF	Timo Gebhart
14	MF	Patrick Funk
15	DF	Arthur Boka

No.		Position	Player
16		MF	Mauro Camoranesi
17		DF	Matthieu Delpierre *(captain)*
18		FW	Cacau *(vice-captain)*
20		MF	Christian Gentner
21		DF	Khalid Boulahrouz
23		GK	Marc Ziegler
24		MF	Mamadou Bah
25		MF	Élson
26		MF	Daniel Didavi
27		DF	Stefano Celozzi
29		FW	Pavel Pogrebnyak
35		MF	Christian Träsch

Players out on loan

Note: Flags indicate national team as has been defined under FIFA eligibility rules. Players may hold more than one non-FIFA nationality.

No.		Position	Player
39		FW	Julian Schieber *(at Nuremberg until June 2011)*

Coaches

Current coaching staff

Jens Keller	Head coach
Jürgen Kramny	Assistant coach
Eberhard Trautner	Goalkeeping coach
Christian Kolodziej	Fitness coach

Coaches since 1920

Name	Period	Honors
Grünwald	1920	
Edward Tom Hanney (1889–1964)	July 1, 1924 - January 1927	Württemberg/Baden champions 1927
Lajos Kovács (b. 1894)	September 1927 - December 31, 1929	Württemberg champions 1929/30
Emil Friz (1904–1966)	January 1, 1930 - June 15, 1930	
Karl Preuß	June 15, 1930–1933	
Willi Rutz (1907–1993)	July 1933 - 1934	
Emil Gröner (b. 1892)	1934–1935	
Fritz Teufel (b. 1910)	1935 - June 30, 1936	German championship runners-up 1935, Gauliga Württemberg champions 1935
Leonhard "Lony" Seiderer (1895–1940)	July 1, 1936 - June 30, 1939	Gauliga Württemberg champions 1937, 1938
Karl Becker (1902–1942)	March 1939 - April 1939	
Josef Pöttinger (1903–1970)	May 1, 1939 - October 1939	
Fritz Teufel	July 1, 1945 - June 30, 1947	Oberliga Süd champions 1946
Georg Wurzer (1907–1982)	July 1, 1947 - April 30, 1960	German champions 1950, 1952, Runners-up 1953, Oberliga Süd champions 1952, 1954, German Cup 1954, 1958
Kurt Baluses (1914–1972)	May 1, 1960 - February 24, 1965	
Franz Seybold (1912–1978)	February 25, 1965 - March 7, 1965	
Rudi Gutendorf (b. 1926)	March 8, 1965 - December 6, 1966	
Albert Sing (1917–2008)	December 7, 1966 - June 30, 1967	
Gunther Baumann (1921–1998)	July 1, 1967 - June 30, 1969	
Franz Seybold	Juli 1, 1969 - June 30, 1970	

Branko Zebec (1929–1988)	July 1, 1970 - April 18, 1972	
Karl Bögelein (b. 1927)	April 19, 1972 - June 30, 1972	
Hermann Eppenhoff (1919–1992)	July 1, 1972 - December 1, 1974	
Fritz Millinger	December 2, 1974 - December 13, 1974	
Albert Sing	December 14, 1974 - June 30, 1975	
István Sztani (b. 1937)	July 1, 1975 - March 31, 1976	
Karl Bögelein	April 1, 1976 - June 30, 1976	
Hans-Jürgen Sundermann (b. 1940)	July 1, 1976 - June 30, 1979	Bundesliga runners-up 1979
Lothar Buchmann (b. 1936)	July 1, 1979 - June 30, 1980	
Hans-Jürgen Sundermann	July 1, 1980 - June 30, 1982	
Helmut Benthaus (b. 1935)	July 1, 1982 - June 30, 1985	German champions 1984
Otto Barić (b. 1932)	July 1, 1985 - March 4, 1986	
Willi Entenmann (b. 1943)	March 5, 1986 - June 30, 1986	German Cup runners-up 1986
Egon Coordes (b. 1944)	July 1, 1986 - June 30, 1987	
Arie Haan (b. 1948)	July 1, 1987 - March 26, 1990	UEFA Cup runners-up 1989
Willi Entenmann	March 27, 1990 - November 19, 1990	
Christoph Daum (b. 1953)	November 20, 1990 - December 10, 1993	German champions 1992
Jürgen Röber (b. 1953)	Dezember 15, 1993 - April 25, 1995	
Jürgen Sundermann	April 26, 1995 - June 30, 1995	
Rolf Fringer (b. 1957)	July 1, 1995 - August 13, 1996	
Joachim Löw (b. 1960)	August 14, 1996 - June 30, 1998	German Cup 1997, Cup Winners' Cup runners up 1998
Winfried Schäfer (b. 1950)	July 1, 1998 - December 4, 1998	
Wolfgang Rolff (b. 1959)	December 5, 1998 - Dezember 31, 1998	
Rainer Adrion (b. 1953)	January 1, 1999 - May 2, 1999	
Ralf Rangnick (b. 1958)	May 3, 1999 - February 23, 2001	
Felix Magath (b. 1953)	February 24, 2001 - June 30, 2004	Bundesliga runners-up 2003

Matthias Sammer (b. 1967)	July 1, 2004 - June 3, 2005	
Giovanni Trapattoni (b. 1939)	June 17, 2005 - February 9, 2006	
Armin Veh (b. 1961)	February 10, 2006 - November 23, 2008	German champions 2007, German Cup runners-up 2007
Markus Babbel (b. 1972)	November 23, 2008 - December 6, 2009	
Christian Gross (b. 1954)	December 6, 2009 - October 13, 2010	
Jens Keller (b. 1970)	October 13, 2010 - *incumbent*	

Bundesliga Position

- 1963/64 - 5th place
- 1964/65 - 12th place
- 1965/66 - 11th place
- 1966/67 - 12th place
- 1967/68 - 8th place
- 1968/69 - 5th place
- 1969/70 - 7th place
- 1970/71 - 12th place
- 1971/72 - 8th place
- 1972/73 - 6th place
- 1973/74 - 9th place
- 1974/75 - 16th place *(relegated to the 2. Bundesliga)*
- 1975/76 - 2. Bundesliga, 11th place
- 1976/77 - 2. Bundesliga, 1st place *(promoted to the 1. Bundesliga)*
- 1977/78 - 4th place
- 1978/79 - 2nd place
- 1979/80 - 3rd place
- 1980/81 - 3rd place
- 1981/82 - 9th place
- 1982/83 - 3rd place
- 1983/84 - 1st *(German champions)*
- 1984/85 - 10th place
- 1985/86 - 5th place
- 1986/87 - 12th place
- 1987/88 - 4th place
- 1988/89 - 5th place
- 1989/90 - 6th place
- 1990/91 - 6th place
- 1991/92 - 1st *(German champions)*
- 1992/93 - 7th place
- 1993/94 - 7th place
- 1994/95 - 12th place
- 1995/96 - 10th place
- 1996/97 - 4th place
- 1997/98 - 4th place
- 1998/99 - 11th place
- 1999/00 - 8th place
- 2000/01 - 15th place
- 2001/02 - 8th place
- 2002/03 - 2nd place
- 2003/04 - 4th place
- 2004/05 - 5th place
- 2005/06 - 9th place
- 2006/07 - 1st *(German champions)*
- 2007/08 - 6th place
- 2008/09 - 3rd place
- 2009/10 - 6th place

External links

- VfB Stuttgart 1893e.V. - Official team site [2]
- HefleswetzKick - VfB Stuttgart Team and History Site [3]
- photos of the party in the streets of Stuttgart after the championship victory 2007 [4]
- Abseits Guide to German Soccer [5]
- f-archiv - The German Soccer-Archiv [6] historical German football league tables (in German)
- eufo.de [7] European football club profiles
- Team statistics [8]

Stuttgarter Kickers

Full name	Sportverein Stuttgarter Kickers e.V.
Nickname(s)	*Die Kickers*, *Die Blauen* (The Blues), *Die Blauen-Götter* (The Blue-Gods).
Founded	21 September 1899
Ground	Gazi-Stadion auf der Waldau (Capacity: 11,436)
Chairman	Edgar Kurz
Manager	Dirk Schuster
League	Regionalliga Süd (IV)
2009-10	Regionalliga Süd (IV), 9th
Home colours	**Away colours**

Stuttgarter Kickers is a German football club that plays in Stuttgart, Baden-Württemberg, founded on 21 September 1899 as *FC Stuttgarter Cickers*. Its members made a deliberate and emphatic choice early on to play football exclusively and to turn their backs on rugby – their chosen sport's close cousin – at a time when both of these new English games were still evolving.

History

In its early years the club had a decent local squad that played in the *Südkreis-Liga*, *Kreisliga Württemberg* and then in the *Bezirksliga Württemberg*. With the reorganization of German football during the Third Reich in 1933, the team – now known as *SV Stuttgarter Kickers* – found itself in the *Gauliga Württemberg*, one of sixteen top tier regional leagues established in the country during that time. It continued to have good results locally, but was unable to impress beyond its own area. In the final year of World War II the Kickers fielded a combined wartime squad with *Sportfreunde Stuttgart*.

After the war the club resumed play in the Oberliga Süd and performed as a mid-table team early on. By 1950 it had slipped to the lower half of the table with a seemingly solid grip on 14th place, constantly struggling to avoid relegation throughout the decade. *Kickers* spent the early 60's in tier II football, but after the formation of the Bundesliga, Germany's new professional league, in 1963, the club was moved to the Regionalliga Süd. In 1974 that league went professional and became the

2.Bundesliga. Between 1963 and the late 1980s the team had varying results, but finally stabilized in the upper half of the standings toward the end of that period. It has one losing appearance to its credit in the German Cup in 1987 and in 1988-89 it made it to the Bundesliga for the first time. It ended a run of 28 years as a second division outfit. The team was immediately relegated after a 17th place finish, but continued to deliver some of its best performances. *Die Blauen* advanced to the semi-finals of the 2000 German Cup and then had a second turn in the Bundesliga in 1991-92, but with the same result as its earlier time up. Over the next decade the club played largely in the second division, before slipping to the *Regionalliga Süd (III)* in 2001, where they remained until 2008, when a tenth place finish narrowly qualified them for the new 3rd Liga. They finished last (20th) in the 3rd Liga and were relegated to the Regionalliga Süd, where they finished in the Season 2009/10 with a 9th place..

The *Stuttgarter Kickers* also have handball, athletics, table tennis, cheerleading, and Lacrosse departments. The association is also recognized for its training of football referees and other game officials. They had a hockey department too, which in 1957 got independent under the name of HTC Stuttgarter Kickers.

Reserve team

The *Stuttgarter Kickers II*, historically also known as *Stuttgarter Kickers Amateure*, are playing in the *Oberliga Baden-Württemberg* since 2000. Previously, the team fluctuated between the *Landesliga* and *Verbandsliga Württemberg*.

Current squad

See also List of Stuttgarter Kickers players

Note: Flags indicate national team as has been defined under FIFA eligibility rules. Players may hold more than one non-FIFA nationality.

No.	Position	Player
1	GK	Daniel Wagner
3	DF	Patrick Auracher
4	DF	Simon Köpf
6	MF	Demis Jung
7	MF	Marcel Ivanusa
8	MF	Michele Rizzi
9	FW	Daniel Reule
10	MF	Enzo Marchese

No.	Position	Player
11	FW	Marcel Brandstetter
13	MF	Oliver Stierle
15	DF	Marcel Rapp
17	DF	Fabian Gerster
19	DF	Alessandro Abruscia
20	MF	Ali Pala
21	GK	Günay Güvenc
23	FW	Dirk Prediger
24	MF	Mahir Savranlioglu
25	FW	Denis Videc
28	DF	Andreas Wonschick

Honours

Traditionally a strong local club, the *Kickers* hold 24 Württemberg championships.

- Southern German championship: 1908, 1913, 1917
- Südkreis-Liga (I) champions: 1913, 1914, 1917
- Kreisliga Württemberg (I) champions: 1921, 1923
- Bezirksliga Württemberg-Baden (I) champions: 1924, 1925
- Bezirksliga Württemberg (I) champions: 1928, 1933
- Gauliga Württemberg (I) champions: 1936, 1939, 1940, 1941, 1942
- 2nd Oberliga Süd (II) champions: 1951, 1959
- 2nd Bundesliga champions: 1988
- Regionalliga Süd champions: 1995
- DFB-Pokal finalist: 1987
- DFB-Pokal semi-finalist: 2000
- Württemberg Cup winners: 2005, 2006

The club's youth teams have enjoyed quite a bit of success on the national scene.

- German Under 19 champions: 1979
- German Cup Junior champions: 1990

Recent seasons

Stuttgarter Kickers

Year	Division	Position
1999-2000	2nd Bundesliga (II)	15th
2000-01	2nd Bundesliga	17th ↓
2001-02	Regionalliga Süd (III)	12th
2002-03	Regionalliga Süd	15th
2003-04	Regionalliga Süd	9th
2004-05	Regionalliga Süd	9th
2005-06	Regionalliga Süd	8th
2006-07	Regionalliga Süd	4th
2007-08	Regionalliga Süd	10th
2008-09	3rd Liga (III)	20th ↓
2009-10	Regionalliga Süd (IV)	9th

Stuttgarter Kickers II

Year	Division	Position
1999-2000	Verbandsliga Württemberg (V)	2nd ↑
2000-01	Oberliga Baden-Württemberg (IV)	11th
2001-02	Oberliga Baden-Württemberg	8th
2002-03	Oberliga Baden-Württemberg	7th
2003-04	Oberliga Baden-Württemberg	12th
2004-05	Oberliga Baden-Württemberg	10th
2005-06	Oberliga Baden-Württemberg	13th
2006-07	Oberliga Baden-Württemberg	9th
2007-08	Oberliga Baden-Württemberg	15th
2008-09	Oberliga Baden-Württemberg (V)	7th
2009-10	Oberliga Baden-Württemberg	12th

Manager History

- 07.01.1945 - 06.30.1946 Ossi Müller
- 07.01.1946 - 06.30.1947 Albert Cozza
- 07.01.1947 - 06.30.1948 Albert Cozza, Josef "Seppl" Müller and Lory Polster
- 07.01.1948 - 06.30.1950 Emil Melcher
- 07.01.1950 - 06.30.1951 Kuno Krügel
- 07.01.1951 - 06.30.1952 Fritz Kerr
- 07.01.1952 - 06.30.1953 Kuno Krügel
- 07.01.1953 - 06.30.1954 Viktor Havliczek
- 07.01.1954 - 06.30.1956 Georg Bayerer
- 07.01.1956 - 06.30.1958 Oswald Pfau
- 07.01.1958 - 06.30.1960 Benda Hügel
- 07.01.1960 - 06.30.1962 Karl-Heinz Grindler
- 07.01.1961 - 04.30.1962 Jenö Csaknady
- 05.01.1962 - 06.30.1962 Albert Sing
- 07.01.1962 - 06.30.1966 Hans Eberle
- 07.01.1966 - 06.30.1969 Georg Wurzer
- 07.01.1969 - 11.30.1969 Gerd Menne
- 12.01.1969 - 06.30.1971 Georg Wurzer
- 07.01.1971 - 06.30.1972 Barthel Thomas
- 07.01.1972 - 06.30.1973 Willibald Hahn
- 07.01.1973 - 09.15.1974 Fritz Millinger
- 09.16.1974 - 06.30.1975 Georg Wurzer and Rudolf Kröner
- 07.01.1975 - 06.30.1977 Rudolf Kröner
- 07.01.1977 - 06.30.1978 Hans Cieslarczyk
- 07.01.1978 - 10.26.1980 Hans-Dieter Roos
- 10.27.1981 - 06.30.1982 Slobodan Cendic
- 07.01.1982 - 01.23.1983 Jürgen Sundermann
- 01.24.1983 - 10.21.1984 Horst Buhtz
- 10.22.1984 - 06.30.1987 Dieter Renner
- 07.01.1987 - 05.02.1990 Manfred Krafft
- 05.02.1990 - 06.30.1992 Rainer Zobel
- 07.01.1992 - 08.23.1992 Frieder Schömezler
- 08.25.1992 - 06.30.1993 Rolf Schafstall
- 07.01.1993 - 02.28.1994 Lorenz-Günther Köstner
- 03.01.1994 - 06.30.1994 Günter Sebert
- 07.01.1994 - 10.26.1994 Paul Sauter
- 10.26.1994 - 02.18.1998 Wolfgang Wolf

- 02.18.1998 - 02.24.1998 Frieder Schömezler
- 02.25.1998 - 05.17.1999 Paul Linz
- 05.18.1999 - 06.30.1999 Ralf Vollmer
- 07.01.1999 - 03.28.2000 Michael Feichtenbeiner
- 03.30.2000 - 06.30.2000 Dragoslav Stepanović
- 07.01.2000 - 09.25.2000 Hans-Jürgen Boysen
- 09.27.2000 - 08.26.2001 Rainer Zobel
- 08.27.2001 - 03.09.2003 Markus Sorg
- 03.10.2001 - 10.27.2003 Rainer Adrion
- 10.27.2003 - 06.30.2007 Robin Dutt
- 07.01.2007 - 11.04.2007 Peter Zeidler
- 11.05.2007 - 09.21.2008 Stefan Minkwitz
- 09.21.2008 - 04.14.2009 Edgar Schmitt
- 04.14.2009 - 06.30.2009 Rainer Kraft
- 07.01.2009 - present Dirk Schuster

External links

- Official website [1] (German)
- The Abseits Guide to German Soccer [2]

Stuttgart Scorpions

Stuttgart Scorpions	
Founded:	1982
Headcoach:	Matthias Mecherlein
League:	German Football League (1. Bundesliga)
Stadium	
Name:	GAZI-Stadion auf der Waldau
Address:	Guts-Muths-Weg 4 70597 Stuttgart
End of Season Standings for Last 5 Years	
2007:	1st Place GFL South; Deutsche Vizemeister
2006:	2nd Place GFL South
2005:	3rd Place GFL South
2004:	3rd Place GFL South
2003:	4th Place GFL South
2002:	2nd Place GFL South
Contact	
Internet:	www.stuttgart-scorpions.de [1]

The **Stuttgart Scorpions** are an American football-team in Stuttgart, Germany, currently the 11th ranked team in Europe. The Scorpions will celebrate the 25th Anniversary of existence in 2007.

See also

- List of American football teams in Germany
- Stuttgart

External links

- Stuttgart Scorpions Official Website [1]
- Red Poison Cheerleader Website [2]
- German Football League Website [3]
- American Football Verband Deutschland Website [4]
- German Bowl XXVIII Website [5]

Gazi-Stadion auf der Waldau

View from the Fernsehturm Stuttgart

Location	Guts-Muths Weg 4 70597 Stuttgart Germany
Coordinates	48°45′14.2″N 9°11′18.3″E
Built	1905
Opened	18 June 1905
Renovated	1913, 1975, 1982, 1997, 2000, 2009
Owner	City of Stuttgart
Operator	City of Stuttgart
Surface	Grass
Capacity	11,436 (Total) 10,368 (Stands) + 1,068 (Seats)
Tenants	
Stuttgarter Kickers, Stuttgart Scorpions, VfB Stuttgart II	

The **Gazi-Stadion auf der Waldau** (previously Waldau-Stadion, initially Kickers-Platz) is a multi-use stadium in the Degerloch district in Stuttgart, Germany. The stadium is situated approximately 200m besides the Fernsehturm Stuttgart and holds 11,436 spectators (of these, 1,068 canopied seats and 4,949 canopied stands), which makes it the second biggest stadium in Stuttgart.. It is home to the Stuttgarter Kickers, currently playing in the Regionalliga Süd. The American Football team Stuttgart Scorpions uses the stadium in the German Football League and, since 2008, the VfB Stuttgart II, playing in the 3. Liga, plays its home games here.

History

The football section of Stuttgarter Kickers plays their home games in the stadium since its inauguration in 1905, thereby being the German club that plays for the longest time in the same stadium.

Until 1975, the stadium featured a wooden terrace that was built after one of FC Arsenal's in scale 1:3. Due to various requirements imposed by the German Football Association, a new main stand was built in 1976 and is in use until today. After having the names **Kickers-Platz** and **Kickers-Stadium** since 1905, the stadium was officially renamed to **Waldau-Stadion** in 1987.

The Stuttgart Scorpions use the stadium since their promotion to the German Football League in 1995.

In 2001, the MTV HipHop Open took place in the stadium. This was the only occurrence of the music festival in the stadium as it moved to the **Reitstadion** in the next year and has been moved to Mannheim since 2009.

In June 2004 the name of the stadium was sold to the German main sponsor Garmo AG for 10 years. Garmo sells its products with the brand name GAZi and renamed the stadium accordingly to GAZi-Stadion auf der Waldau.

On 6 October 2007, the final of the German Bowl, the German championship in American Football, between the Stuttgart Scorpions and the Braunschweig Lions took place in the GAZi-Stadion. Braunschweig won the championship for the third time in a row, defeating Stuttgart 27:6 in front of 8.152 spectators.

On 17 July 2008, Stuttgart's council decided to remodel the stadium for 5.4 million Euro in order to fulfill the requirements imposed by the DFB for the new 3. Liga. It was planned to increase the capacity to 12,000 spectators (2,000 canopied seats and 10.000 stands in total). Beginning of the construction work was planned for January 2009 and should be finished by July 2009. In the end of 2008, however, the council decided to postpone the remodeling for a unknown time span. Following the relegation of Stuttgarter Kickers to the fourth-tier Regionalliga Süd, the remodeling would not have been necessary. VfB Stuttgart II, however, for now continues to host its home games in the 3. Liga in the stadium with a special approval by the DFB.

Hanns-Martin-Schleyer-Halle

Hanns-Martin-Schleyer-Halle is an indoor sporting arena located in Stuttgart, Germany. The capacity of the arena is 15,500 people. The hall was built in 1983 and is named for Hanns Martin Schleyer, a German employer representative, and former SS Officer and Nazi activist, who was kidnapped and killed by the terrorist Red Army Faction. It has a 265-metre (869 ft) track made of wood.

The arena hosted the final phase of the 1985 European basketball championship.

It also hosted the Stuttgart Masters when it was a ATP Super 9 event between 1996 and 2001.

The arena is also used as a velodrome and was used as the host for the 2003 UCI Track Cycling World Championships.

Geographical coordinates: 48°47′38″N 9°13′37″E

External links

- Official Site [1]

Porsche Arena

Location	Stuttgart, Baden-Württemberg Germany
Coordinates	48°47′35″N 9°13′42″E
Broke ground	April, 2005
Opened	May 27, 2006
Construction cost	€ 31,16 million
Architect	'asp' architekten Stuttgart
Capacity	7,849 (Boxing) 7,576 (Stage shows) 6,181 (basketball, handball) 6,042 (concerts) 5,068 (hockey)
Tenants	
Porsche Tennis Grand Prix (Tennis) (2006-present) Handball World Championship, (handball) (2007) Table Tennis European (Table tennis) (Sep 2009)	

Porsche Arena is a multi-purpose arena, located in Stuttgart, Germany. The seating capacity of the arena varies, from 5,100 to 8,000 people and it was opened in 2006, after 14 months of construction.

To fund the construction, costs had already been pre-construction sales of the name rights planned. Dr. Ing h.c. F. Porsche AG bought the name rights, for a ten million euro, for a term of 20 years.

The arena is part of a sport complex that includes the adjacent Mercedes-Benz Arena and Schleyerhalle.

It is the venue for the Porsche Tennis Grand Prix, a WTA Tour event and also hosted some matches at the 2007 World Men's Handball Championship.

Anton Hunger: "The tournament is now at home in Stuttgart. We knew we'd make mistakes at the first edition. But we didn't promise too much last year and have eliminated almost all the mistakes in 2007. A total of more than 36,000 spectators were in the arena. The number was up on the previous year even though seating was slightly reduced to improve comfort."

Bob Dylan performed at the arena during his 2007 European Tour on April 20, 2007.

Gallery

Logo

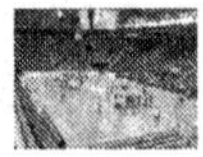

Inside view

Mercedes-Benz Arena, Porsche-Arena, Hanns-Martin-Schleyer-Halle

External links

- Homepage Porsche-Arena [1]
- City of Stuttgart [2]
- Image Web site: Stadionwelt [3]
- Transportation Plan with [4], PDF
- Porsche Arena detail [5], PDF
- Photos of the finished Porsche Arena [6]
- Wikimapia Official site [7]
- Porsche Arena imagne 1 (2007) [8]
- Porsche Arena imagne 2 (07 October 2006) [9]
- Porsche Arena imagne 3 [10]
- Porsche Arena Germany Brazil volleyball 1 [11]
- Porsche Arena Germany Brazil volleyball 2 [12]

Mercedes-Benz Arena

Location	Stuttgart, Baden-Württemberg, Germany
Built	1933
Renovated	2006 ('asp' architekten Stuttgart) 2009-2011 ('asp' architekten Stuttgart)
Construction cost	€ 63,5 million (2009-11 renovated) € 58 million (2006 renovated) € 5,2 million (2001)
Architect	'asp' architekten Stuttgart [1] (2006, 2009-11)
Capacity	52,000 (football) (present) 60,000 (football) (December 2011)
Tenants	
VfB Stuttgart (football) (1933-present)	

The **Mercedes-Benz Arena** is a stadium located in Stuttgart, Germany. Before 1993 it was called **Neckarstadion**, named after the nearby river Neckar and between 1993 and July 2008 it was called **Gottlieb-Daimler-Stadion**. From the 2008-09 season, the stadium was renamed the **Mercedes-Benz Arena**, starting with a pre-season friendly against Arsenal on 30 July 2008.

History

The stadium was originally built in 1933 after designs by German architect Paul Bonatz. After It was built, it was named "Adolf-Hitler-Kampfbahn". From 1945 to 1949 it was called Century Stadium and later Kampfbahn and was used by US Troops to play baseball.The name Neckarstation was used since 1949. It is home to VfB Stuttgart in the Bundesliga (and to the Stuttgarter Kickers when they played in the Bundesliga)

After a major refurbishment in the late 1980s and early 1990s partly financed by Daimler-Benz, the Stuttgart town council dedicated the stadium to Gottlieb Daimler. The inventor had tested both the first motorcycle and the first 4-wheel automobile there in the 1880s, on the road from Cannstatt to

Untertürkheim (now called Mercedesstraße). The new museum, the headquarters and a factory of Mercedes-Benz are nearby.

The stadium capacity is currently around 41,000, after one stand (*Untertürkheimer Kurve*) has been demolished during summer 2009 in the process of converting it to a pure football arena. The rebuilt arena will be finished in December 2011 with a new capacity of 60,000.

It is divided into four sections,

- the *Haupttribüne* (main stands), adjacent to Mercedesstraße, housing VIP-lounges and press seats
- the *EnBW-Tribüne* (formerly *Gegentribüne*, lit: opposite stands), currently named after VfB Stuttgart's main sponsor EnBW
- the *Cannstatter Kurve* (Cannstatt Curve), to the left of the *Haupttribüne*, housing Blocks A and B, occupied by the most devoted home fans, and one of two video walls
- the *Untertürkheimer Kurve* (Untertürkheim Curve), to the right of the *Haupttribühne*, housing the guest team's fans (C and D-Block) and the second video wall

The Gottlieb-Daimler-Stadion features a unique roof construction, making it easily recognizable. Made of precision-tailored membranes of PVC-coated polyester, the roof tissue is durable enough to withstand 1,000kg of weight per square decimeter. It is suspended from an aesthetic steel frame that runs around the entire stadium weighing approximately 2,700 metric tons. The steel cables connecting the roof to the frame alone weigh about 420 tons. The roof wasn't added until the refurbishment preceding the 1993 World Athletics Championships.

International matches

The Gottlieb-Daimler-Stadion hosted four matches of the 1974 FIFA World Cup, two matches of the 1988 UEFA European Football Championship (a 1st Round match and a semi-final) and six games of the 2006 FIFA World Cup, including a Round of 16 game and the third-place playoff match (see below for details).

The stadium also hosted the finals of the European Cup (now known as UEFA Champions League) in 1959 (Real Madrid vs. Stade de Reims) and 1988 (PSV Eindhoven vs. S.L. Benfica).

Trivia

- As Stuttgart is located relatively close to Germany's southern neighbors Switzerland, it has hosted a total of seven international football matches versus the Swiss since 1911.
- Germany's first international football match after World War II in 1950 (against Switzerland) was played at the stadium. The match attendance of 103,000 is the stadium record. The first match after the German reunification in 1990 (also versus Switzerland) took place at Neckarstadion Stadium as well.

- Klaus Fischer scored Germany's "ARD Goal of the Century" here against the Swiss in 1977, with a bicycle kick ("Fallrückzieher"), his trademark move with which he also scored the important 3:3 equalizer in extra time (108th minute) at the 1982 FIFA World Cup vs France, but this was not among the Top 10 of the WC Goal of the Century.
- With 115 m² each, the stadium's two video walls are the largest in Europe.
- The Gottlieb-Daimler-Stadion was the one of the four stadium hosting games during the 2006 FIFA World Cup whose name was *not* changed to *FIFA World Cup Stadium XYZ*, as the dedication to Gottlieb Daimler was not interpreted as advertisement (i.e. for DaimlerChrysler). All others, such as the Allianz-Arena in Munich or the AOL-Arena in Hamburg were obliged to remove all visual references to their stadiums' name sponsors.

Sports other than football

The 1986 European Athletics Championships in which the legendary hammer throw world record by Yuriy Sedykh was set, and the 1993 World Athletics Championships were held there, and the Daimler-Stadium was the host the IAAF World Athletics final from 2006 to 2008. The arena has also been the venue of several Eurobowl finals of American Football in the 1990s. The last athletics event took place in September 2008, after which the stadium undergoes redevelopment in order to build a football-only arena.

Redevelopment

Starting in 2009, the Mercedes-Benz-Arena will be redeveloped into a football-only stadium. It is planned that new stands will be constructed by the summer of 2011, with pitch level being lowered by 1,30 metres in time for the beginning of the 2009-2010 season. Once all the interior redevelopment is finished, the roof will be expanded to cover new rows of seats. The entire construction is expected to be finished by the end of the year 2011. The redevelopment was announced along with the stadium's name change in late March 2008. The first computer images of the new arena were released at the same time, also showing a large cube with four video scoreboards above the centre circle, similar to the one in the Commerzbank-Arena in Frankfurt.

Within the first couple of weeks of the redevelpment, 18 undetonated bombs left over from air raids on Stuttgart during the Second World War were found on the construction site.

International tournaments matches

1974 FIFA World Cup

Stuttgart hosted the following matches at the 1974 FIFA World Cup:

Date	Time(CET)	Team #1	Res.	Team #2	Round	Spectators
1974-06-15	18.00	Poland	3-2	Argentina	1st round, Group 4	31,500
1974-06-19	19.30	Argentina	1-1	Italy	1st round, Group 4	68,900
1974-06-23	16.00	Poland	2-1	Italy	1st round, Group 4	68,900
1974-06-26	19.30	Sweden	0-1	Poland	2nd round, Group B	43,755

UEFA Euro 1988

Date	Time(CET)	Team #1	Res.	Team #2	Round	Spectators
1988-06-12	15.30	England	0-1	Republic of Ireland	1st round, Group B	51,573
1988-06-22	20.15	Soviet Union	2-0	Italy	Semi-finals	61,606

2006 FIFA World Cup

The following games were played at the stadium during the 2006 FIFA World Cup:

Date	Time(CET)	Team #1	Res.	Team #2	Round	Spectators
2006-06-13	18.00	France	0-0	Switzerland	Group G	52,000
2006-06-16	18.00	Netherlands	2-1	Côte d'Ivoire	Group C	52,000
2006-06-19	21.00	Spain	3-1	Tunisia	Group H	52,000
2006-06-22	21.00	Croatia	2-2	Australia	Group F	52,000
2006-06-25	17.00	England	1-0	Ecuador	Round of 16	52,000
2006-07-08	21.00	Germany	3-1	Portugal	Third place match	52,000

External links

- Stadium website [2]
- Mercedes-Benz Arena at Footballmatch [3]

Geographical coordinates: 48°47′32.17″N 9°13′55.31″E

Transportation

Stuttgart Airport

Stuttgart Airport Flughafen Stuttgart	

IATA: STR – ICAO: EDDS 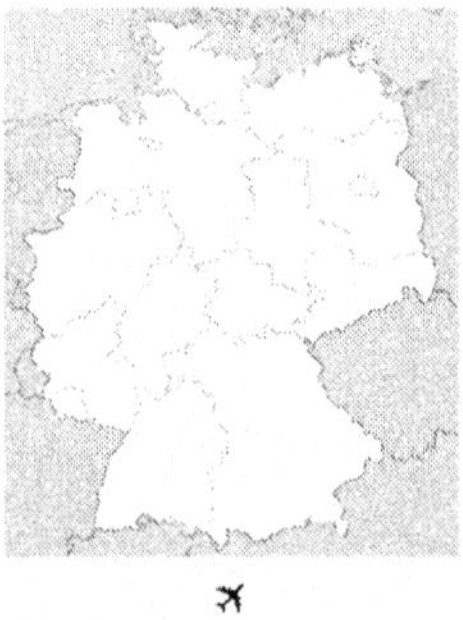 Stuttgart Airport Location of airport in Germany	
Summary	
Airport type	Public
Operator	Flughafen Stuttgart GmbH
Location	Stuttgart, Germany
Hub for	• Germanwings • TUIfly
Elevation AMSL	1,276 ft / 389 m
Coordinates	48°41′24″N 009°13′19″E

Website	www.stuttgart-airport.com [1]		
Runways			
Direction	Length		Surface
	m	ft	
07/25	3,345	10,974	Concrete
Helipads			
Number	Length		Surface
	m	ft	
H1	30	98	Concrete
Source: German AIP at EUROCONTROL			

Stuttgart Airport (in German *Flughafen Stuttgart*, formerly *Flughafen Stuttgart-Echterdingen*) (IATA: **STR**, ICAO: **EDDS**) is an international airport located approximately 13 km (8.1 mi) (10 km (6.2 mi) in a straight line) south of Stuttgart city centre, Germany.

The airport lies on the boundary between the nearby town of Leinfelden-Echterdingen, Filderstadt and Stuttgart itself. It is the 7th most important airport in Germany and the main airport of the *Bundesland* Baden-Württemberg with 8,900,000 passengers in 2009.

It is an important hub for the German low cost carriers Germanwings and TUIfly; and global headquarters for car parking company APCOA Parking.

In 2007 Stuttgart Trade Fair - the ninth biggest exhibition centre in Germany moved to grounds directly next to the airport, raising the profile of the airport and strengthening calls for a second runway.

History

The airport was built in 1939 to replace Böblingen airport. In 1945 the US Air Force took over the airport and the US Army still maintains a helicopter base on the southern side of the airport which it shares with the Baden-Württemberg State Police helicopter wing. The police helicopter wing falls under the control of Stuttgart Police Department and has six modern helicopters based at Stuttgart and two in Söllingen. In 1948 the airport was returned to German authorities.

The airport was expanded after World War II. The runway was extended to 1,800 metres in 1948, then to 2,250 metres in 1961 and finally to 3,345 metres in 1996.

The original 1938 terminal was finally replaced in 2004 and there are now four terminals with a maximum capacity of approximately 12 million passengers.

Expansion

Politicians, town planners and nearby residents have been arguing for years about the construction of a second runway. However, on 25 June 2008 Minister-President Günther Oettinger announced that for the next 8–12 years no second runway will be built and that the restrictions for night operations stay in place.

Terminals, airlines and destinations

Airlines	Destinations	Terminal
Aegean Airlines	Athens, Thessaloniki	1
Air Berlin	Barcelona, Bari [ends 25 March], Berlin-Tegel, Catania, Düsseldorf, Florence, Hamburg, Hanover, Hurghada, Malaga, Milan-Malpensa, Naples, Palermo, Palma de Mallorca, Thessaloniki, Valencia [ends 31 October], Venice-Marco Polo **Seasonal**: Alicante, Bodrum, Dubrovnik, Heringsdorf, Ibiza, Lamezia Terme, Las Palmas de Gran Canaria [begins 7 November], Nice, Olbia, Preveza, Reykjavik-Keflavik, Rijeka, Rimini, Tenerife-South [begins 6 November], Westerland/Sylt	3
Air France	Paris-Charles de Gaulle	3
Air France operated by Régional	Lyon	3
Air Malta	Malta	1
Air Via	Burgas **Seasonal**: Varna	4
Austrian Airlines	Vienna	1
Austrian Airlines operated by Tyrolean Airways	Graz, Vienna	1
Belle Air	Tirana	4
Blue Air	Bucharest-Băneasa, Sibiu	3
British Airways	London-Heathrow	1
Bulgarian Air Charter	Burgas **Seasonal**: Varna	4
Carpatair	Timişoara	3
Cirrus Airlines	Münster/Osnabrück	1

Condor	Fuerteventura, Funchal, Hurghada, Lanzarote, Larnaca, Las Palmas de Gran Canaria, Marsa Alam, Santa Cruz de la Palma, Sharm el-Sheikh, Tenerife-South **Seasonal**: Antalya, Burgas, Chania, Dalaman, Djerba, Heraklion, Ibiza, Jerez de la Frontera, Kos, Palma de Mallorca, Rhodes, Santorini	3
Corendon Airlines	Antalya	4
Czech Airlines	Prague	3
Delta Air Lines	Atlanta	3
Eurocypria Airlines	Larnaca	4
Finnair operated by Finncomm Airlines	Helsinki	1
Flybe	Birmingham	3
Freebird Airlines	Antalya	4
Germania	Hatay, Pristina	4
Germanwings	Barcelona, Bari [begins 27 March], Belgrade, Berlin-Schönefeld, Bucharest-Băneasa, Budapest, Cagliari [begins 14 April], Corfu [seasonal], Dresden, Hamburg [ends 30 October], Hanover, Heraklion [ends 30 October], Leipzig/Halle, Madrid [ends 25 March], Malaga, Pristina, Rome-Fiumicino, Rostock/Laage, Split, Thessaloniki, Vienna, Zagreb **Seasonal**: Ankara, Antalya, Athens, Bastia, Faro, Ibiza, Istanbul-Sabiha Gökçen, Izmir, Kavala, Kraków, Lamezia Terme, Lisbon, Palma de Mallorca, Reykjavik-Keflavik, Zadar	2
Germanwings	London-Stansted, Moscow-Vnukovo, Sarajevo [seasonal]	1
Hamburg International	Adana, Ankara, Antalya, Bodrum, Elazig, Gaziantep, Hatay, Samsun, Trabzon	3
Jat Airways	Belgrade	3
KLM	Amsterdam	3
Koral Blue	**Seasonal**: Hurghada	4
KLM operated by KLM Cityhopper	Amsterdam	3
Lufthansa	Berlin-Tegel, Frankfurt, Hamburg	1
Lufthansa Regional operated by Augsburg Airways	Munich	1
Lufthansa Regional operated by Contact Air	Athens, Bilbao, Bremen, Hamburg, Milan-Malpensa	1

Lufthansa Regional operated by Eurowings	Düsseldorf, Frankfurt	1
Lufthansa Regional operated by Lufthansa CityLine	Brussels, Düsseldorf, Frankfurt, London-Heathrow, Manchester, Munich	1
Onur Air	Antalya	4
Malév Hungarian Airlines	Budapest	1
Nouvelair	Monastir	4
Pegasus Airlines	Ankara, Istanbul-Sabiha Gökçen, Kayseri	4
Pegasus operated by IZair	Izmir	4
Qatar Airways	Doha [begins 9 March]	1
Scandinavian Airlines	Copenhagen	1
Scandinavian Airlines operated by Cimber Sterling	Copenhagen	1
Sky Airlines	Antalya	4
SunExpress	Antalya, Izmir, Istanbul-Sabiha Gökçen	4
Swiss International Air Lines operated by Swiss European Air Lines	Zürich	1
Swiss operated by Contact Air	Zürich	1
Tailwind Airlines	Antalya, Istanbul-Sabiha Gökçen	3
TUIfly	Fuerteventura, Hurghada, Lanzarote, Las Palmas de Gran Canaria, Palma de Mallorca, Sharm el-Sheikh, Tenerife-South **Seasonal**: Antalya, Araxos/Patras, Corfu, Dalaman, Faro, Funchal, Heraklion, Jerez de la Frontera, Kos, Minorca, Rhodes	3
Tunisair	Djerba, Monastir	3
Turkish Airlines	Istanbul-Atatürk	1
XL Airways Germany	Antalya, Pristina	3

Statistics

Passengers and Operations

	Passengers	Operations
1999	7,688,951	119,904
2000	8,141,020	150,451
2001	7,642,409	146,771
2002	7,284,319	144,208
2003	7,595,286	144,903
2004	8,831,216	156,885
2005	9,413,671	160,405
2006	10,111,346	164,735
2007	10,328,120	164,531
2008	9,932,887	160,243
2009	8,941,990	141,572

Busiest Routes out of Stuttgart Airport (2009) (percentage of total passengers)

Rank	Airport	%
1	Berlin Airports (Schönefeld Airport and Tegel Airport)	10,9%
2	Hamburg Airport	8,8%
3	Palma de Mallorca Airport	6,1%
4	London Airports (Heathrow Airport and Stansted Airport)	4,2%
5	Istanbul Airports (Atatürk Airport and Sabiha Gökçen Airport)	4,1%
5	Antalya Airport	4,1%
7	Vienna Airport	3,3%
8	Paris-Charles de Gaulle Airport	2,6%
8	Düsseldorf Airport	2,6%
10	Frankfurt Airport	2,5%
10	Thessaloniki Airport	2,5%
12	Zurich International Airport	2,3%
13	Hanover Airport	2,1%

14	Amsterdam International Airport	1,9%
15	Munich Airport	1,5%
15	Barcelona International Airport	1,5%
15	Hurghada Airport	1,5%
18	Budapest Airport	1,4%
18	Atlanta International Airport	1,4%
18	Dresden Airport	1,4%
21	Las Palmas Airport	1,1%
21	Leipzig Halle Airport	1,1%
23	Tenerife South Airport	1,0%
24	Pristina Airport	0,9%
24	Izmir Airport	0,9%
24	Heraklion Airport	0,9%
24	Fuerteventura Airport	0,9%
24	Rome Fiumicino Airport	0,9%
24	Copenhagen Airport	0,9%

Wide-body aircraft in Stuttgart

Airberlin has a daily service to Palma de Mallorca flown with A330-200 or -300. Condor serves some destinations in Turkey with Boeing 767-300 during the summer season. Delta Air Lines serves its flights with Boeing 767-300. Turkish Airlines serves some flights between Stuttgart and Istanbul-Atatürk with A330/A340. Mainly because of the holiday season or during the Hajj.

Public transportation and access

Stuttgart Airport can be easily reached within 30 minutes from the city's central railway station using the Stuttgart suburban railway S2 or S3. The airport lies right next to the Autobahn A8 that connects the cities of Karlsruhe, Stuttgart and Munich.

The motorway leading to the Airport

A large car park belonging to Stuttgart Messe spans the A8 Autobahn leading to the airport.

interior

Accidents and incidents

- On 19 January 2010, BinAir Swearingen SA-227-C Metro D-CKPP was damaged when the right main undercarriage collapsed on landing.

See also

- United States Air Forces in Europe
- United States Air Force In Germany

Gallery

Airport Interior

Terminal

External links

- Media related to Stuttgart Airport at Wikimedia Commons
- Stuttgart Airport Homepage [2]
- Webcam at Stuttgart [3]

Stuttgarter Straßenbahnen AG

Stuttgarter Straßenbahnen AG (SSB) is the principal public transport operating company in the German city of Stuttgart. The SSB operates light rail lines, bus lines, a rack railway, and a funicular railway.

Colour

Since the coat of arms of Stuttgart shows a *black*, rampant horse on a *yellow* or golden field, the Stuttgart Stadtbahn as well as all the buses come in yellow with black window frames.

Light rail system

Main article: Stuttgart Stadtbahn

The Stadtbahn or (light rail system) covers 17 lines. The system is operated with 164 cars, operates on standard gauge track, and is electrified at 750 volts DC.

Tram system used until December 2007

The last remaining tram line (15) ceased to operate on December, 8th, 2007 and was replaced by the Stadtbahn line U15 on the same day. The old tram system was operated by 38 cars of type GT4. Unlike the city's light rail system, the tram system operated on metre gauge track. The conversion of tram lines to light rail lines was thus a complex procedure, and necessitates mixed gauge track where both systems operated over the same track.

There are also two heritage tram lines, which are operated on the second Sunday of each month and on the last Saturday of each month by the Stuttgarter Historische Straßenbahnen society.

Bus system

The bus network of the SSB covers Stuttgart and many neighbouring cities, with 54 different routes. Bus routes are operated by both SSB itself, and by other operators under contract to SSB.

SSB's own bus fleet consists of approximately 250 vehicles, of which about 160 are articulated buses. The buses are predominantly of Mercedes Benz manufacture, although there are 36 made by MAN in the years 2001 and 2002. The bus fleet is operated from depots and yards at Gaisburg, Möhringen, Sielmingen, and Zuffenhausen.

Other modes

Besides the light rail, tram and bus networks, the SSB operates two more unusual forms of transport:

- The Stuttgart Rack Railway connects the urban districts of Stuttgart South (Marienplatz) and Degerloch (Albplatz). This line operates as SSB route 10, and connects light rail lines U1 and U14 at Marienplatz with lines U5, U6 and U8 at Albplatz.
- The Standseilbahn Stuttgart, a funicular railway, links Südheimer Platz with the Degerloch forest cemetery. This line, which operates as SSB route 20, connects with light rail lines U1 and U14 at Südheimer Platz.

Fares and ticketing

The SSB is part of the regional transport cooperative, the Verkehrs- und Tarifverbund Stuttgart (VVS), which coordinates tickets and fares among all transport operators in the metropolitan area. Besides the SSB's Stadtbahn, tram and bus networks, this coordination includes the Stuttgart S-Bahn, operated by a subsidiary of Deutsche Bahn AG (DBAG), and DBAG's RegionalBahn regional train services within the VVS area.

External links

- Official web site of the SSB [1]

Geographical coordinates: 48°43′26″N 9°07′48″E

Stuttgart Stadtbahn

The **Stuttgart Stadtbahn** is a light rail system in Stuttgart, Germany. It is operated by the Stuttgarter Straßenbahnen AG (SSB), which also operates the bus systems in that city. The system covers much of Stuttgart and also reaches the neighbouring towns of Fellbach, Gerlingen, Leinfelden-Echterdingen, Ostfildern and Remseck am Neckar.

Stuttgart Rathaus Stadtbahn underground station

A sign at a light rail stop in Stuttgart which includes information advising passengers whether services will be formed of single or double / twin light rail vehicles.

Lines

Line	Route
U1	Fellbach – S.-Bad Cannstatt – S.-Charlottenplatz – S.-Heslach – S.-Vaihingen
	S.-Neugereut – S.-Bad Cannstatt – S.-Charlottenplatz – S.-Hölderlinplatz
	S.-Plieningen – S.-Möhringen – S.-Vaihingen
	S.-Untertürkheim – S.-Ostendplatz – S.-Charlottenplatz – S.-Vogelsang – S.-Botnang
U5	S.-Mönchfeld – S.-Zuffenhausen – S.-Hauptbahnhof – S.-Degerloch – S.-Möhringen – Leinfelden
	Gerlingen – S.-Weilimdorf – S.-Feuerbach – S.-Hauptbahnhof – S.-Degerloch – S.-Möhringen
U7	S.-Höhenpark Killesberg – S.-Hauptbahnhof – S.-Ruhbank – S.-Heumaden – Ostfildern-Nellingen
	S.-Vaihingen – S.-Möhringen – S.-Degerloch – Ostfildern-Nellingen
U9	S.-Hedelfingen – S.-Raitelsberg – S.-Hauptbahnhof – S.-Vogelsang
	S.-Hauptbahnhof – S.-Cannstatter Wasen / Gottlieb-Daimler-Stadion / Hanns-Martin-Schleyer-Halle only during the Volksfest, sporting events and music concerts
	S.-Giebel – S.-Feuerbach - S.-Pfostenwäldle – S.-Pragsattel – S.-Bad Cannstatt – S.-Hedelfingen
U14	Remseck-Neckargröningen – S-Münster – S-Hauptbahnhof – S-Rotebühlplatz – S-Heslach
	S.-Mönchfeld - S.-Zuffenhausen – S.-Nordbahnhof – S.-Hauptbahnhof – S.-Eugensplatz – S.-Ruhbank - S.-Heumaden Extension from Zuffenhausen to Stammheim under construction, will be put into operation on December 12, 2010 (estimated).
	S.-Feuerbach - S.-Pfostenwäldle – S.-Pragsattel – S.-Gottlieb-Daimler-Stadion only during sporting events, operation ceased in August 2006
	S.-Degerloch Albstraße – S.-Hauptbahnhof – S.-Höhenpark Killesberg
	S.-Vaihingen – S.-Möhringen – S.-Waldau only during sporting events
	S.-Neugereut – S.-Bad Cannstatt – S.-Daimler-Stadion only during sporting events, since August 2006

History

Stuttgart Stadtbahn, now all standard gauge (1435 mm), has been developed out of a traditional tramway system, which in Stuttgart had metre gauge. In 1961 the city council of Stuttgart decided a general modernization of the municipal tram system; in central areas, the tram should be led underground, in peripheral areas it should get new tracks, separate from road traffic. Intercurrent ideas for a totally new subway were rejected in 1976. At the same time it was decided to enhance modernization of the existing tram in combination with a change from metre gauge to standard gauge. For this reason, Stuttgart made the intermediate effort of rebuilding almost all its tracks with mixed-gauge, on which old streetcars (SSB GT4, built 1959–1965) could run as well as new metro cars

(SSB DT 8, in regular service since 1985).

Current regular operation

The Stadtbahn system runs over 192 km of lines. In the city centre as well as in other densely built-up districts of the city, the Stadtbahn runs underground. The Stadtbahn uses the "U" logo like the underground systems *(U-Bahnen)* in other German cities. However, here the "U" does not stand for *untergrund* (underground) but for *unabhängig* (independent, meaning independent of other traffic infrastructure). Outside the densely built up areas, the Stadtbahn runs on the surface, often along roads with level crossings, though on a separate right-of-way. In a few places, Stadtbahn trains run on street sharing space with other traffic.

The system is operated with 164 cars, operates on standard gauge track, and is electrified at 750 volts DC. On December, 8th, 2007 the ongoing replacement of the city's tram lines was finally completed after 27 years.

The Stuttgart Stadtbahn operates from 04:45 - 01:15, with trains every 10 minutes on all lines during daytime service, and every 15–20 minutes after 20:00 as well as before 12:00 on weekends. Most routes are served by two or more lines in the city centre, so there is a train every few minutes at most stations.

Fares and ticketing

The Stadtbahn is part of the regional transport cooperative, the Verkehrs- und Tarifverbund Stuttgart (VVS), which coordinates tickets and fares among all transport operators in the metropolitan area. Besides the Stadtbahn, these include the SSB's bus networks, together with the Stuttgart S-Bahn, operated by a subsidiary of Deutsche Bahn AG (DBAG), and DBAG's RegionalBahn regional train services within the VVS area.

Colour

Since the coat of arms of Stuttgart shows a *black*, rampant horse on a *yellow* or golden field, the Stuttgart Stadtbahn (as well as all the buses and the last old trams) comes in yellow with black window frames.

External links

- Official web site of the SSB [1]
- Stadtbahn map (pdf) [1]
- Stuttgart Stadtbahn from UrbanRail.Net [2]

Stuttgart Hauptbahnhof

Stuttgart Hauptbahnhof	

Stuttgart Hauptbahnhof (2004)	
Operations	
Category	Long-distance railway hub (*Fernverkehrsknoten*)
Type	Terminal station
Station tracks	17 (1a and 1 to 16)
Passengers	220.000
Daily train services	590
Abbreviation	TS
Construction and location	
Opened	1922
Architect	Paul Bonatz und Friedrich Eugen Scholer
City/town	Stuttgart
Federal state	Baden-Württemberg
Country	Germany
Coordinates: DE-BW	48°47′02″N 9°10′54″E
Route information	
see below	
List of railway stations in Baden-Württemberg	

Stuttgart Hauptbahnhof (usually translated from German as *Stuttgart Central Station*, short form: **Stuttgart Hbf**) is the Hauptbahnhof of the city of Stuttgart, the capital of the Land (state) of Baden-Württemberg, in southwestern Germany. It is the largest regional and long-distance railway station in Stuttgart, the main node of the Stuttgart S-Bahn network, and, together with the halt at

Charlottenplatz, the main node of the Stuttgart Stadtbahn.

Located at the northeastern end of the *Königstraße*, the main pedestrian zone of the city centre, the main line station is a terminus, whilst the subterranean S-Bahn and Stadtbahn stations are through stations. The station is well known for its 12-storey tower with a large, rotating and illuminated Mercedes-Benz star insignia on top; the tower and station building are city landmarks.

Plans for the controversial Stuttgart 21 project to convert the main line terminus station into an underground through station include the demolition of the side wings of the building, together with the elimination of the platforms, tracks, and apron of the terminus station. The planned underground through station is configured at a 90 degree angle to the present station. Construction is scheduled from 2010 to 2019.

An alternative plan, called *Kopfbahnhof 21*, envisions keeping and extensively modernizing the existing terminus station. This plan has the support of architecture experts, who name the present structure as a unique example of the architecture of the 1920s. They particularly criticize the demolition plans of the side wings of the building, since this would drastically alter the character of the building as a whole.

On November 25, 2009, UNESCO preservationists nominated the building for inclusion in their World Cultural Heritage list, urging the city and Deutsche Bahn authorities to stop the *Stuttgart 21* plans to demolish parts of the complex designed by Paul Bonatz.[1]

History

First and second Centralbahnhof

The Centralbahnhof in 1900

Until 1922, the central station was located on the Schlosstrasse (the precise location of the former station is on what is today called the Bolzstrasse), near the Schlossplatz. The first station building, a terminus station with 4 tracks, was built by Karl Etzel for the opening of the Zentralbahn (Württemberg), with its two branches to Ludwigsburg and Esslingen. The building was not remarkable at the time, with the station hall, made of wood, covering the four tracks. On 26 September 1846, the first train, arriving from Canstatt, visited the station. By 1854, the first phase of railway construction in the Kingdom of Württemberg, with routes to Heilbronn, Bretten, Ulm, and Friedrichshafen, was completed.

The former Centralbahnhof building in 2004

Due to increasing railway traffic, the first building was replaced by new construction in the same spot in the 1860s. Between 1863 and 1867, the engineers Klein, Morlok, and Abel created this second station, with 8 tracks, featuring a building with grandiose arches in the Renaissance-style. By 1900, this station had already proven to be too small again. Parts of the facade of this building are today part of an event center and cinema, the *Metropol.*

The Hauptbahnhof of today

The station tower of the Hauptbahnhof in 2004

The present Hauptbahnhof was built between 1914 and 1928, only about 500 meters east of the former station, on the Arnulf-Klett-Platz.

In 1910, the Royal Württemberg State Railways (*Königlich Württembergischen Staats-Eisenbahnen* or *K.W.St.E.*) underwrote an architecural contest, which saw 70 participants. The competition was won by the architects Paul Bonatz and Friedrich Eugen Scholer with their plans for *umbilicus sueviae* - the Navel of Swabia. After undergoing numerous changes, including moving the station tower from the main facade to the wing at the Schlossgarten, construction began in 1914 on the Cannstatter Strasse. Due to the track routing to the old station, construction needed to be done in two phases, with the first phase going into service on 22 October 1922, and the second part being completed in 1928.

In addition to its great architectural quality, the new building was well incorporated into the other structures in the city center. The massive building deals with the steep terrain almost unnoticeably - there are nearly 5 meters from highest to lowest elevation between the tower and the so-called north exit. Bonatz put the tower directly on the axis of the Königstrasse as an optical point of aim, and another axis along the tower and the wing on the Schlossgarten continues on to the Neckar valley. The original plans called for a road leading directly to the building, but Bonatz eliminated this in favor of the Lautenschlagerstraße, as it is known today, which meets the *Kleine Schalterhalle* (small counter hall). Behind this hall are the tracks for the local commuter traffic, and in between this hall and the main building is the central exit, which is beneficial for the control of traffic flow. Underneath the tracks area, three tunnel at right angles to the tracks provide highly functional access points: The mail tunnel runs from the post office annex to the northwestern station area, a personnel tunnel eases the task of changing tracks, and a third tunnel is meant for the transit of express freight.

The construction has some highly regarded features. The facade is made of lime stone, which was covered with bricks; on the inside, sandstone, tuff, and bricks form the walls. The roof structures are partially flat wood roofing, and partially constructed as reinforced concrete roofing. The use of exposed concrete on the pillars lends a modern flair to the main hall. The structure features conservative elements, shown in the monumentality and reserved decorations, as well as progressive elements, as shown by the flat roof structures, for example. The building is one of the most important architectural achievements in southern Germany.

On 15 May 1933, the electrification of all 17 tracks was completed. During World War II, the building was severely damaged on several occasions, even though the fake structure built to look like the Hauptbahnhof near Lauffen am Neckar successfully prevented further destruction. Reconstruction took several years after the end of the war. On 20 August 1987, the building was given the designation of a cultural monument of special significance.

The Hauptbahnhof under threat

As part of the famous Stuttgart 21 project, the two wings are expected to be demolished anytime soon.Wikipedia:Manual_of_Style_(dates_and_numbers)#Chronological_itemsWikipedia:Cleanup Widespread resentment of the entire project to bring the train station underground is expressed by increasing mobilization of the Stuttgart citizenry. In particular the felling of some 260 huge and old trees has nurtured a resistance hitherto unknown in Stuttgart politics. More than 18,000 people have registered as *Parkschützer* (Park Guardians); about a thousand have vowed to stay in the path of demolition crews while chaining themselves to the trees. The colourful resistance has led to nearly daily demonstrations and has raised the spectre of a political landslide during the forthcoming provincial elections.

S-Bahn, Stadtbahn and Stuttgart 21

Between 1971 and 1978, a tunnel was dug under the Hauptbahnhof for the Verbindungsbahn of the S-Bahn network of the middle Neckar area, and an underground station was constructed. This station features two tracks, with the platform in the middle, and was put into service on 1 October 1978.

The underground station for the U-Bahn and Strassenbahn, called *Hauptbahnhof (Arnulf-Klett-Platz)*, went into operation on 9 April 1976. Today, there are seven lines of the Stadtbahn which use this station. The last remaining Strassenbahn line, number 15, was converted to the Stadtbahn service on 9 December 2007. The lower Strassenbahn platform is no longer used for regular service, but may sometimes see special or nostalgia trains.

The connected freight station, which featured a marshaling hump and rail brakes, was closed, due to both the reduction in freight traffic, and in preparation for the Stuttgart 21 project. Construction on the new underground station as part of Stuttgart 21 was originally to be started in 2005 and completed in 2012; the revised schedule now envisions a start in 2010, and completion, including the new Wendlingen–Ulm high-speed railway, in 2019, at a total cost of 4.8 billion Euros.

Building/structure details

The station building was constructed using reinforced concrete, which was then covered with roughly hewn shell limestone ashlar, sourced from the area around Crailsheim. The station tower is 56 meters high, with a rotating Mercedes-Benz star, measuring 5 meters in radius, on the visitor's terrace on the 9th level, right above the *Bistro21*. Also on the tower is a clock, whose radius measures 5.5 meters. Inside the tower is the *TurmForum Stuttgart 21*, which provides information and media to do with the Stuttgart 21 project.

The station tower of the Hauptbahnhof, seen from the middle of the Schlossgarten

The front of the building features a quote by Georg Wilhelm Friedrich Hegel in the form of a lit inscription - the quote reads *... daß diese Furcht zu irren schon der Irrtum selbst ist.* - loosely translated as "...to be fooled by this fear is foolishness itself." The inscription is a work by the artist Joseph Kosuth from the early 1990s.

The Hauptbahnhof, seen from the TV tower

Long-distance trains end their run in the above-ground terminus station at one of 17 tracks (1-16 and 1a), which is located on the second floor of the main hall, with the main entrance and service counters on the ground floor. Also in the main hall, near the south exit, a DB Lounge for first-class passengers and members of frequent-traveller programs, such as bahn.comfort, AIRail, or Miles & More, may be found. In the underground S-Bahn station, which is on the 3rd underground floor, all S-Bahn traffic, which is managed by the Verkehrs- und Tarifverbund Stuttgart (VVS), stops at one of two tracks (numbered 101 and 102).

Under the station forecourt, the seven lines of the Stadtbahn traverse the 2nd underground floor. A personnel passage on the 1st underground floor, which features many stores and boutiques, serves as the pedestrian connection between the Hauptbahnhof and the city center. A part of this 1st underground floor is taken up by an underground parking garage, and a multi-use shelter. In case of a civil emergency, a section of the garage would turn into a shelter with beds, separated from the rest of the garage by pressurized doors; the control room, kitchen, sanitation equipment, and water-and air conditioning for the shelter are located in the 2nd underground floor.

As part of the Stuttgart 21 project, both wings of the Bonatz-designed main building, as well as the track apron, are to be demolished, starting at the end of 2009, notwithstanding the status of the structure as a cultural monument. The Stuttgart architect and Bonatz expert Matthias Roser initiated an international call for the preservation of the Hauptbahnhof, including the wings, and over 400 architects, building historians, monument conservators, art historians, and city planners, such as the Pritzger Prize recipient Richard Meier or David Chipperfield, have joined this effort. This groups views the Bonatz-designed building as one of the most significant railway station structures of the 20th century in Germany and Europe as a whole, and are opposed to any structural changes.

Operations

Routes

The Hauptbahnhof is a traffic node for these routes:

- Mannheim–Stuttgart high-speed railway to Mannheim
- Württemberg Western Railway (*Westbahn*) to Mühlacker – Karlsruhe/Heidelberg
- Franconia Railway (*Frankenbahn*) to Bietigheim-Bissingen – Heilbronn – Würzburg
- Black Forest Railway (*Schwarzwaldbahn*) to Leonberg – Weil der Stadt [– Calw]
- Murr Railway (*Murrbahn*) to direction of Backnang – Nürnberg
- Rems Railway (*Remsbahn*) to Schorndorf – Aalen
- Fils Valley Railway (*Filstalbahn*) to Plochingen – Göppingen – Ulm
- Neckar-Alb railway (*Neckar-Alb-Bahn*) to Plochingen – Tübingen
- Gäubahn to Herrenberg – Rottweil/Freudenstadt - Singen

Long-distance connections

The most significant long-distance connections available at the Stuttgart Hauptbahnhof are listed here:

Connection	Route	Frequency
ICE *11*	Berlin – Frankfurt (Main) – **Stuttgart** – Munich– (Innsbruck)	every 2 hours
ICE *22*	Kiel/Hamburg – Hannover – Göttingen – Kassel – Fulda – Frankfurt (Main) Hbf – Frankfurt (Main) Flughafen – Mannheim – **Stuttgart**	every 2 hours
ICE *42*	Dortmund – Essen – Düsseldorf – Köln – Siegburg/Bonn – Frankfurt (Main) Flughafen – Mannheim – **Stuttgart** – Ulm – Augsburg – Munich	every 2 hours
83	Paris – Straßburg – Karlsruhe – **Stuttgart**	4 trains
ICE *87*	(Frankfurt (Main)) – **Stuttgart** – Horb – Rottweil – Tuttlingen – Singen (Htw.) – Schaffhausen – Bülach – Zurich	every 2 hours
IC *30*	Westerland (Sylt)/Ostseebad Binz – Hamburg – Bremen – Münster (Westf.) – Dortmund – Essen – Köln – Bonn – Koblenz – Mainz – Mannheim – Heidelberg – Vaihingen (Enz) – **Stuttgart**	every 2 hours
IC *32*	Berlin – Hannover – Bielefeld – Dortmund – Köln – Koblenz – Mainz – Mannheim – Heidelberg – Vaihingen (Enz) – **Stuttgart** – Ulm – Friedrichshafen – Lindau – Bregenz – Innsbruck	1 train
IC *35*	Norddeich – Emden – Münster (Westf.) – Duisburg – Köln – Bonn – Koblenz – Mainz – Mannheim – Heidelberg – **Stuttgart**	1 train
IC *55*	Leipzig – Magdeburg – Braunschweig – Hannover – Dortmund – Köln – Bonn – Koblenz – Mainz – Mannheim – Heidelberg – **Stuttgart** – Göppingen – Ulm – Memmingen – Kempten – Oberstdorf	1 train
IC *60*	Karlsruhe – **Stuttgart** – Göppingen – Ulm – Günzburg – Augsburg – Munich	every 2 hours
IC *61*	Karlsruhe – Pforzheim – **Stuttgart** – Aalen – Crailsheim – Ansbach – Nürnberg	every 2 hours
IC *62*	Saarbrücken/Frankfurt (Main) – Heidelberg – **Stuttgart** – Ulm – Günzburg – Augsburg – Munich– Rosenheim – Salzburg – Klagenfurt/Graz/Linz	every 2 hours

Preceding station	DB AG	Following station

Regional connections

	Route	Frequency
R1	**Stuttgart** - Plochingen - Göppingen - Geißlingen (Steige) - Ulm - Biberach - Friedrichshafen - Lindau	every 2 hours
R5	**Stuttgart** - Vaihingen (Enz) - Mühlacker - Pforzheim - Karlsruhe	every 2 hours (plus additional trains Stuttgart - Vaihingen)
R8	**Stuttgart** - Reutlingen - Tübingen - Hechingen - Albstadt - Sigmaringen - Aulendorf	every 2 hours (occasional splitting of trains in Tübingen to Horb)
R1	**Stuttgart** - Esslingen (N) - Plochingen - Göppingen - Geislingen (Steige) - Ulm	every hour
R2	**Stuttgart** - Waiblingen - Schorndorf - Schwäbisch Gmünd - Aalen	every hour (from noon until evening every 30 minutes)
R3	**Stuttgart** - Waiblingen - Backnang - Schwäbisch Hall-Hessental - Crailsheim - Ansbach - Nürnberg	every 2 hours (Mon-Fri between Stuttgart and Schwäb. Hall every hour, at rush hour every 30 minutes, Sat and Sun Stuttgart-Schwäb. Hall requires change of trains in Backnang)
R4	**Stuttgart** - Ludwigsburg - Bietigheim-Bissingen - Heilbronn - Bad Friedrichshall - Osterburken - Würzburg	every 2 hours
R5	**Stuttgart** - Ludwigsburg - Bietigheim-Bissingen - Vaihingen (Enz) - Mühlacker - Pforzheim - Karlsruhe	every 2 hours
R5	**Stuttgart** - Ludwigsburg - Bietigheim-Bissingen - Vaihingen (Enz) - Mühlacker - Bretten - Bruchsal - Heidelberg	every 2 hours
R7	**Stuttgart** - Böblingen - Herrenberg - Eutingen im Gäu - Horb - Rottweil - Tuttlingen - Singen (Hohentwiehl)	every 2 hours
R7	**Stuttgart** - Böblingen - Herrenberg - Eutingen im Gäu - Horb - Rottweil	every 2 hours (shares train between Stuttgart and Eutingen with RegionalExpress train Stuttgart–Freudenstadt)
R7	**Stuttgart** - Böblingen - Herrenberg - Eutingen im Gäu - Freudenstadt	every 2 hours (shares train between Stuttgart and Eutingen with RegionalExpress train Stuttgart–Rottweil)
R8	**Stuttgart** - Esslingen (N) - Plochingen - Nürtingen - Metzingen - Reutlingen - Tübingen	every hour (from noon until evening every 30 minutes)
R1	**Stuttgart** - Esslingen - Plochingen - Göppingen - Geislingen (Steige)	every 2 hours
R1	**Stuttgart** - Ludwigsburg - Bietigheim-Bissingen - Heilbronn - Bad Friedrichshall - Mosbach-Neckarelz	every hour (between Stuttgart and Heilbronn every 30 minutes)

In most cases, these connection start or end in Stuttgart. This means that for most connections that go through Stuttgart Hauptbahnhof, a change of trains is necessary. As part of the Stuttgart 21 project, with Stuttgart Hbf becoming a through-station, most regional connections would no longer require the change of trains.

A frequent topic of discussion is the reactivation of the section Weil der Stadt – Calw on the Schwarzwaldbahn (Württemberg), which would mean the addition of a Regionalbahn or Regional-Express train with the route Stuttgart – Leonberg – Weil der Stadt – Calw.

S-Bahn connections

Line No.	Route
	Kirchheim unter Teck - Plochingen – Esslingen – Neckarpark – Bad Cannstatt – Hauptbahnhof – Schwabstraße – Vaihingen – Rohr – Böblingen – Herrenberg (additional trains on work days between Esslingen and Schwabstraße or Böblingen.)
	Schorndorf – Weinstadt – Waiblingen – Bad Cannstatt – Hauptbahnhof – Schwabstraße – Vaihingen – Rohr – Flughafen/Messe – Filderstadt (additional trains on work days between Schorndorf and Vaihingen.)
	Backnang – Winnenden – Waiblingen – Bad Cannstatt – Hauptbahnhof – Vaihingen – Rohr – Flughafen/Messe (due to the opening of the new exhibition center, trains run to the airport on weekends; late evening traffic only goes to Vaihingen; additional trains on work days between Backnang and Vaihingen).
	Schwabstraße – Hauptbahnhof – Zuffenhausen – Ludwigsburg – Marbach
	Schwabstraße – Hauptbahnhof – Zuffenhausen – Ludwigsburg – Bietigheim
	Schwabstraße – Hauptbahnhof – Zuffenhausen – Leonberg – Weil der Stadt

The abbreviation for the Hauptbahnhof S-Bahn station underground is *TST*.

Freight traffic

In addition to the passenger station, there used to be a closed and already demolished freight station and small shunting station, which featured a marshaling hump with rail brakes.

The station from the inside in 2004

Stadtbahn

Under the Arnulf-Klett-Platz (the station forecourt), the largest and most important node of the Stadtbahn features these routes:

A view of the tracks from the tower in 2005

The station as viewed from the west
(bottom center)

Line No.	Route
U5	Mönchfeld – Zuffenhausen – Hauptbahnhof – Degerloch – Möhringen – Leinfelden Every other train ends in Möhringen Bahnhof, or Mon to Fri between 8:30 and 15:30 at the halt Degerloch Albstraße.
	Gerlingen – Weilimdorf – Feuerbach – Hauptbahnhof – Degerloch – Möhringen (– Vaihingen)
U7	Killesberg – Hauptbahnhof – Ruhbank/Fernsehturm – Heumaden – Ostfildern-Nellingen
U9	Hedelfingen – Raitelsberg – Hauptbahnhof – Vogelsang (– Botnang) During summer break and outside of rush hours only between Hedelfingen and Vogelsang.
U14	Remseck-Neckargröningen – Münster – Hauptbahnhof – Rotebühlplatz – Heslach Vogelrain
	(Mönchfeld –) Zuffenhausen – Nordbahnhof – Hauptbahnhof – Eugensplatz – Ruhbank/Fernsehturm (– Heumaden)

In addition, in case of events at the NeckarPark and Cannstatter Wasen

Line No.	Route
	Hauptbahnhof – Rotebühlplatz – Mineralbäder – Cannstatter Wasen – Neckarpark (Stadion)

Noteworthy

The Hauptbahnhof has been assigned the IATA code *ZWS*, because the station is used by Lufthansa in the AIRail concept. Passengers may travel in ICE trains, which are also assigned flight numbers, to Frankfurt Airport in Frankfurt am Main, instead of using a short-distance flight. For this reason, Lufthansa has a check-in counter near the entrance from the Arnulf-Klett-Platz. Passengers were able to both check and receive their baggage at this counter until 2007; since then, only check-in is possible.

See also

- History of the railway in Württemberg

Literature

- Matthias Roser: Der Stuttgarter Hauptbahnhof - Vom Kulturdenkmal zum Abrisskandidaten ? 1. Auflage, 2008, Schmetterling Verlag, Stuttgart, 151 Seiten, ISBN 3-89657-133-8
- Matthias Roser: *Der Stuttgarter Hauptbahnhof – ein vergessenes Meisterwerk der Architektur.* 1. Auflage, 1987, Silberburg-Verlag Stuttgart, 60 Seiten, ISBN 3-925344-13-6
- Kurt Seidel: *65 Jahre Stuttgarter Hauptbahnhof 1922 bis 1987.* Herausgegeben von der Bundesbahndirektion Stuttgart, 1987, 160 Seiten
- Egon Hopfenzitz und Klaus Fischer: *Chronik Stuttgarter Hauptbahnhof 1846 bis 1998.* Herausgegeben von der DB Station&Service AG, Stuttgart, 1999, 381 Seiten
- Werner Willhaus (Herausgeber): *Verkehrsknoten Stuttgart.* EK-Verlag, Freiburg 2006, ISBN 978-3-88255-251-5

References

This article incorporates information from the equivalent article on the German Wikipedia.

Geographical coordinates: 48°47′02″N 9°10′54″E

Stuttgart Rack Railway

Rack Railway at Haigst

The **Stuttgart Rack Railway** (German: *Zahnradbahn*) is an electric rack railway in Stuttgart, Germany. It is the only urban rack railway in Germany.

Affectionately called *Zacke* (*spike*) by the residents of Stuttgart, the line was opened on 23 August 1884. It connects the urban districts of Stuttgart South (Marienplatz) and Degerloch (Albplatz). The route runs along the *Alte Weinsteige*, which was historically the main route to the *Filder* towns until the *Neue Weinsteige* was built in 1826.

Over its 2.2 km route the line climbs a height of 205 m (from 260 m to 465 m AMSL). The maximum incline on the route is 17.5% (between Liststrasse and Pfaffenweg). On the branch line to the depot of the (old) rack railway yard, the maximum incline is 20.0%. Between the stops at Pfaffenweg and Wielandshöhe there is a view of Stuttgart's city centre.

The rack railway is integrated with the metropolitan railway network of the Stuttgarter Straßenbahnen AG (SSB) as Line 10. At Marienplatz it connects with Stuttgart Stadtbahn lines U1 and U14 and at Albplatz it connects with lines U5, U6 and U8.

The line is one of two working railway lines that are tourist attractions in Stuttgart; the other being the Stuttgart funicular railway that leads to the forest cemetery, and operates as SSB line 20.

The rack railway train includes a wagon at the front or back for transporting bicycles.

History

- 23 August 1884: Opening of the Stuttgart - Degerloch rack railway, the first section of the *Filderbahn* line, as a narrow gauge (1000 mm (3 ft 3 $^{3}/_{8}$ in)) steam-operated railway with a Riggenbach system. The Filderbahn Company operated the route from Stuttgart to Degerloch station.
- 1902: Electrification of the rack railway and the adhesion routes from Degerloch to Hohenheim and from Möhringen to Vaihingen. Electrification of the rack railway line was delayed by two years due to technical problems.
- 1903: Relocation of the passing track from Haigst to Wielandshöhe.
- 1904: Electrical operation begins on the rack railway, steam operation limited to Sunday excursions.

- 1918: Two additional steam engines taken over second-hand from the Swiss *Brünigbahn* railway for steam services which had increased due to the war.
- 1920: *Filderbahn* taken over by the city of Stuttgart and its management transferred to the *Stuttgarter Straßenbahnen* (Stuttgart Tramways).
- 1921: Steam operations ended.
- 1926: All passenger coaches on the rack railway and *Filderbahn* repainted to SSB livery. However, to distinguish SSB-owned vehicles from *Filderbahn*-owned vehicles, the latter provisionally prefixed their vehicle numbers with the letter "F".
- 1934: *Filderbahn* and the rack railway transfer to the ownership of the *Stuttgarter Straßenbahnen.*
- 1935: First two railcars with 3 axles are delivered, number 101 (in service until 1982) and 102 (scrapped due to damage in 1974).
- 1936: Relocation of the rack railway's Stuttgart terminal station from the valley to Marienplatz to improve transfers to the trams.
- 1937: Motor coach 103 was the first vehicle built entirely of steel to be delivered to the SSB.
- 1950: Last two coaches of the second generation railcars delivered, number 104 (today a museum railcar) and 105 (dismantled in 1995).
- 1954: Last railcar of the first generation, number 109, is taken out of service.
- 1956: Transfer of trailer(s) from the *Filderbahn* to the rack railway to handle the increased school traffic. This was however extremely rarely done and then only up to 1965 when the practice was discontinued.
- 1965: Replacement of the old cast iron bridge (commonly called the Turkish bridge because its manufacturer, Maschinenfabrik Esslingen, originally intended to deliver the bridge to Turkey.) over the *Neue Weinsteige* by the present-day reinforced concrete bridge.
- 1971: As a result of changes to the track layout at Marienplatz and the construction of the underground station the double-tracked valley station at Marienplatz was replaced by a single-tracked station, half of which is located on the bridge across a water reservoir (later filled in).
- 1974: Railcar number 102, recently taken out of service, is paraded in the Stuttgart Shrove Tuesday procession as an attraction.
- 1977: As a result of the rebuilding of the rack railway's Degerloch station, the connecting track to the adhesion railway was lifted and the rack railway became isolated from the rest of the SSB network.
- 1978: Cessation of routine three-coach working.
- 1980: Refurbishing of the complete rack railway track for use with newly commissioned railcars of type ZT4.
- 1982: Introduction of modern ZT4 motor coaches into the metropolitan railway network. Trials on transporting bicycles on the inclined line in a demonstration wagon designed by the company.
- 1984: Centenary celebrations and last school run on the traditional rack railway route by motor coach 104 and demonstration car 120.

- 1989: Replacement of the former swinging leaf doors on the ZT4 by appropriate external swing out doors on the DT8.
- 1992: Sale of display car 117 (built 1896) to the Härtsfeld Museum Railway (HMB) in Neresheim. Hitherto it had been displayed by a private collector as a monument. The museum employs it today as narrow gauge passenger vehicle on its own line.
- 1994: Extension of the route at the top of the line to the *Albplatz* to improve the connexion to the metropolitan railway.
- 2002: Reopening of the rebuilt terminal and bridge at the entirely redesigned and modernized *Marienplatz* (6 December).
- 2004: Replacement of the track superstructure; partial laying of a new, slightly narrower rack rail.

See also

- Passenger railways

External links

- http://www.trampicturebook.de/tram/germany/stuttgar/zacke.htm

Geographical coordinates: 48°45′19″N 9°10′20″E

Standseilbahn Stuttgart

Car number 1 in the upper station

The **Standseilbahn Stuttgart** or **Stuttgart Cable Car** is a funicular railway in the city of Stuttgart, Germany. The line links the Südheimer valley station with the Stuttgart Degerloch forest cemetery in the south quarters of Heslach. Operated by Stuttgarter Straßenbahnen AG (SSB), it was opened on 30 October 1929 to facilitate visitors to the forest cemetery which is 90 metres (300 ft) above Stuttgart Heslach. At Südheimer, the funicular connects to Stuttgart Stadtbahn lines U1 and U14.

The funicular has the following technical parameters:

- Length: 536 metres (1759 ft)
- Height: 87 metres (285 ft)
- Maximum steepness: 28.3%
- Journey time: 3 minutes
- Cars: 2
- Capacity: 74 passengers per car

- Traction: Electricity
- Track Gauge: 1000 mm (3 ft 3 $^3/_8$ in)

The two cars, constructed of teak, were manufactured by Esslingen Engine Works. In December 1999, one of the cars was damaged by an uprooted tree as a result of a thunderstorm, but was afterwards restored. The line was modernised in 2004 in order to meet the new European Union safety guidelines. Since 24 July 2004, it is again running on schedule.

The line is one of two active transport tourist attractions in Stuttgart, the other being the Stuttgart Rack Railway (line 10).

The line sometimes is referred to as 'Erbschleicherexpress' which translates as legacy hunter express.

References

Specific

General

1. Hans-Joachim Knupfer: *Hoch über Heslach - Die Stuttgarter Seilbahn. 75 Jahre Technik- und Verkehrsgeschichte.* Stuttgarter Straßenbahnen AG, Stuttgart 2004, ISBN 3-00-013868-4
2. G. Bauer, U. Theurer, C. Jeanmaire: *Stuttgarter Straßenbahnen. Eine Dokumentation über die Straßenbahnlinien von 1868 - 1975.* Verlag Eisenbahn Gut Vorhard, Villigen AG 1976, ISBN 3856490264, page 232
3. Gottfried Bauer, Ulrich Theurer: *Von der Straßenbahn zur Stadtbahn Stuttgart 1975-2000. Eine Dokumentation über den Schienenverkehr der Stuttgarter Straßenbahnen AG (SSB) zwischen 1975 und 2000.* Stuttgarter Straßenbahnen AG, Stuttgart 2000, ISBN 3-00-006615-2, pages 167,204-205

External links

- http://www.trampicturebook.de/tram/germany/stuttgar/seilbahn.htm
- Description of the heslach round walk which incorporates a ride with the Standseilbahn Stuttgart [1]

This article incorporates information from the German Wikipedia.

Geographical coordinates: 48°45′21″N 9°08′32″E

Article Sources and Contributors

History of Germany *Source*: http://en.wikipedia.org/?oldid=390484629 *Contributors*: StAnselm

Geography of Germany *Source*: http://en.wikipedia.org/?oldid=390237226 *Contributors*: Happysailor

Politics of Germany *Source*: http://en.wikipedia.org/?oldid=378678790 *Contributors*: 1 anonymous edits

Economy of Germany *Source*: http://en.wikipedia.org/?oldid=390106943 *Contributors*: Wavelength

Foreign relations of Germany *Source*: http://en.wikipedia.org/?oldid=387786876 *Contributors*: John of Reading

Culture of Germany *Source*: http://en.wikipedia.org/?oldid=389310693 *Contributors*: Kantianer

Neuschwanstein Castle *Source*: http://en.wikipedia.org/?oldid=390397081 *Contributors*:

Brandenburg Gate *Source*: http://en.wikipedia.org/?oldid=389726674 *Contributors*: 1 anonymous edits

Black Forest *Source*: http://en.wikipedia.org/?oldid=384441635 *Contributors*: Ryn78

Cologne Cathedral *Source*: http://en.wikipedia.org/?oldid=389824106 *Contributors*: Amandajm

Bavarian State Archaeological Collection *Source*: http://en.wikipedia.org/?oldid=376441116 *Contributors*: Jpbowen

Stuttgart *Source*: http://en.wikipedia.org/?oldid=389792258 *Contributors*: Shortride

State Museum of Natural History Stuttgart *Source*: http://en.wikipedia.org/?oldid=364697071 *Contributors*: BredoteauU2

Württemberg Mausoleum *Source*: http://en.wikipedia.org/?oldid=382924669 *Contributors*:

Kunstmuseum Stuttgart *Source*: http://en.wikipedia.org/?oldid=377292182 *Contributors*: Aygulka

Porsche Museum, Stuttgart *Source*: http://en.wikipedia.org/?oldid=377292397 *Contributors*: Aygulka

Landesmuseum Württemberg *Source*: http://en.wikipedia.org/?oldid=389317849 *Contributors*: Nick Number

Mercedes-Benz Museum *Source*: http://en.wikipedia.org/?oldid=384457684 *Contributors*:

Linden Museum *Source*: http://en.wikipedia.org/?oldid=372034540 *Contributors*:

Staatsgalerie Stuttgart *Source*: http://en.wikipedia.org/?oldid=377495718 *Contributors*: Djfarmo

Neue Staatsgalerie *Source*: http://en.wikipedia.org/?oldid=390644960 *Contributors*: Elekhh

Stiftskirche (Stuttgart) *Source*: http://en.wikipedia.org/?oldid=372923501 *Contributors*:

Evangelical-Lutheran Church in Württemberg *Source*: http://en.wikipedia.org/?oldid=371527040 *Contributors*: Ulf Heinsohn

Blaubeuren Abbey *Source*: http://en.wikipedia.org/?oldid=289436512 *Contributors*:

Wilhelm Palais *Source*: http://en.wikipedia.org/?oldid=383288480 *Contributors*: Mertinger

Hohenheim *Source*: http://en.wikipedia.org/?oldid=385909437 *Contributors*: Neddyseagoon

Old Castle (Stuttgart) *Source*: http://en.wikipedia.org/?oldid=377292366 *Contributors*: Aygulka

New Castle (Stuttgart) *Source*: http://en.wikipedia.org/?oldid=382265227 *Contributors*: BurgererSF

Castle Solitude *Source*: http://en.wikipedia.org/?oldid=382265291 *Contributors*: BurgererSF

Rosenstein Castle *Source*: http://en.wikipedia.org/?oldid=341783741 *Contributors*: HMallison

Hegel House *Source*: http://en.wikipedia.org/?oldid=383278689 *Contributors*:

Schillerplatz (Stuttgart) *Source*: http://en.wikipedia.org/?oldid=382425061 *Contributors*: TIY

Schlossplatz, Stuttgart *Source*: http://en.wikipedia.org/?oldid=377292340 *Contributors*: Aygulka

Staatstheater Stuttgart *Source*: http://en.wikipedia.org/?oldid=255666460 *Contributors*:

Stuttgart Ballet *Source*: http://en.wikipedia.org/?oldid=375262605 *Contributors*: Mirokado

Birkenkopf *Source*: http://en.wikipedia.org/?oldid=353122443 *Contributors*: Droll

Stuttgart Observatory *Source*: http://en.wikipedia.org/?oldid=315017621 *Contributors*: Cantons-de-l'Est

Observation Tower Burgholzhof *Source*: http://en.wikipedia.org/?oldid=383292370 *Contributors*: Pjt56

Tagblatt-Turm *Source*: http://en.wikipedia.org/?oldid=353702309 *Contributors*: Histech

Fernsehturm Stuttgart *Source*: http://en.wikipedia.org/?oldid=377292059 *Contributors*: Aygulka

Cannstatter Wasen *Source*: http://en.wikipedia.org/?oldid=384493765 *Contributors*:

Cannstatter Volksfest *Source*: http://en.wikipedia.org/?oldid=390071114 *Contributors*: 1 anonymous edits

Fruit Column *Source*: http://en.wikipedia.org/?oldid=295600641 *Contributors*:

Stuttgart Spring Festival *Source*: http://en.wikipedia.org/?oldid=347999436 *Contributors*:

Stuttgart Trade Fair *Source*: http://en.wikipedia.org/?oldid=320235247 *Contributors*: Creet

Christmas Market, Stuttgart *Source*: http://en.wikipedia.org/?oldid=339328075 *Contributors*: Esowteric

Schocken Department Store, Stuttgart *Source*: http://en.wikipedia.org/?oldid=381925533 *Contributors*: LilHelpa

Killesbergpark *Source*: http://en.wikipedia.org/?oldid=352406237 *Contributors*: Pjt56

Schönbuch *Source*: http://en.wikipedia.org/?oldid=356032263 *Contributors*: 1 anonymous edits

Landesarboretum Baden-Württemberg *Source*: http://en.wikipedia.org/?oldid=317915961 *Contributors*: Daderot

Botanischer Garten der Universität Hohenheim *Source*: http://en.wikipedia.org/?oldid=348521560 *Contributors*: Deor

Wilhelma *Source*: http://en.wikipedia.org/?oldid=387790959 *Contributors*: 1 anonymous edits

VfB Stuttgart *Source*: http://en.wikipedia.org/?oldid=390582854 *Contributors*: Yoda1893

Stuttgarter Kickers *Source*: http://en.wikipedia.org/?oldid=387659032 *Contributors*:

Stuttgart Scorpions *Source*: http://en.wikipedia.org/?oldid=368441965 *Contributors*: John of Reading

Gazi-Stadion auf der Waldau *Source*: http://en.wikipedia.org/?oldid=379193618 *Contributors*: Jared Preston

Hanns-Martin-Schleyer-Halle *Source*: http://en.wikipedia.org/?oldid=364796962 *Contributors*: Woohookitty

Porsche Arena *Source*: http://en.wikipedia.org/?oldid=390239392 *Contributors*:

Mercedes-Benz Arena *Source*: http://en.wikipedia.org/?oldid=386708753 *Contributors*:

Stuttgart Airport *Source*: http://en.wikipedia.org/?oldid=390469660 *Contributors*: Bad.taste.in.music

Stuttgarter Straßenbahnen AG *Source*: http://en.wikipedia.org/?oldid=332185891 *Contributors*: Peter Horn

Stuttgart Stadtbahn *Source*: http://en.wikipedia.org/?oldid=358293546 *Contributors*: Blarf

Stuttgart Hauptbahnhof *Source*: http://en.wikipedia.org/?oldid=390530967 *Contributors*: AMackenzie

Stuttgart Rack Railway *Source*: http://en.wikipedia.org/?oldid=358624025 *Contributors*: 1 anonymous edits

Standseilbahn Stuttgart *Source*: http://en.wikipedia.org/?oldid=382555269 *Contributors*: Joseolgon

Image Sources, Licenses and Contributors

File:Coat of Arms of Germany.svg *Source*: http://bibliocm.bibliolabs.com/mwAnon/index.php?title=File:Coat_of_Arms_of_Germany.svg *License*: unknown *Contributors*: -

file:Europa Germanen 50 n Chr.svg *Source*: http://bibliocm.bibliolabs.com/mwAnon/index.php?title=File:Europa_Germanen_50_n_Chr.svg *License*: unknown *Contributors*: -

file:Pforzen Inschrift.JPG *Source*: http://bibliocm.bibliolabs.com/mwAnon/index.php?title=File:Pforzen_Inschrift.JPG *License*: unknown *Contributors*: -

File:Empire carolingien 768-811.jpg *Source*: http://bibliocm.bibliolabs.com/mwAnon/index.php?title=File:Empire_carolingien_768-811.jpg *License*: GNU Free Documentation License *Contributors*: cyberprout

file:Balduineum Wahl Heinrich VII.jpg *Source*: http://bibliocm.bibliolabs.com/mwAnon/index.php?title=File:Balduineum_Wahl_Heinrich_VII.jpg *License*: unknown *Contributors*: -

file:HRR 10Jh.jpg *Source*: http://bibliocm.bibliolabs.com/mwAnon/index.php?title=File:HRR_10Jh.jpg *License*: unknown *Contributors*: -

file:Marienburg19001.jpg *Source*: http://bibliocm.bibliolabs.com/mwAnon/index.php?title=File:Marienburg19001.jpg *License*: unknown *Contributors*: -

file:HRR 14Jh.jpg *Source*: http://bibliocm.bibliolabs.com/mwAnon/index.php?title=File:HRR_14Jh.jpg *License*: unknown *Contributors*: -

File:Holbein-death.png *Source*: http://bibliocm.bibliolabs.com/mwAnon/index.php?title=File:Holbein-death.png *License*: unknown *Contributors*: -

File:Lutherrose.svg *Source*: http://bibliocm.bibliolabs.com/mwAnon/index.php?title=File:Lutherrose.svg *License*: unknown *Contributors*: -

File:Luther46c.jpg *Source*: http://bibliocm.bibliolabs.com/mwAnon/index.php?title=File:Luther46c.jpg *License*: unknown *Contributors*: Aavindraa, CTSWyneken, David Levy, Hahnchen, Ixfd64, Joakao, Rosenzweig, Schmelzle, Shakko, Shizhao, Wst, 1 anonymous edits

File:Grotepier TN.JPG *Source*: http://bibliocm.bibliolabs.com/mwAnon/index.php?title=File:Grotepier_TN.JPG *License*: unknown *Contributors*: -

file:Reichskarte1705.jpg *Source*: http://bibliocm.bibliolabs.com/mwAnon/index.php?title=File:Reichskarte1705.jpg *License*: unknown *Contributors*: Lotje, Michail, RobNS, Skim, 2 anonymous edits

file:Acprussiamap2.gif *Source*: http://bibliocm.bibliolabs.com/mwAnon/index.php?title=File:Acprussiamap2.gif *License*: unknown *Contributors*: -

File:1french-empire1811.jpg *Source*: http://bibliocm.bibliolabs.com/mwAnon/index.php?title=File:1french-empire1811.jpg *License*: unknown *Contributors*: -

File:Nationalversammlung.jpg *Source*: http://bibliocm.bibliolabs.com/mwAnon/index.php?title=File:Nationalversammlung.jpg *License*: unknown *Contributors*: -

File:Reichsgründung1871-AW.jpg *Source*: http://bibliocm.bibliolabs.com/mwAnon/index.php?title=File:Reichsgründung1871-AW.jpg *License*: unknown *Contributors*: -

File:Map-deutsches-kaiserreich.png *Source*: http://bibliocm.bibliolabs.com/mwAnon/index.php?title=File:Map-deutsches-kaiserreich.png *License*: unknown *Contributors*: -

File:Otto von Bismarck.JPG *Source*: http://bibliocm.bibliolabs.com/mwAnon/index.php?title=File:Otto_von_Bismarck.JPG *License*: unknown *Contributors*: Evert A. Duykinck, A Portrait Gallery of Eminent Men and Women of Europe and America, with Biographies. New York: Johnson, Wilson and Company.

File:Karolinen-stamp.jpg *Source*: http://bibliocm.bibliolabs.com/mwAnon/index.php?title=File:Karolinen-stamp.jpg *License*: unknown *Contributors*: Original uploader was Delpino at en.wikipedia

File:Deutsches Reich2.png *Source*: http://bibliocm.bibliolabs.com/mwAnon/index.php?title=File:Deutsches_Reich2.png *License*: Creative Commons Attribution 2.5 *Contributors*: kgberger

File:Germanborders.svg *Source*: http://bibliocm.bibliolabs.com/mwAnon/index.php?title=File:Germanborders.svg *License*: Public Domain *Contributors*: User:Renata3

File:Bundesarchiv Bild 183-1990-0123-021, Berlin, Abriss der Mauer.jpg *Source*: http://bibliocm.bibliolabs.com/mwAnon/index.php?title=File:Bundesarchiv_Bild_183-1990-0123-021,_Berlin,_Abriss_der_Mauer.jpg *License*: unknown *Contributors*: -

File:MerkelEU50 2.jpg *Source*: http://bibliocm.bibliolabs.com/mwAnon/index.php?title=File:MerkelEU50_2.jpg *License*: unknown *Contributors*: -

File:Deutsche Post - 1 Reichsmark.jpg *Source*: http://bibliocm.bibliolabs.com/mwAnon/index.php?title=File:Deutsche_Post_-_1_Reichsmark.jpg *License*: unknown *Contributors*: -

File:HRR 1789.png *Source*: http://bibliocm.bibliolabs.com/mwAnon/index.php?title=File:HRR_1789.png *License*: Creative Commons Attribution 2.5 *Contributors*: ziegelbrenner

File:Deutscher Bund.png *Source*: http://bibliocm.bibliolabs.com/mwAnon/index.php?title=File:Deutscher_Bund.png *License*: unknown *Contributors*: -

File:Deutsches Reich1.png *Source*: http://bibliocm.bibliolabs.com/mwAnon/index.php?title=File:Deutsches_Reich1.png *License*: Creative Commons Attribution-Sharealike 2.5 *Contributors*: kgberger

File:DR 1941 785 Adolf Hitler.jpg *Source*: http://bibliocm.bibliolabs.com/mwAnon/index.php?title=File:DR_1941_785_Adolf_Hitler.jpg *License*: unknown *Contributors*: -

File:NS administrative Gliederung 1944.png *Source*: http://bibliocm.bibliolabs.com/mwAnon/index.php?title=File:NS_administrative_Gliederung_1944.png *License*: GNU Free Documentation License *Contributors*: User:Exec

File:Map-Germany-1947.svg *Source*: http://bibliocm.bibliolabs.com/mwAnon/index.php?title=File:Map-Germany-1947.svg *License*: unknown *Contributors*: -

File:Deutschland Bundeslaender 1957.png *Source*: http://bibliocm.bibliolabs.com/mwAnon/index.php?title=File:Deutschland_Bundeslaender_1957.png *License*: GNU Free Documentation License *Contributors*: David Kernow, Disposable.Heroes, Jed, Koavf, OwenBlacker, Trockennasenaffe, W-j-s, 1 anonymous edits

File:LocationGermany.png *Source*: http://bibliocm.bibliolabs.com/mwAnon/index.php?title=File:LocationGermany.png *License*: unknown *Contributors*: -

File:Germany general map.png *Source*: http://bibliocm.bibliolabs.com/mwAnon/index.php?title=File:Germany_general_map.png *License*: unknown *Contributors*: -

File:Deutschland Landschaften.png *Source*: http://bibliocm.bibliolabs.com/mwAnon/index.php?title=File:Deutschland_Landschaften.png *License*: unknown *Contributors*: -

File:Hintersee.jpg *Source*: http://bibliocm.bibliolabs.com/mwAnon/index.php?title=File:Hintersee.jpg *License*: unknown *Contributors*: -

File:Germanymap2.png *Source*: http://bibliocm.bibliolabs.com/mwAnon/index.php?title=File:Germanymap2.png *License*: unknown *Contributors*: -

File:Kanzler21a.jpg *Source*: http://bibliocm.bibliolabs.com/mwAnon/index.php?title=File:Kanzler21a.jpg *License*: unknown *Contributors*: -

Image:Reichstag mit Wiese2.jpg *Source*: http://bibliocm.bibliolabs.com/mwAnon/index.php?title=File:Reichstag_mit_Wiese2.jpg *License*: unknown *Contributors*: -

File:Bundesarchiv Bild 183-P0619-306, Trabant 601.jpg *Source*: http://bibliocm.bibliolabs.com/mwAnon/index.php?title=File:Bundesarchiv_Bild_183-P0619-306,_Trabant_601.jpg *License*: unknown *Contributors*: -

Image:BASF1.jpg *Source*: http://bibliocm.bibliolabs.com/mwAnon/index.php?title=File:BASF1.jpg *License*: unknown *Contributors*: -

File:ICE 3M KRM.jpg *Source*: http://bibliocm.bibliolabs.com/mwAnon/index.php?title=File:ICE_3M_KRM.jpg *License*: unknown *Contributors*: -

Image:European union emu map en.png *Source*: http://bibliocm.bibliolabs.com/mwAnon/index.php?title=File:European_union_emu_map_en.png *License*: unknown *Contributors*: -

File:Flag of Austria.svg *Source*: http://bibliocm.bibliolabs.com/mwAnon/index.php?title=File:Flag_of_Austria.svg *License*: Public Domain *Contributors*: User:SKopp

File:Flag of Belarus.svg *Source*: http://bibliocm.bibliolabs.com/mwAnon/index.php?title=File:Flag_of_Belarus.svg *License*: unknown *Contributors*: -

File:Flag of Belgium (civil).svg *Source*: http://bibliocm.bibliolabs.com/mwAnon/index.php?title=File:Flag_of_Belgium_(civil).svg *License*: unknown *Contributors*: -

File:Flag of Croatia.svg *Source*: http://bibliocm.bibliolabs.com/mwAnon/index.php?title=File:Flag_of_Croatia.svg *License*: unknown *Contributors*: -

File:Flag of Cyprus.svg *Source*: http://bibliocm.bibliolabs.com/mwAnon/index.php?title=File:Flag_of_Cyprus.svg *License*: unknown *Contributors*: -

File:Flag of the Czech Republic.svg *Source*: http://bibliocm.bibliolabs.com/mwAnon/index.php?title=File:Flag_of_the_Czech_Republic.svg *License*: unknown *Contributors*: -

File:Flag of Denmark.svg *Source*: http://bibliocm.bibliolabs.com/mwAnon/index.php?title=File:Flag_of_Denmark.svg *License*: unknown *Contributors*: -

File:Flag of the United Kingdom.svg *Source*: http://bibliocm.bibliolabs.com/mwAnon/index.php?title=File:Flag_of_the_United_Kingdom.svg *License*: unknown *Contributors*: -

File:Flag of France.svg *Source*: http://bibliocm.bibliolabs.com/mwAnon/index.php?title=File:Flag_of_France.svg *License*: unknown *Contributors*: -

File:Flag of Greece.svg *Source*: http://bibliocm.bibliolabs.com/mwAnon/index.php?title=File:Flag_of_Greece.svg *License*: unknown *Contributors*: -

File:Flag of Hungary.svg *Source*: http://bibliocm.bibliolabs.com/mwAnon/index.php?title=File:Flag_of_Hungary.svg *License*: unknown *Contributors*: -

File:Flag of Italy.svg *Source*: http://bibliocm.bibliolabs.com/mwAnon/index.php?title=File:Flag_of_Italy.svg *License*: unknown *Contributors*: -

File:Flag of the Netherlands.svg *Source*: http://bibliocm.bibliolabs.com/mwAnon/index.php?title=File:Flag_of_the_Netherlands.svg *License*: unknown *Contributors*: -

File:Flag of Kosovo.svg *Source*: http://bibliocm.bibliolabs.com/mwAnon/index.php?title=File:Flag_of_Kosovo.svg *License*: GNU Free Documentation License *Contributors*: User:Cradel, User:Ningyou

File:Flag of Latvia.svg *Source*: http://bibliocm.bibliolabs.com/mwAnon/index.php?title=File:Flag_of_Latvia.svg *License*: unknown *Contributors*: -

File:Flag of Malta.svg *Source*: http://bibliocm.bibliolabs.com/mwAnon/index.php?title=File:Flag_of_Malta.svg *License*: unknown *Contributors*: -

File:Flag of Moldova.svg *Source*: http://bibliocm.bibliolabs.com/mwAnon/index.php?title=File:Flag_of_Moldova.svg *License*: unknown *Contributors*: -

File:Flag of Lithuania.svg *Source*: http://bibliocm.bibliolabs.com/mwAnon/index.php?title=File:Flag_of_Lithuania.svg *License*: unknown *Contributors*: -

File:Flag of Poland.svg *Source*: http://bibliocm.bibliolabs.com/mwAnon/index.php?title=File:Flag_of_Poland.svg *License*: unknown *Contributors*: -

File:Flag of Romania.svg *Source*: http://bibliocm.bibliolabs.com/mwAnon/index.php?title=File:Flag_of_Romania.svg *License*: Public Domain *Contributors*: User:AdiJapan

File:Flag of Russia.svg *Source*: http://bibliocm.bibliolabs.com/mwAnon/index.php?title=File:Flag_of_Russia.svg *License*: unknown *Contributors*: -

File:Flag of Serbia.svg *Source*: http://bibliocm.bibliolabs.com/mwAnon/index.php?title=File:Flag_of_Serbia.svg *License*: Public Domain *Contributors*: ABF, Avala, B1mbo, Denelson83, EDUCA33E, Fry1989, Herbythyme, Homo lupus, Imbris, Maks Stirlitz, Mormegil, Nightstallion, Nikola Smolenski, Nuno Gabriel Cabral, Odder, R-41, Rainman, Rokerismoravee, Sasa Stefanovic, Siebrand, TFCforever, ThomasPusch, Túrelio, Zscout370, 7 anonymous edits

File:Flag of Slovakia.svg *Source*: http://bibliocm.bibliolabs.com/mwAnon/index.php?title=File:Flag_of_Slovakia.svg *License*: unknown *Contributors*: -

File:Flag of Turkey.svg *Source*: http://bibliocm.bibliolabs.com/mwAnon/index.php?title=File:Flag_of_Turkey.svg *License*: Public Domain *Contributors*: User:Dbenbenn

File:Flag of Ukraine.svg *Source*: http://bibliocm.bibliolabs.com/mwAnon/index.php?title=File:Flag_of_Ukraine.svg *License*: unknown *Contributors*: -

File:Flag of Bolivia.svg *Source*: http://bibliocm.bibliolabs.com/mwAnon/index.php?title=File:Flag_of_Bolivia.svg *License*: unknown *Contributors*: -

File:Flag of Canada.svg *Source*: http://bibliocm.bibliolabs.com/mwAnon/index.php?title=File:Flag_of_Canada.svg *License*: unknown *Contributors*: -

File:Flag of Paraguay.svg *Source*: http://bibliocm.bibliolabs.com/mwAnon/index.php?title=File:Flag_of_Paraguay.svg *License*: unknown *Contributors*: -

File:Flag of the United States.svg *Source*: http://bibliocm.bibliolabs.com/mwAnon/index.php?title=File:Flag_of_the_United_States.svg *License*: unknown *Contributors*: -

File:Flag of Uruguay.svg *Source*: http://bibliocm.bibliolabs.com/mwAnon/index.php?title=File:Flag_of_Uruguay.svg *License*: unknown *Contributors*: -

File:Flag of Armenia.svg *Source*: http://bibliocm.bibliolabs.com/mwAnon/index.php?title=File:Flag_of_Armenia.svg *License*: unknown *Contributors*: -

File:Flag of Georgia.svg *Source*: http://bibliocm.bibliolabs.com/mwAnon/index.php?title=File:Flag_of_Georgia.svg *License*: unknown *Contributors*: -

File:Flag of India.svg *Source*: http://bibliocm.bibliolabs.com/mwAnon/index.php?title=File:Flag_of_India.svg *License*: unknown *Contributors*: -

File:Flag of Iraq.svg *Source*: http://bibliocm.bibliolabs.com/mwAnon/index.php?title=File:Flag_of_Iraq.svg *License*: unknown *Contributors*: -

File:Flag of Japan.svg *Source*: http://bibliocm.bibliolabs.com/mwAnon/index.php?title=File:Flag_of_Japan.svg *License*: unknown *Contributors*: -

File:Flag of Pakistan.svg *Source*: http://bibliocm.bibliolabs.com/mwAnon/index.php?title=File:Flag_of_Pakistan.svg *License*: unknown *Contributors*: -

File:Flag of the People's Republic of China.svg *Source*: http://bibliocm.bibliolabs.com/mwAnon/index.php?title=File:Flag_of_the_People's_Republic_of_China.svg *License*: unknown *Contributors*: -

File:Flag of Egypt.svg *Source*: http://bibliocm.bibliolabs.com/mwAnon/index.php?title=File:Flag_of_Egypt.svg *License*: unknown *Contributors*: -

File:Flag of Libya.svg *Source*: http://bibliocm.bibliolabs.com/mwAnon/index.php?title=File:Flag_of_Libya.svg *License*: unknown *Contributors*: -

File:Flag of Namibia.svg *Source*: http://bibliocm.bibliolabs.com/mwAnon/index.php?title=File:Flag_of_Namibia.svg *License*: unknown *Contributors*: -

Image:Goethecut.png *Source*: http://bibliocm.bibliolabs.com/mwAnon/index.php?title=File:Goethecut.png *License*: unknown *Contributors*: -

Image:Printing3 Walk of Ideas Berlin.JPG *Source*: http://bibliocm.bibliolabs.com/mwAnon/index.php?title=File:Printing3_Walk_of_Ideas_Berlin.JPG *License*: unknown *Contributors*: -

Image:Immanuel Kant (painted portrait).jpg *Source*: http://bibliocm.bibliolabs.com/mwAnon/index.php?title=File:Immanuel_Kant_(painted_portrait).jpg *License*: unknown *Contributors*: -

Image:Martin Luther 3.jpg *Source*: http://bibliocm.bibliolabs.com/mwAnon/index.php?title=File:Martin_Luther_3.jpg *License*: unknown *Contributors*: -

Image:Berliner (pastry).jpg *Source*: http://bibliocm.bibliolabs.com/mwAnon/index.php?title=File:Berliner_(pastry).jpg *License*: unknown *Contributors*: -

Image:AllianzArenaSunset.jpg *Source*: http://bibliocm.bibliolabs.com/mwAnon/index.php?title=File:AllianzArenaSunset.jpg *License*: unknown *Contributors*: -

Image:Inglehart Values Map.svg *Source*: http://bibliocm.bibliolabs.com/mwAnon/index.php?title=File:Inglehart_Values_Map.svg *License*: unknown *Contributors*: -

File:Schloss Hohenschwangau IMG 6920.JPG *Source*: http://bibliocm.bibliolabs.com/mwAnon/index.php?title=File:Schloss_Hohenschwangau_IMG_6920.JPG *License*: unknown *Contributors*: -

File:Burg Hohenzollern ak.jpg *Source*: http://bibliocm.bibliolabs.com/mwAnon/index.php?title=File:Burg_Hohenzollern_ak.jpg *License*: unknown *Contributors*: -

File:Schloss Stolzenfels Sammlung Duncker.jpg *Source*: http://bibliocm.bibliolabs.com/mwAnon/index.php?title=File:Schloss_Stolzenfels_Sammlung_Duncker.jpg *License*: unknown *Contributors*: -

File:Wartburg19001.jpg *Source*: http://bibliocm.bibliolabs.com/mwAnon/index.php?title=File:Wartburg19001.jpg *License*: unknown *Contributors*: -

File:Ludwig II king of Bavaria.jpg *Source*: http://bibliocm.bibliolabs.com/mwAnon/index.php?title=File:Ludwig_II_king_of_Bavaria.jpg *License*: unknown *Contributors*: -

File:Johannes Bernhard Neuschwanstein Baustelle 1882-85 (01).jpg *Source*: http://bibliocm.bibliolabs.com/mwAnon/index.php?title=File:Johannes_Bernhard_Neuschwanstein_Baustelle_1882-85_(01).jpg *License*: unknown *Contributors*: -

File:Neuschwanstein - Blick in den oberen Schlosshof.jpg *Source*: http://bibliocm.bibliolabs.com/mwAnon/index.php?title=File:Neuschwanstein_-_Blick_in_den_oberen_Schlosshof.jpg *License*: unknown *Contributors*: -

File:Neuschwanstein castle.jpg *Source*: http://bibliocm.bibliolabs.com/mwAnon/index.php?title=File:Neuschwanstein_castle.jpg *License*: unknown *Contributors*: -

File:Schloss Neuschwanstein2, Germany.jpg *Source*: http://bibliocm.bibliolabs.com/mwAnon/index.php?title=File:Schloss_Neuschwanstein2,_Germany.jpg *License*: unknown *Contributors*: -

File:Schloss Neuschwanstein 6862.jpg *Source*: http://bibliocm.bibliolabs.com/mwAnon/index.php?title=File:Schloss_Neuschwanstein_6862.jpg *License*: unknown *Contributors*: -

File:NeuschwansteinGrundriss.PNG *Source*: http://bibliocm.bibliolabs.com/mwAnon/index.php?title=File:NeuschwansteinGrundriss.PNG *License*: unknown *Contributors*: -

File:Neuschwanstein Gang.jpg *Source*: http://bibliocm.bibliolabs.com/mwAnon/index.php?title=File:Neuschwanstein_Gang.jpg *License*: unknown *Contributors*: -

File:Neuschwanstein Boden.jpg *Source*: http://bibliocm.bibliolabs.com/mwAnon/index.php?title=File:Neuschwanstein_Boden.jpg *License*: unknown *Contributors*: -

File:Neuschwanstein throne room_00180u.jpg *Source*: http://bibliocm.bibliolabs.com/mwAnon/index.php?title=File:Neuschwanstein_throne_room_00180u.jpg *License*: unknown *Contributors*: -

File:Neuschwanstein study 00181u.jpg *Source*: http://bibliocm.bibliolabs.com/mwAnon/index.php?title=File:Neuschwanstein_study_00181u.jpg *License*: unknown *Contributors*: -

File:Neuschwanstein dining room_00184u.jpg *Source*: http://bibliocm.bibliolabs.com/mwAnon/index.php?title=File:Neuschwanstein_dining_room_00184u.jpg *License*: unknown *Contributors*: -

File:Neuschwanstein Kueche.jpg *Source*: http://bibliocm.bibliolabs.com/mwAnon/index.php?title=File:Neuschwanstein_Kueche.jpg *License*: unknown *Contributors*: -

File:Neuschwanstein.jpg *Source*: http://bibliocm.bibliolabs.com/mwAnon/index.php?title=File:Neuschwanstein.jpg *License*: unknown *Contributors*: -

File:Ludwig auf dem Totenbett Koppay.jpg *Source*: http://bibliocm.bibliolabs.com/mwAnon/index.php?title=File:Ludwig_auf_dem_Totenbett_Koppay.jpg *License*: unknown *Contributors*: -

File:Neuschwanstein Castle LOC print rotated.jpg *Source*: http://bibliocm.bibliolabs.com/mwAnon/index.php?title=File:Neuschwanstein_Castle_LOC_print_rotated.jpg *License*: unknown *Contributors*: -

File:DBP 1977 916 Schloss Neuschwanstein.jpg *Source*: http://bibliocm.bibliolabs.com/mwAnon/index.php?title=File:DBP_1977_916_Schloss_Neuschwanstein.jpg *License*: unknown *Contributors*: -

Image:Brandenburger Tor abends.jpg *Source*: http://bibliocm.bibliolabs.com/mwAnon/index.php?title=File:Brandenburger_Tor_abends.jpg *License*: unknown *Contributors*: -

Image:ZLB-Berliner Ansichten-Januar.jpg *Source*: http://bibliocm.bibliolabs.com/mwAnon/index.php?title=File:ZLB-Berliner_Ansichten-Januar.jpg *License*: unknown *Contributors*: -

File:Bundesarchiv Bild 183-85417-0002, Berlin, Mauerbau, Brandenburger Tor.jpg *Source*: http://bibliocm.bibliolabs.com/mwAnon/index.php?title=File:Bundesarchiv_Bild_183-85417-0002,_Berlin,_Mauerbau,_Brandenburger_Tor.jpg *License*: unknown *Contributors*: -

File:Bundesarchiv Bild 183-1990-0305-347, Berlin, Brandenburger Tor.jpg *Source*: http://bibliocm.bibliolabs.com/mwAnon/index.php?title=File:Bundesarchiv_Bild_183-1990-0305-347,_Berlin,_Brandenburger_Tor.jpg *License*: unknown *Contributors*: -

File:U2 at the Brandenburg Gate.jpg *Source*: http://bibliocm.bibliolabs.com/mwAnon/index.php?title=File:U2_at_the_Brandenburg_Gate.jpg *License*: unknown *Contributors*: -

Image:SedanBrandenburgerTor.jpg *Source*: http://bibliocm.bibliolabs.com/mwAnon/index.php?title=File:SedanBrandenburgerTor.jpg *License*: unknown *Contributors*: -

Image:Brandenburger tor 1871.jpg *Source*: http://bibliocm.bibliolabs.com/mwAnon/index.php?title=File:Brandenburger_tor_1871.jpg *License*: unknown *Contributors*: -

Image:2005-10-26 Brandenburger-Tor.JPG *Source*: http://bibliocm.bibliolabs.com/mwAnon/index.php?title=File:2005-10-26_Brandenburger-Tor.JPG *License*: unknown *Contributors*: -

Image:Brandenburg Gate Quadriga at Night.jpg *Source*: http://bibliocm.bibliolabs.com/mwAnon/index.php?title=File:Brandenburg_Gate_Quadriga_at_Night.jpg *License*: unknown *Contributors*: -

File:Bundesarchiv Bild 183-85417-0003, Berlin, Mauerbau, Brandenburger Tor.jpg *Source*: http://bibliocm.bibliolabs.com/mwAnon/index.php?title=File:Bundesarchiv_Bild_183-85417-0003,_Berlin,_Mauerbau,_Brandenburger_Tor.jpg *License*: unknown *Contributors*: -

File:Bundesarchiv Bild 173-1282, Berlin, Brandenburger Tor, Wasserwerfer.jpg *Source*: http://bibliocm.bibliolabs.com/mwAnon/index.php?title=File:Bundesarchiv_Bild_173-1282,_Berlin,_Brandenburger_Tor,_Wasserwerfer.jpg *License*: unknown *Contributors*: -

File:13.8 scharf.png *Source*: http://bibliocm.bibliolabs.com/mwAnon/index.php?title=File:13.8_scharf.png *License*: unknown *Contributors*: -

Image:Berlin-Baby-Wall-1968.jpg *Source*: http://bibliocm.bibliolabs.com/mwAnon/index.php?title=File:Berlin-Baby-Wall-1968.jpg *License*: unknown *Contributors*: -

File:Bundesarchiv Bild 175-V00-02081, Berlin, Brandenburger Tor, Luftbild.jpg *Source*: http://bibliocm.bibliolabs.com/mwAnon/index.php?title=File:Bundesarchiv_Bild_175-V00-02081,_Berlin,_Brandenburger_Tor,_Luftbild.jpg *License*: unknown *Contributors*: -

Image:Reagan_vor_dem_Brandenburger_Tor.png *Source*: http://bibliocm.bibliolabs.com/mwAnon/index.php?title=File:Reagan_vor_dem_Brandenburger_Tor.png *License*: unknown *Contributors*: -

Image:Berlin wall Brandenburger Tor graffiti.jpg *Source*: http://bibliocm.bibliolabs.com/mwAnon/index.php?title=File:Berlin_wall_Brandenburger_Tor_graffiti.jpg *License*: unknown *Contributors*: -

Image:Thefalloftheberlinwall1989.JPG *Source*: http://bibliocm.bibliolabs.com/mwAnon/index.php?title=File:Thefalloftheberlinwall1989.JPG *License*: unknown *Contributors*: -

File:BrandenburgerTorDezember1989.jpg *Source*: http://bibliocm.bibliolabs.com/mwAnon/index.php?title=File:BrandenburgerTorDezember1989.jpg *License*: unknown *Contributors*: -

File:Bundesarchiv Bild 183-1989-1115-023, Berlin, Brandenburger Tor, vor Grenzöffnung.jpg *Source*: http://bibliocm.bibliolabs.com/mwAnon/index.php?title=File:Bundesarchiv_Bild_183-1989-1115-023,_Berlin,_Brandenburger_Tor,_vor_Grenzöffnung.jpg *License*: unknown *Contributors*: -

Image:Crane removed part of Wall Brandenburg Gate.jpg *Source*: http://bibliocm.bibliolabs.com/mwAnon/index.php?title=File:Crane_removed_part_of_Wall_Brandenburg_Gate.jpg *License*: unknown *Contributors*: -

File:Bundesarchiv Bild 183-1989-1222-016, Berlin, Grenzöffnung Brandenburger Tor.jpg *Source*: http://bibliocm.bibliolabs.com/mwAnon/index.php?title=File:Bundesarchiv_Bild_183-1989-1222-016,_Berlin,_Grenzöffnung_Brandenburger_Tor.jpg *License*: unknown *Contributors*: -

File:BrandeburgGateOpening.jpg *Source*: http://bibliocm.bibliolabs.com/mwAnon/index.php?title=File:BrandeburgGateOpening.jpg *License*: unknown *Contributors*: -

File:Bundesarchiv Bild 183-1989-1222-034, Berlin, Grenzöffnung Brandenburger Tor.jpg *Source*: http://bibliocm.bibliolabs.com/mwAnon/index.php?title=File:Bundesarchiv_Bild_183-1989-1222-034,_Berlin,_Grenzöffnung_Brandenburger_Tor.jpg *License*: unknown *Contributors*: -

File:Bundesarchiv Bild 183-1989-1223-004, Berlin, Grenzübergang Brandenburger Tor.jpg *Source*: http://bibliocm.bibliolabs.com/mwAnon/index.php?title=File:Bundesarchiv_Bild_183-1989-1223-004,_Berlin,_Grenzübergang_Brandenburger_Tor.jpg *License*: unknown *Contributors*: -

File:Volkspolizei_at_the_official_opening_of_the_Brandenburg_Gate.jpg *Source*: http://bibliocm.bibliolabs.com/mwAnon/index.php?title=File:Volkspolizei_at_the_official_opening_of_the_Brandenburg_Gate.jpg *License*: unknown *Contributors*: -

File:Bundesarchiv Bild 183-1990-0429-411, Berlin, Abriss der Mauer am Brandenburger Tor.jpg *Source*: http://bibliocm.bibliolabs.com/mwAnon/index.php?title=File:Bundesarchiv_Bild_183-1990-0429-411,_Berlin,_Abriss_der_Mauer_am_Brandenburger_Tor.jpg *License*: unknown *Contributors*: -

File:Visa Brandenburger Tor.jpg *Source*: http://bibliocm.bibliolabs.com/mwAnon/index.php?title=File:Visa_Brandenburger_Tor.jpg *License*: unknown *Contributors*: -

File:Mauer hinter Reichstag.jpg *Source*: http://bibliocm.bibliolabs.com/mwAnon/index.php?title=File:Mauer_hinter_Reichstag.jpg *License*: unknown *Contributors*: -

File:BrandenburgerTor.1.jpg *Source*: http://bibliocm.bibliolabs.com/mwAnon/index.php?title=File:BrandenburgerTor.1.jpg *License*: unknown *Contributors*: -

Image:Windbuchencom.jpg *Source*: http://bibliocm.bibliolabs.com/mwAnon/index.php?title=File:Windbuchencom.jpg *License*: unknown *Contributors*: -

Image:Feldberg.JPG *Source*: http://bibliocm.bibliolabs.com/mwAnon/index.php?title=File:Feldberg.JPG *License*: unknown *Contributors*: -

Image:Auf dem Teisenkopf.jpg *Source*: http://bibliocm.bibliolabs.com/mwAnon/index.php?title=File:Auf_dem_Teisenkopf.jpg *License*: unknown *Contributors*: -

Image:titisee winter.jpg *Source*: http://bibliocm.bibliolabs.com/mwAnon/index.php?title=File:Titisee_winter.jpg *License*: unknown *Contributors*: -

Image:clock_forest.jpg *Source*: http://bibliocm.bibliolabs.com/mwAnon/index.php?title=File:Clock_forest.jpg *License*: unknown *Contributors*: -

Image:Mummelsee.jpg *Source*: http://bibliocm.bibliolabs.com/mwAnon/index.php?title=File:Mummelsee.jpg *License*: unknown *Contributors*: -

Image:Bodensee vor Ueberlingen.jpg *Source*: http://bibliocm.bibliolabs.com/mwAnon/index.php?title=File:Bodensee_vor_Ueberlingen.jpg *License*: unknown *Contributors*: -

Image:Avg-853-02.jpg *Source*: http://bibliocm.bibliolabs.com/mwAnon/index.php?title=File:Avg-853-02.jpg *License*: unknown *Contributors*: -

Image:Burg Hohenzollern mit Schwarzwald2.JPG *Source*: http://bibliocm.bibliolabs.com/mwAnon/index.php?title=File:Burg_Hohenzollern_mit_Schwarzwald2.JPG *License*: unknown *Contributors*: -

Image:Cologne Cathedral.jpg *Source*: http://bibliocm.bibliolabs.com/mwAnon/index.php?title=File:Cologne_Cathedral.jpg *License*: unknown *Contributors*: -

File:Flag of Germany.svg *Source*: http://bibliocm.bibliolabs.com/mwAnon/index.php?title=File:Flag_of_Germany.svg *License*: unknown *Contributors*: -

Image:Cologne Cathedral Altarpiece of Magi by Stephan Lochner.jpg *Source*: http://bibliocm.bibliolabs.com/mwAnon/index.php?title=File:Cologne_Cathedral_Altarpiece_of_Magi_by_Stephan_Lochner.jpg *License*: unknown *Contributors*: -

Image:Warning sign in cologne.jpg *Source*: http://bibliocm.bibliolabs.com/mwAnon/index.php?title=File:Warning_sign_in_cologne.jpg *License*: unknown *Contributors*: -

Image:Cologne - Panoramic Image of the old town at dusk.jpg *Source*: http://bibliocm.bibliolabs.com/mwAnon/index.php?title=File:Cologne_-_Panoramic_Image_of_the_old_town_at_dusk.jpg *License*: unknown *Contributors*: -

Image:Koelner Dom Innenraum.jpg *Source*: http://bibliocm.bibliolabs.com/mwAnon/index.php?title=File:Koelner_Dom_Innenraum.jpg *License*: unknown *Contributors*: -

Image:Cologne Cathedral Shrine of Magi.jpg *Source*: http://bibliocm.bibliolabs.com/mwAnon/index.php?title=File:Cologne_Cathedral_Shrine_of_Magi.jpg *License*: unknown *Contributors*: -

Image:CologneCathedralBell02.jpg *Source*: http://bibliocm.bibliolabs.com/mwAnon/index.php?title=File:CologneCathedralBell02.jpg *License*: unknown *Contributors*: -

Image:Plan.cathedrale.Cologne.png *Source*: http://bibliocm.bibliolabs.com/mwAnon/index.php?title=File:Plan.cathedrale.Cologne.png *License*: unknown *Contributors*: -

Image:Detail, Cologne Cathedral Tower.jpg *Source*: http://bibliocm.bibliolabs.com/mwAnon/index.php?title=File:Detail,_Cologne_Cathedral_Tower.jpg *License*: unknown *Contributors*: -

image:Koelner-dom-spire.jpg *Source*: http://bibliocm.bibliolabs.com/mwAnon/index.php?title=File:Koelner-dom-spire.jpg *License*: unknown *Contributors*: -

image:CologneCathedralInSpire.JPG *Source*: http://bibliocm.bibliolabs.com/mwAnon/index.php?title=File:CologneCathedralInSpire.JPG *License*: unknown *Contributors*: -

Image:Dom-Koeln-IMG 4518.JPG *Source*: http://bibliocm.bibliolabs.com/mwAnon/index.php?title=File:Dom-Koeln-IMG_4518.JPG *License*: unknown *Contributors*: -

Image:Cathedral main entrance.jpg *Source*: http://bibliocm.bibliolabs.com/mwAnon/index.php?title=File:Cathedral_main_entrance.jpg *License*: unknown *Contributors*: -

Image:Cathedral 1 by andy205.jpg *Source*: http://bibliocm.bibliolabs.com/mwAnon/index.php?title=File:Cathedral_1_by_andy205.jpg *License*: unknown *Contributors*: -

Image:Koelner Dom Dach.jpg *Source*: http://bibliocm.bibliolabs.com/mwAnon/index.php?title=File:Koelner_Dom_Dach.jpg *License*: unknown *Contributors*: -

File:Cologne Cathedral interior.JPG *Source*: http://bibliocm.bibliolabs.com/mwAnon/index.php?title=File:Cologne_Cathedral_interior.JPG *License*: unknown *Contributors*: -

Image:Gerokreuz full 20050903.jpg *Source*: http://bibliocm.bibliolabs.com/mwAnon/index.php?title=File:Gerokreuz_full_20050903.jpg *License*: unknown *Contributors*: -

Image:Koelner dom neue orgel.jpg *Source*: http://bibliocm.bibliolabs.com/mwAnon/index.php?title=File:Koelner_dom_neue_orgel.jpg *License*: unknown *Contributors*: -

Image:Bayerfenster Ss Peter and Virgin Mary.jpg *Source*: http://bibliocm.bibliolabs.com/mwAnon/index.php?title=File:Bayerfenster_Ss_Peter_and_Virgin_Mary.jpg *License*: unknown *Contributors*: -

Image:Koelnerdomlightshow.jpg *Source*: http://bibliocm.bibliolabs.com/mwAnon/index.php?title=File:Koelnerdomlightshow.jpg *License*: unknown *Contributors*: -

Image:Koelner Dom bei Nacht 1 RB.JPG *Source*: http://bibliocm.bibliolabs.com/mwAnon/index.php?title=File:Koelner_Dom_bei_Nacht_1_RB.JPG *License*: unknown *Contributors*: -

Image:Neues Schloss.jpg *Source*: http://bibliocm.bibliolabs.com/mwAnon/index.php?title=File:Neues_Schloss.jpg *License*: unknown *Contributors*: -

File:Coat of arms of Stuttgart.svg *Source*: http://bibliocm.bibliolabs.com/mwAnon/index.php?title=File:Coat_of_arms_of_Stuttgart.svg *License*: unknown *Contributors*: -

File:Germany location map.svg *Source*: http://bibliocm.bibliolabs.com/mwAnon/index.php?title=File:Germany_location_map.svg *License*: GNU Free Documentation License *Contributors*: User:NordNordWest

File:Red pog.svg *Source*: http://bibliocm.bibliolabs.com/mwAnon/index.php?title=File:Red_pog.svg *License*: unknown *Contributors*: -

File:Stuttgart Panorama 2007.jpg *Source*: http://bibliocm.bibliolabs.com/mwAnon/index.php?title=File:Stuttgart_Panorama_2007.jpg *License*: unknown *Contributors*: -

File:Stuttgart_at_night_.jpg *Source*: http://bibliocm.bibliolabs.com/mwAnon/index.php?title=File:Stuttgart_at_night_.jpg *License*: unknown *Contributors*: -

File:AltesSchlossStuttgart.JPG *Source*: http://bibliocm.bibliolabs.com/mwAnon/index.php?title=File:AltesSchlossStuttgart.JPG *License*: unknown *Contributors*: -

File:Neues Schloss Stuttgart.jpg *Source*: http://bibliocm.bibliolabs.com/mwAnon/index.php?title=File:Neues_Schloss_Stuttgart.jpg *License*: unknown *Contributors*: -

File:Stuttgart Rathaus Marktplatz 1907.jpg *Source*: http://bibliocm.bibliolabs.com/mwAnon/index.php?title=File:Stuttgart_Rathaus_Marktplatz_1907.jpg *License*: unknown *Contributors*: -

File:Stuttgart wappen alt.jpg *Source*: http://bibliocm.bibliolabs.com/mwAnon/index.php?title=File:Stuttgart_wappen_alt.jpg *License*: unknown *Contributors*: -

File:Stiftskirche Stuttgart.jpeg *Source*: http://bibliocm.bibliolabs.com/mwAnon/index.php?title=File:Stiftskirche_Stuttgart.jpeg *License*: unknown *Contributors*: -

File:Stuttgart Schillerplatz.jpg *Source*: http://bibliocm.bibliolabs.com/mwAnon/index.php?title=File:Stuttgart_Schillerplatz.jpg *License*: unknown *Contributors*: -

File:Stuttgart AlteKanzlei01.JPG *Source*: http://bibliocm.bibliolabs.com/mwAnon/index.php?title=File:Stuttgart_AlteKanzlei01.JPG *License*: unknown *Contributors*: -

File:Stuttgart-haus-der-wirtschaft.jpg *Source*: http://bibliocm.bibliolabs.com/mwAnon/index.php?title=File:Stuttgart-haus-der-wirtschaft.jpg *License*: unknown *Contributors*: -

File:Stuttgart-Feuersee.jpg *Source*: http://bibliocm.bibliolabs.com/mwAnon/index.php?title=File:Stuttgart-Feuersee.jpg *License*: unknown *Contributors*: -

File:Stuttgart Staatsoper.jpg *Source*: http://bibliocm.bibliolabs.com/mwAnon/index.php?title=File:Stuttgart_Staatsoper.jpg *License*: unknown *Contributors*: -

File:Cannstatter-fruchtsaeule-2004.jpg *Source*: http://bibliocm.bibliolabs.com/mwAnon/index.php?title=File:Cannstatter-fruchtsaeule-2004.jpg *License*: unknown *Contributors*: -

File:Stuttgart alte staatsgalerie.jpg *Source*: http://bibliocm.bibliolabs.com/mwAnon/index.php?title=File:Stuttgart_alte_staatsgalerie.jpg *License*: unknown *Contributors*: -

File:Stiftskirche stuttgart.jpg *Source*: http://bibliocm.bibliolabs.com/mwAnon/index.php?title=File:Stiftskirche_stuttgart.jpg *License*: unknown *Contributors*: -

File:Stuttgart Rathaus01.JPG *Source*: http://bibliocm.bibliolabs.com/mwAnon/index.php?title=File:Stuttgart_Rathaus01.JPG *License*: unknown *Contributors*: -

File:Koenigsbau Stuttgart 20060901.jpg *Source*: http://bibliocm.bibliolabs.com/mwAnon/index.php?title=File:Koenigsbau_Stuttgart_20060901.jpg *License*: unknown *Contributors*: -

File:Zuckerle.jpg *Source*: http://bibliocm.bibliolabs.com/mwAnon/index.php?title=File:Zuckerle.jpg *License*: unknown *Contributors*: -

File:Stuttgart HochschuleFuerMusikUndDarstellendeKunst.jpg *Source*: http://bibliocm.bibliolabs.com/mwAnon/index.php?title=File:Stuttgart_HochschuleFuerMusikUndDarstellendeKunst.jpg *License*: unknown *Contributors*: -

File:Stadtbahn Stuttgart - Hst Rathaus.jpg *Source*: http://bibliocm.bibliolabs.com/mwAnon/index.php?title=File:Stadtbahn_Stuttgart_-_Hst_Rathaus.jpg *License*: unknown *Contributors*: -

File:Zahnradbahn stuttgart 1917.jpg *Source*: http://bibliocm.bibliolabs.com/mwAnon/index.php?title=File:Zahnradbahn_stuttgart_1917.jpg *License*: unknown *Contributors*: -

File:stuttgart hbf1.jpg *Source*: http://bibliocm.bibliolabs.com/mwAnon/index.php?title=File:Stuttgart_hbf1.jpg *License*: unknown *Contributors*: -

File:EDDS - 001.jpg *Source*: http://bibliocm.bibliolabs.com/mwAnon/index.php?title=File:EDDS_-_001.jpg *License*: unknown *Contributors*: -

File:Bosch-Parkhaus02.jpg *Source*: http://bibliocm.bibliolabs.com/mwAnon/index.php?title=File:Bosch-Parkhaus02.jpg *License*: unknown *Contributors*: -

File:Gottlieb-daimler-stadion.jpg *Source*: http://bibliocm.bibliolabs.com/mwAnon/index.php?title=File:Gottlieb-daimler-stadion.jpg *License*: unknown *Contributors*: -

File:Flag of England.svg *Source*: http://bibliocm.bibliolabs.com/mwAnon/index.php?title=File:Flag_of_England.svg *License*: unknown *Contributors*: -

File:Flag of Wales 2.svg *Source*: http://bibliocm.bibliolabs.com/mwAnon/index.php?title=File:Flag_of_Wales_2.svg *License*: unknown *Contributors*: -

File:Flag of Tunisia.svg *Source*: http://bibliocm.bibliolabs.com/mwAnon/index.php?title=File:Flag_of_Tunisia.svg *License*: unknown *Contributors*: -

File:Stuttgart, Blickrichtung Nord von der Weinsteige aus, Innenstadt.jpg *Source*: http://bibliocm.bibliolabs.com/mwAnon/index.php?title=File:Stuttgart,_Blickrichtung_Nord_von_der_Weinsteige_aus,_Innenstadt.jpg *License*: unknown *Contributors*: -

File:Stuttgart SchlossSolitude.jpg *Source*: http://bibliocm.bibliolabs.com/mwAnon/index.php?title=File:Stuttgart_SchlossSolitude.jpg *License*: unknown *Contributors*: -

File:Fernsehturm stuttgart.jpg *Source*: http://bibliocm.bibliolabs.com/mwAnon/index.php?title=File:Fernsehturm_stuttgart.jpg *License*: unknown *Contributors*: -

File:Stuttgart Schlossplatz Nacht new.jpg *Source*: http://bibliocm.bibliolabs.com/mwAnon/index.php?title=File:Stuttgart_Schlossplatz_Nacht_new.jpg *License*: unknown *Contributors*: -

File:Stuttgart-Hegel-Birthplace-2006-04-09a.jpg *Source*: http://bibliocm.bibliolabs.com/mwAnon/index.php?title=File:Stuttgart-Hegel-Birthplace-2006-04-09a.jpg *License*: unknown *Contributors*: -

Image:Grabkapelle fern.jpg *Source*: http://bibliocm.bibliolabs.com/mwAnon/index.php?title=File:Grabkapelle_fern.jpg *License*: unknown *Contributors*: -

Image:Grabkapelle-Rotenberg.jpg *Source*: http://bibliocm.bibliolabs.com/mwAnon/index.php?title=File:Grabkapelle-Rotenberg.jpg *License*: unknown *Contributors*: -

Image:Burg-wirtemberg.jpg *Source*: http://bibliocm.bibliolabs.com/mwAnon/index.php?title=File:Burg-wirtemberg.jpg *License*: unknown *Contributors*: -

File:Neues Porsche-Museum am Porscheplatz Stuttgart-Zuffenhausen 2007 Foto Wolfgang Pehlemann DSCN8511.jpg *Source*: http://bibliocm.bibliolabs.com/mwAnon/index.php?title=File:Neues_Porsche-Museum_am_Porscheplatz_Stuttgart-Zuffenhausen_2007_Foto_Wolfgang_Pehlemann_DSCN8511.jpg *License*: unknown *Contributors*: -

Image:Porsche-Museum-Zuffenhausen.jpg *Source*: http://bibliocm.bibliolabs.com/mwAnon/index.php?title=File:Porsche-Museum-Zuffenhausen.jpg *License*: unknown *Contributors*: -

File:Porsche-Museum Portal Winter.JPG *Source*: http://bibliocm.bibliolabs.com/mwAnon/index.php?title=File:Porsche-Museum_Portal_Winter.JPG *License*: unknown *Contributors*: -

Image:Porsche360.jpg *Source*: http://bibliocm.bibliolabs.com/mwAnon/index.php?title=File:Porsche360.jpg *License*: unknown *Contributors*: -

Image:PorscheNo1.jpg *Source*: http://bibliocm.bibliolabs.com/mwAnon/index.php?title=File:PorscheNo1.jpg *License*: unknown *Contributors*: -

Image:Porsche 917C.jpg *Source*: http://bibliocm.bibliolabs.com/mwAnon/index.php?title=File:Porsche_917C.jpg *License*: unknown *Contributors*: -

Image:Porsche917-30.jpg *Source*: http://bibliocm.bibliolabs.com/mwAnon/index.php?title=File:Porsche917-30.jpg *License*: unknown *Contributors*: -

Image:McLaren TAG Porsche F1.jpg *Source*: http://bibliocm.bibliolabs.com/mwAnon/index.php?title=File:McLaren_TAG_Porsche_F1.jpg *License*: unknown *Contributors*: -

Image:Porsche 911 GT1 '98 -25.jpg *Source*: http://bibliocm.bibliolabs.com/mwAnon/index.php?title=File:Porsche_911_GT1_'98_-25.jpg *License*: unknown *Contributors*: -

File:Altes_Schloss_Stuttgart.jpg *Source*: http://bibliocm.bibliolabs.com/mwAnon/index.php?title=File:Altes_Schloss_Stuttgart.jpg *License*: unknown *Contributors*: -

File:Holzeimer Jungsteinzeit Waldsee-Reute.jpg *Source*: http://bibliocm.bibliolabs.com/mwAnon/index.php?title=File:Holzeimer_Jungsteinzeit_Waldsee-Reute.jpg *License*: unknown *Contributors*: -

File:Samson Fenster aus Alpirsbach.jpg *Source*: http://bibliocm.bibliolabs.com/mwAnon/index.php?title=File:Samson_Fenster_aus_Alpirsbach.jpg *License*: unknown *Contributors*: -

File:Palmesel Veringendorf.jpg *Source*: http://bibliocm.bibliolabs.com/mwAnon/index.php?title=File:Palmesel_Veringendorf.jpg *License*: unknown *Contributors*: -

Image:Stuttgart alte staatsgalerie.jpg *Source*: http://bibliocm.bibliolabs.com/mwAnon/index.php?title=File:Stuttgart_alte_staatsgalerie.jpg *License*: unknown *Contributors*: -

Image:Staatsgalerie1.jpg *Source*: http://bibliocm.bibliolabs.com/mwAnon/index.php?title=File:Staatsgalerie1.jpg *License*: unknown *Contributors*: -

Image:Staatsgalerie Stuttgart bei Nacht.jpg *Source*: http://bibliocm.bibliolabs.com/mwAnon/index.php?title=File:Staatsgalerie_Stuttgart_bei_Nacht.jpg *License*: unknown *Contributors*: -

Image:Stuttgart Staatsgalerie2.jpg *Source*: http://bibliocm.bibliolabs.com/mwAnon/index.php?title=File:Stuttgart_Staatsgalerie2.jpg *License*: unknown *Contributors*: -

Image:Blaubeuren-Hochaltar-SchreinfigurenDetail1.jpg *Source*: http://bibliocm.bibliolabs.com/mwAnon/index.php?title=File:Blaubeuren-Hochaltar-SchreinfigurenDetail1.jpg *License*: unknown *Contributors*: -

File:PD-icon.svg *Source*: http://bibliocm.bibliolabs.com/mwAnon/index.php?title=File:PD-icon.svg *License*: unknown *Contributors*: -

Image:AltesSchlossStuttgart.JPG *Source*: http://bibliocm.bibliolabs.com/mwAnon/index.php?title=File:AltesSchlossStuttgart.JPG *License*: unknown *Contributors*: -

Image:Stuttgart-altes-schloss-innenhof.jpg *Source*: http://bibliocm.bibliolabs.com/mwAnon/index.php?title=File:Stuttgart-altes-schloss-innenhof.jpg *License*: unknown *Contributors*: -

Image:Stuttgart-schlosskapelle.jpg *Source*: http://bibliocm.bibliolabs.com/mwAnon/index.php?title=File:Stuttgart-schlosskapelle.jpg *License*: unknown *Contributors*: -

Image:EberhardI.jpg *Source*: http://bibliocm.bibliolabs.com/mwAnon/index.php?title=File:EberhardI.jpg *License*: unknown *Contributors*: -

IMage:Altes Schloss Stuttgart.jpg *Source*: http://bibliocm.bibliolabs.com/mwAnon/index.php?title=File:Altes_Schloss_Stuttgart.jpg *License*: unknown *Contributors*: -

Image:Neues Schloss Stuttgart.jpg *Source*: http://bibliocm.bibliolabs.com/mwAnon/index.php?title=File:Neues_Schloss_Stuttgart.jpg *License*: unknown *Contributors*: -

Image:StuttgartSchlossPlatz.JPG *Source*: http://bibliocm.bibliolabs.com/mwAnon/index.php?title=File:StuttgartSchlossPlatz.JPG *License*: unknown *Contributors*: -

Image:Stuttgart Schlossplatz Nacht new.jpg *Source*: http://bibliocm.bibliolabs.com/mwAnon/index.php?title=File:Stuttgart_Schlossplatz_Nacht_new.jpg *License*: unknown *Contributors*: -

File:Solitude_pan-pjt.jpg *Source*: http://bibliocm.bibliolabs.com/mwAnon/index.php?title=File:Solitude_pan-pjt.jpg *License*: unknown *Contributors*: -

Image:Stuttgart Schillerplatz.jpg *Source*: http://bibliocm.bibliolabs.com/mwAnon/index.php?title=File:Stuttgart_Schillerplatz.jpg *License*: unknown *Contributors*: -

Image:Stuttgart-schillerplatz-2.jpg *Source*: http://bibliocm.bibliolabs.com/mwAnon/index.php?title=File:Stuttgart-schillerplatz-2.jpg *License*: unknown *Contributors*: -

Image:Stuttgart AlteKanzlei01.JPG *Source*: http://bibliocm.bibliolabs.com/mwAnon/index.php?title=File:Stuttgart_AlteKanzlei01.JPG *License*: unknown *Contributors*: -

Image:Stuttgart StiftsKirche03.JPG *Source*: http://bibliocm.bibliolabs.com/mwAnon/index.php?title=File:Stuttgart_StiftsKirche03.JPG *License*: unknown *Contributors*: -

Image:Stiftskirche stuttgart.jpg *Source*: http://bibliocm.bibliolabs.com/mwAnon/index.php?title=File:Stiftskirche_stuttgart.jpg *License*: unknown *Contributors*: -

Image:Schillerplatz.png *Source*: http://bibliocm.bibliolabs.com/mwAnon/index.php?title=File:Schillerplatz.png *License*: unknown *Contributors*: -

Image:Schillerdenkmal, Schillerplatz Stuttgart.JPG *Source*: http://bibliocm.bibliolabs.com/mwAnon/index.php?title=File:Schillerdenkmal,_Schillerplatz_Stuttgart.JPG *License*: unknown *Contributors*: -

Image:Kunstmuseum-stuttgart-2004.jpg *Source*: http://bibliocm.bibliolabs.com/mwAnon/index.php?title=File:Kunstmuseum-stuttgart-2004.jpg *License*: unknown *Contributors*: -

Image:Stuttgart-kunstgebaeude.jpg *Source*: http://bibliocm.bibliolabs.com/mwAnon/index.php?title=File:Stuttgart-kunstgebaeude.jpg *License*: unknown *Contributors*: -

Image:Stuttgart_Merkur.jpg *Source*: http://bibliocm.bibliolabs.com/mwAnon/index.php?title=File:Stuttgart_Merkur.jpg *License*: unknown *Contributors*: -

Image:Stuttgart Staatsoper.jpg *Source*: http://bibliocm.bibliolabs.com/mwAnon/index.php?title=File:Stuttgart_Staatsoper.jpg *License*: unknown *Contributors*: -

Image:Birkenkopf-Stuttgart.jpg *Source*: http://bibliocm.bibliolabs.com/mwAnon/index.php?title=File:Birkenkopf-Stuttgart.jpg *License*: unknown *Contributors*: -

Image:Stuttgart-Observatory-20060401.jpg *Source*: http://bibliocm.bibliolabs.com/mwAnon/index.php?title=File:Stuttgart-Observatory-20060401.jpg *License*: unknown *Contributors*: -

File:Burgholzhofturm-pjt.jpg *Source*: http://bibliocm.bibliolabs.com/mwAnon/index.php?title=File:Burgholzhofturm-pjt.jpg *License*: unknown *Contributors*: -

Image:Stuttgart-tagblatt-turm2006.jpg *Source*: http://bibliocm.bibliolabs.com/mwAnon/index.php?title=File:Stuttgart-tagblatt-turm2006.jpg *License*: unknown *Contributors*: -

File:Stuttgart TV tower at night.jpg *Source*: http://bibliocm.bibliolabs.com/mwAnon/index.php?title=File:Stuttgart_TV_tower_at_night.jpg *License*: unknown *Contributors*: -

Image:Cannstatter-fruchtsaeule-2004.jpg *Source*: http://bibliocm.bibliolabs.com/mwAnon/index.php?title=File:Cannstatter-fruchtsaeule-2004.jpg *License*: unknown *Contributors*: -

Image:WasenFruitColumn.JPG *Source*: http://bibliocm.bibliolabs.com/mwAnon/index.php?title=File:WasenFruitColumn.JPG *License*: unknown *Contributors*: -

Image:Bosch-Parkhaus02.jpg *Source*: http://bibliocm.bibliolabs.com/mwAnon/index.php?title=File:Bosch-Parkhaus02.jpg *License*: unknown *Contributors*: -

Image:Stuttgarter Weihnachstmarkt 2004.JPG *Source*: http://bibliocm.bibliolabs.com/mwAnon/index.php?title=File:Stuttgarter_Weihnachstmarkt_2004.JPG *License*: unknown *Contributors*: -

Image:Killesbergturm1.jpg *Source*: http://bibliocm.bibliolabs.com/mwAnon/index.php?title=File:Killesbergturm1.jpg *License*: unknown *Contributors*: -

Image:SchoenbuchNaturparkKarte.gif *Source*: http://bibliocm.bibliolabs.com/mwAnon/index.php?title=File:SchoenbuchNaturparkKarte.gif *License*: unknown *Contributors*: -

Image:SchoenbuchBirkensee2.jpg *Source*: http://bibliocm.bibliolabs.com/mwAnon/index.php?title=File:SchoenbuchBirkensee2.jpg *License*: unknown *Contributors*: -

File:Hohenheim-gartenplan.jpg *Source*: http://bibliocm.bibliolabs.com/mwAnon/index.php?title=File:Hohenheim-gartenplan.jpg *License*: unknown *Contributors*: -

Image:WilhelmaNachttierhaus.jpg *Source*: http://bibliocm.bibliolabs.com/mwAnon/index.php?title=File:WilhelmaNachttierhaus.jpg *License*: unknown *Contributors*: -

Image:Wilhelmafant.jpg *Source*: http://bibliocm.bibliolabs.com/mwAnon/index.php?title=File:Wilhelmafant.jpg *License*: unknown *Contributors*: -

Image:Wilhelma Ochsenfrosch 2.jpg *Source*: http://bibliocm.bibliolabs.com/mwAnon/index.php?title=File:Wilhelma_Ochsenfrosch_2.jpg *License*: unknown *Contributors*: -

Image:Schwiegermuttersessel in der Wilhelma.jpg *Source*: http://bibliocm.bibliolabs.com/mwAnon/index.php?title=File:Schwiegermuttersessel_in_der_Wilhelma.jpg *License*: unknown *Contributors*: -

File:Flag of Switzerland.svg *Source*: http://bibliocm.bibliolabs.com/mwAnon/index.php?title=File:Flag_of_Switzerland.svg *License*: unknown *Contributors*: -

File:Flag of Cote d'Ivoire.svg *Source*: http://bibliocm.bibliolabs.com/mwAnon/index.php?title=File:Flag_of_Cote_d'Ivoire.svg *License*: Public Domain *Contributors*: User:Jon Harald Søby

File:Flag of Guinea.svg *Source*: http://bibliocm.bibliolabs.com/mwAnon/index.php?title=File:Flag_of_Guinea.svg *License*: Public Domain *Contributors*: User:SKopp

File:Flag of Brazil.svg *Source*: http://bibliocm.bibliolabs.com/mwAnon/index.php?title=File:Flag_of_Brazil.svg *License*: unknown *Contributors*: -

File:Flag of Hungary (1867-1918).svg *Source*: http://bibliocm.bibliolabs.com/mwAnon/index.php?title=File:Flag_of_Hungary_(1867-1918).svg *License*: unknown *Contributors*: -

File:Flag of SFR Yugoslavia.svg *Source*: http://bibliocm.bibliolabs.com/mwAnon/index.php?title=File:Flag_of_SFR_Yugoslavia.svg *License*: unknown *Contributors*: -

File:Flag of Slovenia.svg *Source*: http://bibliocm.bibliolabs.com/mwAnon/index.php?title=File:Flag_of_Slovenia.svg *License*: unknown *Contributors*: -

File:Waldaustadion Degerloch.jpg *Source*: http://bibliocm.bibliolabs.com/mwAnon/index.php?title=File:Waldaustadion_Degerloch.jpg *License*: unknown *Contributors*: -

Image:Porsche-Arena-Suedfront.jpg *Source*: http://bibliocm.bibliolabs.com/mwAnon/index.php?title=File:Porsche-Arena-Suedfront.jpg *License*: unknown *Contributors*: -

image:Porsche-Arena-Logo.jpg *Source*: http://bibliocm.bibliolabs.com/mwAnon/index.php?title=File:Porsche-Arena-Logo.jpg *License*: unknown *Contributors*: -

image:Porsche-Arena-innen.jpg *Source*: http://bibliocm.bibliolabs.com/mwAnon/index.php?title=File:Porsche-Arena-innen.jpg *License*: unknown *Contributors*: -

image:Luftbild Daimlerstadion Schleyerhalle Porsche-Arena.jpg *Source*: http://bibliocm.bibliolabs.com/mwAnon/index.php?title=File:Luftbild_Daimlerstadion_Schleyerhalle_Porsche-Arena.jpg *License*: unknown *Contributors*: -

Image:Gottlieb-Daimler-Stadion-2007.jpg *Source*: http://bibliocm.bibliolabs.com/mwAnon/index.php?title=File:Gottlieb-Daimler-Stadion-2007.jpg *License*: unknown *Contributors*: -

File:Flag of Argentina.svg *Source*: http://bibliocm.bibliolabs.com/mwAnon/index.php?title=File:Flag_of_Argentina.svg *License*: unknown *Contributors*: -

File:Flag of the Soviet Union.svg *Source*: http://bibliocm.bibliolabs.com/mwAnon/index.php?title=File:Flag_of_the_Soviet_Union.svg *License*: unknown *Contributors*: -

File:Flag of Spain.svg *Source*: http://bibliocm.bibliolabs.com/mwAnon/index.php?title=File:Flag_of_Spain.svg *License*: Public Domain *Contributors*: Pedro A. Gracia Fajardo, escudo de Manual de Imagen Institucional de la Administración General del Estado

File:Flag of Australia.svg *Source*: http://bibliocm.bibliolabs.com/mwAnon/index.php?title=File:Flag_of_Australia.svg *License*: unknown *Contributors*: -

File:Flag of Portugal.svg *Source*: http://bibliocm.bibliolabs.com/mwAnon/index.php?title=File:Flag_of_Portugal.svg *License*: unknown *Contributors*: -

Image:Luftbild EDDS.jpg *Source*: http://bibliocm.bibliolabs.com/mwAnon/index.php?title=File:Luftbild_EDDS.jpg *License*: unknown *Contributors*: -

File:Airplane_silhouette.svg *Source*: http://bibliocm.bibliolabs.com/mwAnon/index.php?title=File:Airplane_silhouette.svg *License*: unknown *Contributors*: -

File:Flughafen Stuttgart - Terminal 3.jpg *Source*: http://bibliocm.bibliolabs.com/mwAnon/index.php?title=File:Flughafen_Stuttgart_-_Terminal_3.jpg *License*: unknown *Contributors*: -

Image:Stuttgart Airport Interior 2005-06-02.jpg *Source*: http://bibliocm.bibliolabs.com/mwAnon/index.php?title=File:Stuttgart_Airport_Interior_2005-06-02.jpg *License*: GNU Free Documentation License *Contributors*: BlackIceNRW, Enslin, JamesBowes, JuergenL, Thuresson

Image:commons-logo.svg *Source*: http://bibliocm.bibliolabs.com/mwAnon/index.php?title=File:Commons-logo.svg *License*: logo *Contributors*: User:3247, User:Grunt

Image:Stadtbahn Stuttgart - Hst Rathaus.jpg *Source*: http://bibliocm.bibliolabs.com/mwAnon/index.php?title=File:Stadtbahn_Stuttgart_-_Hst_Rathaus.jpg *License*: unknown *Contributors*: -

Image:Stuttgart-next-service- describer.jpg *Source*: http://bibliocm.bibliolabs.com/mwAnon/index.php?title=File:Stuttgart-next-service-_describer.jpg *License*: unknown *Contributors*: -

File:Hbf-stuttgart-2004.jpg *Source*: http://bibliocm.bibliolabs.com/mwAnon/index.php?title=File:Hbf-stuttgart-2004.jpg *License*: unknown *Contributors*: -

File:Stg-bahnhof-1900.jpg *Source*: http://bibliocm.bibliolabs.com/mwAnon/index.php?title=File:Stg-bahnhof-1900.jpg *License*: unknown *Contributors*: AnRo0002, Enslin, Fb78, Xenophon, ¡0-8-15!

File:Centralbahnhof-2004.jpg *Source*: http://bibliocm.bibliolabs.com/mwAnon/index.php?title=File:Centralbahnhof-2004.jpg *License*: GNU Free Documentation License *Contributors*: AnRo0002, AndreasPraefcke, BLueFiSH.as, Burts, Enslin, Stefan-Xp, ¡0-8-15!

File:Bahnhofsturm-stuttgart-2004.jpg *Source*: http://bibliocm.bibliolabs.com/mwAnon/index.php?title=File:Bahnhofsturm-stuttgart-2004.jpg *License*: GNU Free Documentation License *Contributors*: AndreasPraefcke, Enslin, HBR, Stefan-Xp, ¡0-8-15!

File:Stuttgart HBF Ost 01.jpg *Source*: http://bibliocm.bibliolabs.com/mwAnon/index.php?title=File:Stuttgart_HBF_Ost_01.jpg *License*: Creative Commons Attribution-Sharealike 2.5 *Contributors*: Ra Boe

File:Stuttgart Hauptbahnhof vom Fernsehturm.jpg *Source*: http://bibliocm.bibliolabs.com/mwAnon/index.php?title=File:Stuttgart_Hauptbahnhof_vom_Fernsehturm.jpg *License*: Creative Commons Attribution 3.0 *Contributors*: Photo: Andreas Praefcke

File:ICE-Logo.svg *Source*: http://bibliocm.bibliolabs.com/mwAnon/index.php?title=File:ICE-Logo.svg *License*: unknown *Contributors*: -

File:Db-schild.svg *Source*: http://bibliocm.bibliolabs.com/mwAnon/index.php?title=File:Db-schild.svg *License*: Public Domain *Contributors*: See below.

File:Stgtbahnhof.jpg *Source*: http://bibliocm.bibliolabs.com/mwAnon/index.php?title=File:Stgtbahnhof.jpg *License*: unknown *Contributors*: -

File:Stuttgart hbf 002.jpg *Source*: http://bibliocm.bibliolabs.com/mwAnon/index.php?title=File:Stuttgart_hbf_002.jpg *License*: unknown *Contributors*: -

File:Hauptbahnhof Stuttgart.jpg *Source*: http://bibliocm.bibliolabs.com/mwAnon/index.php?title=File:Hauptbahnhof_Stuttgart.jpg *License*: unknown *Contributors*: -

Image:Stuttgarter-zahnradbahn-zacke haltestelle-haigst.jpg *Source*: http://bibliocm.bibliolabs.com/mwAnon/index.php?title=File:Stuttgarter-zahnradbahn-zacke_haltestelle-haigst.jpg *License*: unknown *Contributors*: -

Image:Stuttgarter-seilbahn-2004.jpg *Source*: http://bibliocm.bibliolabs.com/mwAnon/index.php?title=File:Stuttgarter-seilbahn-2004.jpg *License*: unknown *Contributors*: -

CPSIA information can be obtained at www.ICGtesting.com
Printed in the USA
BVOW09s2040030516

446614BV00012B/179/P

9 781249 216896